PERSPECTIVES ON UNDERDEVELOPMENT

BANKING
ON
POVERTY

The Global Impact
of the IMF
&
World Bank

Edited by Jill Torrie

with a Foreword by Mel Watkins

between the lines

The **Perspectives on Underdevelopment** Series

Perpetuating Poverty:
The Political Economy of Canadian Foreign Aid
by Robert Carty and Virginia Smith

Ties That Bind:
Canada and the Third World
edited by Robert Clarke and Richard Swift

Bitter Grounds:
Roots of Revolt in El Salvador
by Liisa North

BANKING ON POVERTY

The Global Impact
of the IMF
&
World Bank

"It is important to note that IMF programs are not designed to increase the welfare of the population. They are designed to bring the external payments account into balance. . . . The IMF is the ultimate guardian of the interests of capitalists and bankers doing international business."

— Kari Polyani Levitt

© 1983 by Between The Lines

Published by: Between The Lines
                         427 Bloor Street West
                         Toronto, Ontario, Canada

Typeset by: Dumont Press Graphix
                         97 Victoria Street North
                         Kitchener, Ontario, Canada

Designed by: Dumont Press Graphix

Cover designed by: Moe Lyons and Paula Greenberg

                    Printed and bound in Canada by:
                         The Alger Press Limited

Between The Lines receives financial assistance from the Ontario Arts
Council.

**This book is dedicated to my grandmother, Mabel Blanche
Welland (1885-   ) — J.T**

Canadian Cataloguing in Publication Data

Main entry under title:
Banking on poverty

(Perspectives on underdevelopment)
Papers presented at a conference held at the University of
Toronto, Sept. 7-9, 1982.
Bibliography: p. 330
ISBN 0-919946-38-0 (bound). - ISBN 0-919946-39-9 (pbk.)

1. International Monetary Fund — Congresses. 2. World
Bank — Congresses. 3. International finance — Congresses
4. Developing countries — Economic conditions —
Congresses. I. Torrie, Jill, 1948-   II. Series.

HG3881.B36 1983   332'.042   C83-099044-5

Between The Lines is a joint project of the Development Education
Centre, Toronto, and Dumont Press Graphix, Kitchener.

Table of Contents

Acknowledgements

The development of this book has truly been a co-operative effort. Thirteen organizations representing the interests of church, labour and non-governmental bodies sponsored and planned "The Global Impact of the IMF and World Bank" conference at the University of Toronto in September 1982. They were:
Anglican World Missions; Canada-Asia Working Group; Canadian Catholic Organization for Development and Peace; Group for the Defence of Civil Rights in Argentina; Jesuit Centre for Social Faith and Justice; Latin American Working Group; New Democratic Party Club, University of Toronto; *New Internationalist* magazine; Ontario Federation of Labour; Oxfam-Canada; Students' Administrative Council, University of Toronto; Taskforce on Churches and Corporate Responsibility; and *This Magazine*.

Representatives from these bodies formed the conference organizing committee, and inspired this collection of essays based on papers presented at the conference. I would especially like to thank Robert Carty (LAWG), Wayne Ellwood (NI), Bonnie Green (TCCR), Duncan MacDonald (OFL), Renate Pratt (TCCR), Roger Rolfe (Oxfam), and Virginia Field Smith (GDCRA) for their hard work on the "sounding board". It was a pleasure to work with the other committee members: Mel Watkins (TM), Fr. Jim Webb (JC), Peter Taylor, Rev. Murray MacInnis (ACWM), and Reuban Cusipag (CAWG). The committee benefited from the patient accounting services of Ken Ward of the United Church, while Daphne Anne Garcia (TCCR staff) and Diane Scott (Oxfam volunteer) helped with a great deal of the administrative work. The conference itself could not have run as smoothly as it did without the organizational and diplomatic skills of the chairpersons.

The conference was generously funded by:
Anglican Church of Canada, Primate's World Relief and Development Fund; Canadian Catholic Organization for Development and Peace; Canadian Union of Public Employees, Ontario Division; CISO; Jesuit Fathers of Upper Canada; Labour Council of Metropolitan Toronto; Ontario Federation of Labour; Ontario Public Service Employees Union; Oxfam-Canada; Retail and Wholesale and Department Store Union; Retail and Wholesale and Department Store Union, Local 414; Sisters of St. Joseph of the Diocese of Hamilton; The Sisters, Faithful Companions of Jesus; Taskforce on the Churches and Corporate Responsibility; United Auto Workers; United Church, Division of Mission in Canada; United Church, Division of World Outreach; United Electrical, Radio and Machine Workers of America; United Food and Commercial Workers — Region 18, Canada; Ursuline Generalate; Walter and Duncan Gordon Charitable Foundation.

The Canadian Centre for Policy Alternatives in Ottawa first suggested we put together this book and organized the rough typing of the conference transcripts. During the development of this publication, Renate Pratt and Bob Carty continued to act as a "sounding board". I would like to thank them for an invaluable and enjoyable collaboration. Fortunately, we have had the expert work of Robert Ganton Clarke of Between The Lines for additional editorial work.

Finally, on behalf of all the organizers, sponsors and funders, I would like to thank the group that made both this book and the conference possible — the contributors. For me they became the second sounding board and it has been a personal pleasure to learn from and work with all of them. And given the topic of our collaboration, I believe it is entirely possible we may have such an opportunity again.

J.T.,
Conference co-ordinator,
Toronto, October 1983

Foreword

Mel Watkins

The International Monetary Fund, or IMF, and the World Bank are two of the key institutions of the world economy, and notably of the capitalist sphere to which Canada belongs. Together they hold annual meetings, rotating between Washington in the odd years and the rest of the world in the even. (That half of these meetings take place in the United States tells us something about American predominance in these allegedly global institutions.) For 1982 the site chosen was Toronto, Canada.

It was a wholly sensible choice. Toronto is a major convention centre, with the hotel space needed to accommodate the 10,000 to 15,000 people that would be attracted to the meeting, whether as official delegates from member countries or as camp-followers from the private banks. Furthermore, Toronto is itself the headquarters for large Canadian banks (and increasingly so relative to Montreal), which are themselves heavily involved in the world of international finance.

The choice of Toronto, though understandable, was all the same a matter of concern to some of us, both as citizens and as representatives of a variety of groups: churches, trade unions, progressive publications, Third World solidarity groups. We were not opposed to the meetings being held in Toronto; indeed, the economic activity that would be generated could only be welcomed in the midst of a crisis of unemployment. Rather, what bothered us was that the very fact of this location meant the meetings would receive more coverage in Canada than would otherwise have been the case. The result risked being self-serving publicity for the IMF and the World Bank and for their particular point of view.

The reason we were not happy with that prospect was that we were not enamoured of the track record of these institutions, as evidenced by their willingness to impose harsh conditions on already poor countries and to disregard the state of human rights within countries as a criterion for loans. Nor were we happy with their philosophy, or ideology. In the era of Reagan and Thatcher, their approach was increasingly neoconservative and monetarist: that is, following stringent fiscal and monetary policies — notwithstanding recession and unemployment. To our minds, then, there were important issues of social justice, relevant to people both outside and inside Canada, with respect to which the IMF and the World Bank were mostly worsening matters. We feared specifically that publicity for these institutions would strengthen illiberal tendencies amongst our masters in Canada — in government, in the central bank and in the corporate sector — and legitimize harsh policies to the further disadvantage of ordinary Canadians.

If anyone had any doubts about the latter, they had presumably been removed when, at a luncheon in Toronto on March 10, 1982, the Managing Director of the IMF lauded the Canadian fiscal and monetary authorities "for showing courage and determination in implementing an anti-inflation program even though the economy has been moving into recession". He did not mince words: "Unquestionably, the authorities are following the right course." The IMF chose to weigh in on the side of a most important Canadian debate at a time when trade unionists, farmers, homeowners, small businessmen, etc., etc., all squeezed by usurious interest rates and double-digit unemployment, were increasingly lining up on the other side.

From the outset, the group of us who organized, first, a public conference on the occasion of the World Bank/IMF meetings in September 1982, and now this book, was aware that we had a rare opportunity. We had a chance to link the concerns of people working around both Canadian issues and Third World issues, and to bring people together from otherwise often separate compartments of political work. We therefore set out to gather together speakers from Canada, the Third World and — as the centre of everyone's empire — the United States.

We saw our function as educational. True, we shared a point of view, one of concern and dissent, and we saw the conference as a way of articulating and disseminating that dissent. Bear in mind that we were not the "main event" and that we wanted, unlike the official meetings, to provide a public forum for points of view other than the official and orthodox. At the same time, we did invite spokespersons from the Fund/ Bank and from the Canadian government; we appreciated their coming and we are pleased to include their presentations here.

As well, though the topic of international finance seems frighteningly esoteric, we were resolved to organize a popular conference where people with expertise would present their views in a way accessible to an audience of interested citizens. We think we succeeded in doing that, and that this volume bears us out.

The conference was, to be frank, a great success. There were many excellent presentations to large audiences. This encouraged the conference organizers to put together this book, which consists mostly of presentations to the conference. All have been carefully edited so that they are crisp while remaining accessible. Some have been revised for inclusion here. Tom Naylor, who gave a lively talk at the conference, subsequently wrote a most useful assessment of the actual IMF/World Bank meetings, which we have decided to print because of the feeling it provides for the milieu of the main event. As well as presenting his own paper to the conference, Cranford Pratt has written a special introduction to this book that sets the Bank and the Fund in a global setting.

At the time the conference took place, the world economy had literally skated to the brink of disaster. (There was a suspicion that this was so at the time; there is now something approaching consensus on this matter.) Disaster had stared us in the face because of monetarist policies so beloved to bankers — in some part because high interest rates so effectively line their pockets — and because of the bloated structure of international debt, so burdensome to borrowing countries because of the high interest rates and so worrisome to lending banks, which risked going under themselves if enough countries defaulted. But, someone may insist, is any of this still true? Have we not since seen an economic recovery? Are the papers in this book, mostly prepared in that prior context, still germane?

It is a fact that matters economic are no longer quite as bad as they were a year or so ago, though on the most critical matter, that of jobs, the rate of unemployment has hardly fallen at all. The economy is in a recovery phase, and for that we can be grateful. But the strength and longevity of the recovery remain uncertain. And a key reason for that uncertainty remains those high real rates of interest, which only appear to have fallen and in fact remain very high when we allow for the sharp decline in the rate of inflation. In addition, the structure of international debt still overhangs the world economy and threatens, like a house of cards, to come tumbling down — bringing everything else down with it. So these matters, which so much exercised both the official meetings in September 1982 — albeit from rather different perspectives — and our conference continue to haunt us and to merit our attention.

Beyond that, the presentations remain germane because fundamental issues of social justice and human rights do not go away. These issues were the bottom line for the conference. They were the reason why those who organized the conference came together in the first place, the reason why we were able to attract such outstanding speakers and draw such impressive audiences. They are also the bottom line for this book. In discussing economic issues, it is easy to become bogged down in technicalities and be intimidated by economists. Though an economist, I believe that economic questions are really questions about justice and morality. That view, which was so ably put forth in the 1983 New Year's statement of the Roman Catholic Bishops on the Canadian economy, is the view that permeates this book. We offer no apology for that; rather, we ask you to please read on in the firm hope that you will come to share our concerns.

Introduction

International Bankers and the Crisis of Debt

R. Cranford Pratt

International attention rarely focuses for any length of time on the needs and aspirations of the poor. This is above all true in periods of global economic crisis when the rich and powerful struggle to protect their own advantage. While in more prosperous times those with money and an assumed authority may offer up at least a little generosity of spirit and sense of "global solidarity" (to use a phrase from the Brandt Commission), in periods of economic crisis they tend to pay attention only to those international issues that either threaten them or offer the prospect of benefits. The threat to Western banks from the debt crises of a number of newly industrialized countries; the international consequences of high interest rates and major budgetary deficits in the United States; the rising non-tariff barriers of major industrialized countries; the disagreements over the particulars of East-West trade — these and similar issues dominate Western intergovernmental meetings and academic comment about the international crisis.

This volume has a different preoccupation. It is primarily concerned with the impact of the policies and practices of the International Monetary Fund and World Bank on low-income countries and on the poor within the rest of the Third World. In particular it is concerned with the ways these two international institutions have sought to manage the global economic crisis of the last ten years. The recurrent theme is that the dominant policies of the United States and other Western powers in the ruling councils of the financial insitutions, and the development theories and ideology adhered to by Western officials, have intensified rather than assauged the basic asymmetry of international relations. These factors have led to IMF and World Bank policies that make severe intrusions upon the sovereign responsibilities of many governments of the Third World. Those policies not only often entail major additional cuts in the living standards of the poorest sectors of Third World societies but are also unlikely to produce the economic results claimed on their behalf.

This volume also includes a number of papers that are not about the Third World or the IMF and the World Bank, but are instead about policy options for Canada in the present global economic crisis. Indeed, there is a basic consistency in how Canada and other major capitalist countries have sought to cope with the economic recession and the policies pressed upon Third World governments by the IMF and World Bank. That consistency lies in the consequences those policies have for income distribution. What the IMF and World Bank promote for the Third World and what the Canadian Government pursues are each marked by an emphasis on a need for high interest rates, greater reliance on market forces, wage cuts and budgetary restraint, particularly in expenditures on social services. The policies of both Canada and the international institutions, in other words, ignore important objectives such as job creation, the maintenance of basic levels of welfare and the promotion of greater equity.

This consistency is, in part, a structural feature of capitalism. The most obvious capitalist prescription for coping with an economic crisis is to find ways to increase the rewards for investment and to lower costs. Typically this means greater inducements to invest for the financier and lower real wages for the worker. It, therefore, means widening income inequalities and, if not greater unemployment, then certainly no direct employment creation by government. To ask a capitalist economy to promote recovery by safeguarding the income levels of the poor and by directly generating new employment is to follow the classic Keynesian liberal-capitalist maxims. To those in power in Washington and Ottawa, those policy prescriptions are not acceptable because they inevitably involve state and international intervention — unpopular remedies for those with power in capitalist societies. To those people such remedies would also seem likely to diminish the recovery potential of the major capitalist countries.

This structural (and political) reason for the underlying consistency between the World Bank-IMF policies on the one hand and the Canadian and many other Western governments on the other has been reinforced by the widespread influence in Western governments of the same theories of economic development that hold sway in the international financial institutions. Those who struggle against policies implemented in Canada on the advice of the Bank of Canada and the Treasury are struggling against the same ideology and economic thinking that so strongly influences the IMF and World Bank. The inclusion in this volume of a discussion of major issues as related not only to the international institutions but also to Canadian policy therefore makes good sense.

The Third World in the international economy

In the 25-year period from 1950 to 1975, the overall economic growth-rate of Third World countries compared favourably to that of industrialized countries. This may not be a particularly important fact — it conceals as much as it reveals — but it is true. From 1950 to 1976 the growth-rate of the industrialized developed countries averaged 4.2 per cent; that of the less developed countries (LDCs) was 5 per cent. However, because of higher rates of population growth, these percentages translate into the following growth-rates in per capita incomes.

Category of Countries	Per capita Growth-Rates 1951 - 75
OECD* Countries	3.2 %
All LDCs	3.1 %
Tropical African	2.0 %
South Asian	1.8 %

* Organization for Economic Co-operation and Development

Thus, per capita growth-rates, even in the decades of extended growth, were higher in the rich countries than in the poor. As a result the gap in living standards widened significantly. In 1981, the World Bank projected per capita income levels to the year 1990 on the basis of two scenarios, a high one and a low one. For the low-income countries of Africa these projections show per capita income in constant 1980 dollars as rising from $220 in 1980 by an annual rate of .1 per cent under the high scenario and falling by 1 per cent under the low scenario. For the low-income countries of Asia the 1980 figure was $210 and the two projections involved increases of 2.1 per cent and 1 per cent respectively. In contrast, the 1980 per capita income for industrialized countries was $10,660 and the projections to 1990 were for increases each year of 3.1 per cent or 2.3 per cent depending on whether the high or low scenario was assumed. The gap between income levels in Asia and Africa in contrast to Europe and North America was not only enormous but also expected to continue to widen very significantly.

Some middle-income developing countries, in contrast to these low-income countries, experienced high growth-rates throughout those 25 years. Two quite different types of economies had considerable success: the oil-exporting countries and those newly-industrializing countries that were able to export rapidly rising levels of manufactured goods. For example, during the years 1960 to 1979 Singapore held to a per capita income growth-rate of 8.6 per cent, Korea, 9.5 per cent, Mexico, 6.2 per cent. Malaysia, 7.2 per cent and Brazil 6.6 per cent. With growth-rates this substantial in most of these rapidly developing, newly industrializing countries, income levels of all sectors of the society rose. However, in a few of them, especially countries where property, productive assets and political power were grossly unequal in their distribution, the poor actually were left poorer in absolute terms at the end of the period of "growth".* Moreover, even in cases where

* It is surprisingly difficult to answer the straightforward question, has growth benefited the poor? Conceptual problems and inadequate statistics are the main reasons for this difficulty. One recent overview of the literature concludes that for each of 13 less developed countries where enough information is available, absolute poverty lessened in 10 (Bangladesh, Brazil, Costa Rica, Pakistan, Puerto Rico, Singapore,

income levels rose throughout the society, the rich received disproportionately more of the rising income than did the poor. The growth-rates, therefore, are impressive in these countries but the welfare consequences for the poor are less positive than per capita income averages might suggest.

In any case, this growth pattern in less developed countries during the period from the 1950s to the 1970s was dramatically upset by the late 1970s, when a further round of oil price increases (in 1979-80) and an intensified global recession led to two developments of major consequence for those nations.

First, the oil-importing, less developed countries were particularly hit by the recession of the 1980s. The partially industrialized countries could no longer easily penetrate the markets of the developed world while the poorer countries, dependent for foreign exchange on primary commodity exports, faced declining terms of trade as well as a decline in export values. Real flows in these years of crisis slackened. By 1982 terms of trade were worse than they had been since the 1930s. Per capita income levels in many of the poorest countries had fallen in each of the last four years, bringing with them, inevitably, severe strain on public expenditures as well.

The results of all this have been immediately devastating — lower incomes still, especially for the already very poor, increasing inequalities, reduced levels of health services and education, and falling levels of public investment. Often, as well, a downward spiral began as foreign exchange shortages led to cuts in essential imports of spare parts, intermediate goods and inputs into the local manufacturing sector. These cuts in turn caused a further decline in output and in exports.

There was, therefore, a very substantial need for additional resource transfers from the developed world to call a halt to this spiral and to make possible the economic adjustments required by the permanent changes within the international economic system. The new economic conditions, if uncorrected, would only continue to cause severe balance of pay-

---

Sri Lanka, Taiwan, Thailand and Mexico) and worsened in 3 (Argentina, India and the Philippines): Gary Fields, *Poverty, Inequality and Development*, Cambridge University Press, 1980.

ments deficits. And, as if the additional poverty and human suffering and the complex economic difficulties were not sufficient, further consequences — such as mounting corruption, administrative decay and political disintegration — foreshadowed a lessening of state capability to initiate an effective recovery.

The banks in turn were moved by what Reginald Green, a leading development economist, has called an "animal hunger". With their holdings swollen by deposits from the Organization of Petroleum Exporting Countries (OPEC), the banks were searching the globe for reasonable investment outlets. The still fast-growing middle-income countries in the Third World were natural targets. *Financial Times* writer Hugh O'Shaughnessy has suggested that the U.S. government was content to see very heavy lending by private U.S. banks to these important economies in order thereby to tie these economies and their regimes more closely into the Western orbit.

By the late 1970s the banks were congratulating themselves for successfully recycling oil dollars to everyone's satisfaction, most particularly their own. Returns from their intermediary role were substantial. The rate of interest charged ran from .875 per cent to over 2 per cent above the London inter-bank rate. In the early 1980s, Brazil, for example, paid one of the highest spreads in the world, 2.25 per cent above the inter-bank rate. Increasingly the loans were made at floating interest rates! That is, the rate of interest on the loans was recurrently adjusted as the inter-bank rate itself shifted.

From 1973-74 onward and even more intensely after 1979, a number of Third World countries began as well to borrow from the banks to offset their balance of payments deficits. The banks quickly became a far more important source of balance of payments lending to the LDCs than the IMF. These balance of payments loans were completely seperate from productivity-related investments. And, as the banks became more anxious in 1981 and after, a much increased proportion of the new loans was made up of short-term loans of one to two years.

The loans briefly eased foreign exchange pressures on the regimes involved but, if their problems were not to intensify quickly, the debtors' terms of trade and levels of exports would need to improve rapidly. The foreign debt of Third World countries had soared to a total of over $750 billion by early 1983, according to *The Economist,* with private banks holding over half of this total. This marked a five-fold increase since 1971 and a doubling since 1979. Much of this debt was concentrated in a few countries: Mexico, Brazil, Argentina and South Korea alone accounted for over half of Third World debt to the private banks. Mexico and Brazil each owed approximately $80 billion, and Argentina $38 billion.

By 1982 first Argentina, then Mexico and Brazil with others soon to follow, faced unmanageable foreign exchange problems. Their foreign exchange earnings had remained stagnant while their interest payments had soared both because of continued heavy borrowing and because, with interest rates rising, many of their loans had been granted at floating interest rates. Repayments were heavy not only because of substantial short-term loans but also because the borrowing had not been carefully planned, with the result that repayments fell due in an erratic fashion. For example, in 1982 49 per cent of Mexico's total debt was due for repayment, 35 per cent of Brazil's, 47 per cent of Argentina's and 69 per cent of Venezuela's. In 1981 Morgan Guaranty Trust estimated the total of interest charges and repayments as a percentage of each of these countries' exports: The figures were Mexico 85 per cent, Brazil 67 per cent, Argentina 100 per cent and Venezuela 79 per cent.

Full or even significant repayment was thus out of the question and indeed the "rolling over"* of debt had already occurred for a number of countries. However, even the payment of interest on debts was likely to prove impossible for countries with the heaviest burdens. The threat or at least the risk of a major default was therefore real and immediate. By 1982 the debt crisis facing the middle-income, less developed countries was as pressing in its urgency as the more general economic crisis that had a grip upon many of the least developed.

The World Bank and the IMF: organization and structure

Since its beginnings at Bretton Woods in 1944, the IMF's most important objective has always been the establishment of stable

* When loans coming due are deferred or renewed for a further period of time, usually at a higher interest rate and for heavy additional fees.

exchange rates; the creation of confidence in the reserve currencies in which this liquidity would be denominated; and the provision of access to loans for countries facing short-term deficits in their balance of payments.

The World Bank, in contrast, was created to provide loans for major infrastructural investments for which private bank loans would not be available.

Both of these institutions, it is true, were designed to make international capitalism work. But it is also the case that a mixed international economic system would need institutions to perform similar functions, as indeed would a socialist world system. The organizations' structure and operation reflect an unavoidable feature of inter-state relations in the modern world. International morality and the international capacity to work together for common ends are fragile at best. Even while acting to create international institutions of wide utility, states seek as best they can to maximize their own strategic and economic interests.

With regard to the IMF and the World Bank — as also with the United Nations — the powerful have found ways to ensure that their interests in particular will be looked after. Indeed, the introduction of the international monetary arrangements, though of widespread advantage, did entail major special advantages for the United States, an element that cannot be regarded as unintended. Susan Strange, Professor of International Relations at the London School of Economics, made this same point in an 1981 issue of *International Journal*:

The international monetary system is not just a necessary adjunct to the open trading system that must be made to function efficiently if all are to enjoy ... the benefits of the division of labour. Rather, it is a highly political instrument shaping the world's production structure and redistributing risks and opportunities and costs and benefits.

The charters of both institutions firmly safeguard Western dominance, and more particularly American dominance. Voting in both the IMF and the World Bank is weighted, based on quotas that broadly reflect each member-country's economic strength and determine its contribution. This was the price demanded by the rich for their participation. Thus the United States has always had the largest number of votes in the Bank, initially representing approximately 35 per cent of the total and more recently 20 per cent. The United Kingdom is in second place with 7 per cent of the total voting power. (That the United Kingdom has the second highest number of votes rather than Japan or Germany reflects the fact that the quotas were originally set in 1945 and have been adjusted only inadequately since then.) Some decisions require a 75 per cent vote and others — the most important — require 85 per cent. The United States can veto the most crucial decisions and along with several allies can block any vote on issues requiring a 75 per cent vote. A quite similar concentration of power also exists in the IMF.

By custom, the head of the World Bank is American, while the head of the IMF is European. By charter the headquarters of both institutions are in the United States. Both institutions acquiesced to an American request for location in Washington, rather than in New York along with the United Nations.

The World Bank has an executive board of 20 members: The board's 5 permanent members are the countries with the largest quotas and the 15 others are each elected by a cluster of countries with a more or less equal overall number of votes. In the IMF the arrangements are very similar, with an executive board of 21 members, 6 of them permanent. Canada in each case represents a cluster of countries including Ireland and some of the English Caribbean countries. Within that cluster, Canada controls 85 per cent of the votes.

These structural arrangements were not seriously challenged at the time of the founding of the institutions. More recently there has been no possibility for any major restructuring of power within either institution, this for the same reason that initially gave these institutions their structures: The powerful would not have it otherwise.

The workings of the World Bank

The World Bank — known officially as the International Bank for Reconstruction and Development — was not created with the needs of the Third World in mind. Rather, it was created to assist the economic reconstruction and development of war-damaged Western Europe. Very soon however, the European powers could themselves raise the loans they needed from private banks or in other ways. As a result the Bank extended its lending to credit-worthy Third World countries.* The purpose and form of these loans were the same as for the Bank's first loans to European countries. They were aimed at major infrastructural projects, which could not be financed by bank loans but would generate and facilitate additional local and international investment. From its beginning the purpose of the World Bank was therefore to aid and reinforce international and national capitalism rather than to challenge it.

The loans carried lower interest charges (11.6 per cent in 1981) than many developing countries had to pay for funds borrowed from the international capital market — if indeed they could float their own bonds internationally at all. World Bank loans were also of longer duration than private bank loans and involved a welcome seven-year moratorium before repayment had to begin. Thus, while the most rapidly developing LDCs often chose to borrow from capital markets rather than from the World Bank so as to be free of its interfering supervision, for many others the Bank was an attractive and important source of capital.

However, it quickly became clear that many countries were too poor to pass the Bank's stringent tests of credit-worthiness. These poorer countries, led by India, pressed for the establishment of a new international aid agency linked to the United Nations, one that would for them be a source of concessional finance, that is, a source of low-interest development loans. The Western states, rather than rejecting the Indian proposal outright, supported an alternative arrangement: the creation in 1960 of the International Development Association (IDA) as a subsidiary of the World Bank.

IDA quickly became a major source of concessional finance for the poorest countries. IDA credits are available only to the poorest countries — in recent years those with a per capita annual income of less than $730. In fact the major recipients have been the very poorest countries. Unlike the funds for the regular loans of the World Bank, which are borrowed by the Bank on international capital markets, IDA funds are paid to the Bank by its members as part of the multilateral component of

* The reasons for this extension are discussed in Part One of this book, "The Global Impact of the World Bank".

aid programs. These payments are pledged to IDA on a three-yearly basis, with individual contributions constituting an agreed-upon proportion of the American contribution. The sums involved are substantial: IDA dispersed over $2 billion in 1982. Nevertheless, this aid has never constituted more than 2 per cent of the total domestic investment in the countries receiving it. IDA assistance in 1980 accounted for roughly 9 per cent of the total overseas development assistance received by less developed countries. It has therefore been far less substantial than inter-governmental, bilateral aid and vastly less than —indeed in most countries only a tiny fraction of — locally generated investment funds.

The Bank has been able to exert a major influence on many Third World countries. World Bank and IDA credits were initially, and continue predominantly to be, project loans; that is, loans directly intended to meet the foreign exchange component of specific development projects. The Bank therefore has always had an important influence on the identification and shaping of the projects it has assisted. The combination of the Bank staff's high level of professional expertise and its control over significant funds has given it a major influence in regard to projects backed. That influence gradually extended more widely as Bank officials sought to advise governments as well about macro-economic policies. That advice, as noted already, followed a common pattern, emphasizing the benevolent importance of market forces, foreign investment and increased exports. It thus entailed an uncritical and often ideological acceptance of the view that a full integration into the international economic system was in the best interest of the poorest countries.

There are important ambiguities in even that component of the World Bank, IDA, which is clearly of greatest interest to the poorest countries. Some of the main issues are:
1) The continuing influence of the United States on the policies of the Bank, including the country distribution of its credits;
2) The income-distribution consequences of the development strategy urged upon Third World governments by the World Bank and the increased dependency and exposure to exogenous shocks this strategy is likely to involve;
3) The intrusion by the Bank into important issues of national

policy that are properly the responsibility of sovereign governments;
4) The difficulty that development projects have in reaching
and aiding the poorest people in Third World countries, particularly if the projects are large, capital-intensive infrastructural projects — as the World Bank's have tended to be.

This short check list of issues is an aid to sorting out
approaches to the World Bank. One school, emphasizing the
American influence, questions the worth of many Bank projects, opposes the emphasis on exports and sees the benefits of
many of the projects, as well as of the underlying development
strategy being promoted, as accruing to transnational enterprises. This school advocates that Third World countries abandon the Bank and look to internal revolutionary change and
South-South co-operation.

A second group, though highly critical of the Bank, takes
the view that the day of revolutionary transformation is so far
off that intermediate targets must primarily be emphasized.
Moreover, many people in this group are likely to argue that a
decline in self-aggrandizing economic nationalism and the
development of a greater acceptance of global mutual responsibilities are most likely to be accomplished through meaningful incremental advances towards greater international justice and equity. This group has, therefore, emphasized various
reforms, such as a greater sharing of power with poor countries
within the Bank's governing councils and greater flexibility
aimed at development strategies that seek more self-reliant
economies and greater equity. Those within this group have
often advocated the creation of a new structure — in which
Third World countries would play a substantial directing role.

Members within this second group are divided, however, in
their view of the influence that the Bank should seek to have on
the economic policies of Third World governments. Some,
sceptical that the Bank would in fact use such influence wisely
and mindful of the sensitivity of governments to intrusions on
their sovereignty, would like to see a relaxation of the conditions attached by the Bank to the credits it extends. Others, in
contrast, urge that the Bank use the leverage which it has with
Third World governments to promote land reform, greater
equity, and the recognition of basic human rights.

The main activities of IMF

The division of responsibility between the Bank and the IMF in regard to the foreign exchange needs of member states has been, in theory, clear and straightforward. Where the foreign exchange need is developmental — that is, where it arises from a need for a higher rate of productivity-oriented capital investment — a country should turn to the World Bank. Where a shortfall is due to lasting changes in the position of a country within the international system, both the IMF and the Bank, it can be argued, have a role to play. The primary function of the IMF, however, has been to provide foreign exchange credit to member countries who are experiencing short-term, correctable, balance of payment difficulties usually caused by exogenous factors.

The IMF has extended its credits in a number of rather complicated ways. Each member state was assigned a quota based on its gold and dollar reserves, its average imports, the variability of its exports and their ratio to the national income. The quota is the country's contribution to the loaning resources of the IMF. Each country pays in, initially in gold, 25 per cent of its quota and pledges the balance, if called for, in its own currency. The total value of the quotas, in 1982, was approximately U.S.\$62 billion. A country's quota also determines its voting strength in the IMF. The United States deploys, for example, over 126,000 votes, nearly 20 per cent of the total, in contrast to 40 African countries whose total vote is 34,741.

A country's quota, in turn, determines the total credits it is permitted to draw. A country facing a balance of payments shortfall may draw 25 per cent of its quota, called the first quota tranche, with comparative ease. Until 1981 it could request up to three more such tranches. When a country seeks one of these credits, the IMF and the government in question negotiate a stand-by agreement, which embodies a set of policy proposals intended to correct the imbalance. The agreement also includes a series of monetary targets relating, for example, to the new foreign and domestic credit and the budget deficit that the government is pledged to meet. Credits are often "back-end loaded", that is, the larger portion of the credit is disbursed only after the country has demonstrated that it is able to meet the targets specified in the stand-by agreement. The Fund has always been extremely firm with borrowers, cutting off further payments under a stand-by agreement if the targets, for whatever reason, are not met.

In 1981 there were in place some 34 stand-by agreements involving a total of 14.55 billion SDRs. However 9.8 billion of this remained undrawn and 10 of the agreements had been stopped by the Fund because of non-compliance by the creditor with the terms of the stand-by agreement. The conditions required in a stand-by agreement covering second to fourth tranches are typically very severe, requiring a rapid achievement of very significant cuts in the foreign exchange deficits through the implementation of a series of policy measures that are a part of the IMF's prescription for economies in trouble: devaluation, significant cuts in government welfare expenditures, limitations to wage increases and a fuller reliance on market mechanisms.

It is of course true that countries with foreign exchange deficits must quickly correct them. It is also true that this cannot be accomplished without social cost, because substantial cuts have to be made somewhere in the economy. However, the burden of the adjustments typically required by the IMF fall most heavily on the urban poor. The adjustments, therefore, have an adverse impact on income distribution and often provide the impetus for social unrest.

As we've seen, many middle-income Third World countries much prefer to handle a foreign exchange crisis by borrowing from international private banks in order to avoid these onerous conditions. The least developed countries, however, do not have that option: They are not seen as credit-worthy by the banks. Thus, for the least developed countries, the IMF, far from being a source of last resort for credit to cover a balance of payment crisis, is in fact the only possible source.

Over the last several decades the IMF has provided low and high conditionality funding in a variety of additional ways. The most important of these are:

1) Special Drawing Rights (SDRs): The IMF, in 1970, decided to provide a source of liquidity other than U.S. dollars by distributing 9.3 billion "SDRs" to its members over a three-year period. The SDR is a reserve asset whose value is linked to five major currencies — the dollar, mark, yen, franc and pound. A second distribution of SDRs totalling 12 billion occurred over

three years beginning in 1979. Both distributions in no way favoured the poor countries because they were distributed between countries according to the same ratios as their quotas. Nevertheless the distribution of SDRs did bring the LDCs some additional exchangeable reserves.

2) General Arrangements to Borrow (GAB): created in 1962 by the ten industrialized countries and, at least until 1983, available only to them. Their purpose is to safeguard the regular funds of the IMF which might be overwhelmed if several of the countries with substantial quotas sought credits at the same time.

3) Extended Fund Facility: introduced in 1974 as an additional source of credit for a country in serious difficulty because of a need to accomplish major structural changes in the economy. This facility entails the acceptance of strict conditionalities. Its special feature is that its credits cover three-year periods, as opposed to being issued annually like the stand-by agreements.

4) Supplementary Financing Facility and the enlarged access policy: more recently introduced to help countries that had exhausted their tranches. Credits under them involve high conditionality and high cost. The new facility totalled 7.8 billion SDRs contributed equally by OPEC and industrialized countries; enlarged access policy brought a further 10 billion, mainly contributed by Saudi Arabia. This facility and policy permitted the Fund to extend credit tranches under stand-by agreements to a maximum of 150 per cent of quota in any one year and to a total of 450 per cent in any three-year period.

5) Compensatory Financing Facility: introduced in 1962 to provide credit of three to five years' duration to cover shortfalls due to unforeseen difficulties encountered by countries heavily dependent on resource exports. The first 50 per cent of these credits come with low conditionality.

6) The Trust Fund: Interest-free loans over a ten-year period were made available to developing countries from 1979 to 1981 from this source, created by the sale of one-third of the Fund's gold holdings. Its credits are also low conditionality loans.

7) Finally, there have been several specific facilities to help the developing countries cope with crises entirely beyond their control: For example, in 1974 an oil facility was created, worth 6.9 billion SDRs, to provide low conditionality loans to

countries hard hit by oil price increases. In 1981 a similar facility was created to help developing countries cope with the unexpected heavy increases in cereal prices.

These various facilities illustrate the interaction of two contrary tendencies in the Fund. The first, and lesser one, is a responsiveness to Third World needs, illustrated by the introduction of several low conditionality facilities to help LDCs adjust to the impact of factors entirely beyond their control. Clearly, from their standpoint and indeed from the standpoint of evident fairness these were desirable. However, working in the opposite direction and of greater impact has been the responsiveness of the Fund to U.S. and other vigorous Western government pressures to employ leverage on the LDCs. Illustrating this are the new facilities that provide additional funds to LDCs but always with high levels of conditionality attached.

By the late 1970s there was wide agreement amongst those who wished to see the IMF help Third World countries more effectively. Their proposals have tended to include:

1) A redistribution of voting power in the IMF so that the LDCs would have a greater influence.

2) An easing of the conditions imposed and a lengthening of the period for repayment, at least where the deficits that necessitated IMF assistance were not caused by indulgent or misconceived policies by the country seeking credit.

3) Additional SDR allocations, with the major share going to the least developed countries as an almost painless way to augment their reserves.

4) Increased availability to the LDCs of low conditionality funding. This has been available through private loans for the middle-income countries. In contrast the poorer countries have rapidly been thrust into high conditionality borrowing. Even the limited amounts of low conditionality credit available through the IMF have declined over the years as a ratio of these countries' level of international trade.

5) Greater sensitivity to the adverse social and political consequences of the policies required in stand-by and other credit agreements.

6) An adequate expansion of the quotas, a step widely accepted as involving a 100 per cent increase.

7) The incorporation into stand-by agreements of economic

strategies that express social and political values different from those implicit in the export-oriented capitalist stategy so singlemindedly insisted upon by the IMF. The Fund, of course, must insist upon an adjustment program that promises to eliminate the imbalances that necessitated the approach to the Fund in the first instance. But a strategy that distributes the social cost of the adjustment more equitably and involves a more active role for state institutions should be permitted if, as the economists say, "it has its numbers right"; that is, if it is professionally defensible as an alternative way to achieve the required correction of the foreign exchange shortfall.

Global crisis in the Eighties

Since 1980 the global crisis has become far more severe, with the least developed countries being especially hard hit. At the same time the debt crisis, which came to a head in 1982, has posed a most serious threat to those middle-income countries that had borrowed heavily from the commercial banks. How have the World Bank and IMF responded to these simultaneous challenges?

To begin with, both institutions are seriously short of adequate resources, in each case because of a U.S. desire to limit their activities, particularly with reference to the least developed countries. In the case of the World Bank's IDA, the American government reneged on its 1980 commitment to the sixth replenishment, requiring that its contribution instead be spread over four years. As a result of this and of matching withdrawals by other states, IDA, which had expected to have $4.1 billion available in 1982, instead had $2.6 billion. In constant dollars the value of IDA credits extended fell by 39 per cent from 1980 to 1982. The level of American participation in the seventh replenishment, for 1984-86, was expected to be down once again in constant dollar value. At a time of maximum need for imaginative international aid initiatives towards the least developed, IDA has been very severely cut and its morale and sense of purpose badly undermined.

The United States has also been the main opponent of the proposal to increase IMF quotas by at least 100 per cent, even though this move was otherwise very widely supported. The United States finally accepted an increase in quotas of

approximately 50 per cent — a step unlikely to provide sufficient funds for any major increase in IMF credits through
stand-by agreements. Reinforcing this likelihood have been
several other specific changes ensuring that the least developed would not be able to draw on these funds by a further 50
per cent.* The United States recognizes the importance of IMF
credits to the stability of the international system but wants to
exercise more direct control over those credits. On U.S. insistence therefore, instead of the 100 per cent increase in the
quotas, the General Arrangements to Borrow (GAB) would be
expanded to approximately $20 billion and would be a special
fund from which members could seek crisis assistance when —
but only when — their debt problem threatened a systemic
crisis. However, and this is of central significance, control of
these special funds would not be exercised through the regular
IMF machinery but rather would rest with the contributors to
GAB. Thus, to augment its control of debt crisis management,
the United States has severely undermined the functioning
multilateralism of the Fund.

Although they would be doing less for the least developed
countries, the Bank and the Fund were more insistent than ever
on exercising close control over the development and related
policies of governments receiving their loans and credits. J. de
Larosière, managing director of the Fund, boasted in late 1982
that 80 per cent of the new IMF credits in that year were on high
conditionality terms. This contrasts with a percentage of
approximately 25 per cent in 1974 after the first major oil price
increases. In pursuit of the same objective — closer control —
and on U.S. insistence, there has been no further allocation at
all of SDRs, let alone an allocation primarily directed to the
least developed.

Perhaps the most important relevant development in these
last several years has been the heavy involvement of the IMF in
complex arrangements made to manage the debt crisis facing
Mexico, Brazil, Argentina and other middle-income countries

* Two of these changes can be noted briefly. First, the quotas for many
least developed countries would in fact increase by nearer to 35 per
cent, with 50 per cent being the overall average increase in all quotas.
Second, it was expected that the right to borrow up to a limit of 450
per cent of quota over three years would be significantly cut.

— countries that borrowed very heavily from the commercial banks but hardly at all from the IMF. In the recession following the 1979-80 oil price increases those countries chose to cope with their balance of payment crisis by making additional short-term loans from the commercial banks. When the recession did not rapidly lift, they quickly faced a major debt crisis.

This kind of debt crisis develops through at least three stages:

1) The crisis begins with an inability to repay foreign loans as they fall due — not a new phenomenon for banks dealing with Third World countries. The problem is handled by a negotiated agreement to "roll over" the loans.

2) The private banks, for whatever reason, grow anxious about being over-extended in the Third World and seek ways to cut their commitments. The renegotiation of loans becomes more difficult in these circumstances. However, where debt levels are very high, as with Mexico, Brazil and Argentina, the banks almost have no option. For example, in early 1983 they quietly accepted a unilateral Argentinian decision to convert one and two-year loans into five-year loans. This was preferable to writing off the loans.

3) Finally, a country gets to the point where it needs not only to roll over loans that are due but also must borrow in order to meet the interest payments it owes. This clearly is a genuine crisis: Unless there is an early and substantial improvement in the foreign exchange earnings of the country, the crisis will merely deepen with each new quarter.

Mexico reached this final stage in its debt crisis in September 1982. Brazil and Argentina arrived at it a few months later. That stage, however, proved to be just as much a crisis to its creditors. For example, by 1982 nine U.S. banks had extended no less than $80 billion of loans to Third World countries, an amount far in excess of their total equity capital. Thus not only is the stability of one or several major middle-income countries involved but so also is the viability of some major banks and, therefore as well, the stability of the international financial system.

That system has shown great ingenuity in seeking to avoid catastrophe. The IMF has not played the leading role in this but has been an active participant in the whole operation. The typical pattern is that either the United States or a small group of major creditors extend an additional short-term loan to get the country out of its immediate balance of payments crisis. The major parties involved then assemble an elaborate inter-related package of additional loans. This package usually includes special loans from ad hoc American government sources, for example a loan organized by the U.S. Federal Reserve Bank and participated in by other Western central banks; a loan by the Bank for International Settlement, the international bank serving the central banks; a major stand-by credit by the IMF; and an agreement by the country's creditors that the loans due will be extended, that credit levels will not be cut and that a major new loan will be made.

The debts involved are far too large for an IMF credit by itself to meet the need. The IMF's role, however, is more than merely its contribution of credit, which usually constitutes about 25 per cent of the total package. More important, the conditions that the IMF attaches to its credit, once accepted, are an encouragement to the banks that they dare extend themselves even further. In addition the IMF has several times made its stand-by agreement conditional on an agreement from the private banks to also become further involved.

The example of the Mexican debt crisis shows how these arrangements work. The Mexican arrangements had these components:

1) a $600 million emergency loan by a small number of the most involved U.S. banks;

2) a $1 billion advance by the U.S. Commodity Credit Corporation on future deliveries of Mexican produce;

3) a $1 billion advance by the U.S. government on future delivery of oil;

4) a $1.85 billion credit organized by the U.S. Federal Reserve Bank; this was dependent, however, on

5) a $3.85 billion credit from the IMF Extended Fund Facility; dependent, however, on

6) $4.4 billion in additional loans by the commercial banks that were already Mexico's creditors.

No one should see such an arrangement as other than a rather desperate stopgap to avoid a disastrous default. One would need vast confidence in the omniscience of the Fund to believe that the conditions it attaches to its credit ensure recovery. Indeed, several risks were immediately visible. To begin with, there was a strong possibility that the debtor country would be unable politically to pursue the austerity measures insisted upon by the Fund. In addition, without a real global recovery the country would both fail to meet the IMF targets and again soon face an identical crisis.

However, if you look primarily at the needs of the least developed countries, the importance of this continuing story of debt crisis rests elsewhere. The preoccupation with the crisis in middle-income countries has so overextended the Fund as to lessen its capacity financially and professionally to concern itself effectively with the needs of the least developed. The U.S. government, the commercial banks and central banks have become far more effective than the Fund as intervenors and mobilizers of credit. A structured, institutionalized multilateralism in which some scope exists for the least developed countries has therefore been weakened. Nevertheless, the Fund is still extraordinarily involved in the complex and precarious debt arrangements for some of the largest of the Third World debtors.

Finally, all of this has further reinforced the dominance of the particular ideology embodied in the IMF and World Bank. This ideology offers little to the least developed countries and to the poor in middle-income countries. Despite pressing human need for major and imaginative initiatives to make both institutions more responsive to the needs of the world's poor, the immediate reality is that the Third World and in particular the poorest within it are likely to experience a serious deterioration in the assistance they receive. This is a common refrain in this volume, as it often is in other comment on the World Bank and International Monetary Fund.

Impressions of an IMF/World Bank Meeting

R.T. Naylor

On the surface, the annual IMF-World Bank extravaganza, as held in Toronto in 1982, bore a close affinity to a Shriner's Club convention. But appearances can be deceiving. For there were two separate events of vastly different orders of importance occurring simultaneously.

Certainly the vast majority of the estimated 11,000 officially-recognized participants were lower-order functionaries of the participating governments and financial institutions. They, together with a motley assortment of spies and hustlers, and cheered on by some 850 reporters and media technicians, began arriving after the most important business had been transacted, for a mass meeting that attracted most of the public attention.

But the major power brokers of the world of high finance — private and public — were also represented. They came to attend the other, less well-known but far more important event — the inner sanctum meeting of treasury officials and top international bankers, to which delegates from countries seeking debt relief were periodically summoned to make their pleas and hear the judgements.

However, the annual meetings have other functions besides debating such mundane matters as whether or not the international financial system is likely to survive. The subsidiary events were actually the ones that attracted the most attention and to which the delegates, guests and visitors dedicated the bulk of their time. These other events were largely the creation of the nimble imaginations of the Canadian hosts, private and public, who spared little effort in devising schemes for enlightening the minds and lightening the pockets of their guests.

For the largest Canadian banks the event was a public relations coup, conferring on them *de jure* recognition of their entry into the big leagues and giving them an opportunity to entertain their foreign counterparts, thus establishing both a claim for reciprocity at another time and place and a higher position in the queue for business in the inter-bank market. Bankers' receptions closely resemble potlach ceremonies, both in format and in function, and those sponsored by the Canadian banks — up to their eyeballs in the sovereign lending business — were no exception.

For the Government of Ontario it was a chance to sell the province's virtues, and its hydro giant's bonds, to prospective international investors at a time when unemployment (and its potentially adverse political fallout) was on the rise, and when generally weak bond markets might well be skittish over absorbing more of the burden and waste of the province's nuclear program. The sales pitch took various forms, ranging from giving out free rides on Toronto's "clean, safe" subway system to a massive reception at Queen's Park.

If the meetings had taken place in Montreal one could be sure that its irrepressible mayor would have seized the opportunity to demonstrate the city's solidarity with the developing nations of the world by escalating its debt load in order to leave behind another pharaonic and publicly-funded monument to his own past. But Ontario and Toronto are quite different in character. And provincial premier smiling Bill Davis sees history in terms of the *Guinness Book of Records*. Hence his decision to follow up on the most-people-in-a-telephone-booth caper by staging a reception for all the delegates, guests, visitors and assorted, local party-hacks at once. In an unprecedented effort, while the Toronto press exulted, 10,000 people gathered in the provincial parliament building to drink Ontario wine and consequently, one surmises, to relieve the congestion in city hotels by shifting part of it to local hospitals.

The federal government was not far behind. Indeed, sensing the importance of the Ontario nuclear program for the future of its CANDU reactor, the ruling Liberals apparently chose to collaborate with Premier Davis's Progressive Conservative attempt to massage more money out of the international capital market. Ottawa most agreeably held its grand "Canadian-Gala-Canadien" reception in Toronto's new Roy Thomson Hall — the ghastly grey interior of which resembles nothing more closely than the core of a nuclear reactor, complete with the threat of fuel rods about to descend from the ceiling.

On its own, the federal government also tried its hand at salesmanship. Its Canadian International Development Agency (CIDA), intent on increasing its profile in front of both the Canadian business community and potential buyers of Canadian goods, set up an information trailer across the road from the Sheraton Centre meeting grounds. The purpose was ostensibly not only to inform the visitors about Canadian products but also to try to keep Canadian businesses from inadvertently insulting their foreign guests by, for example, offering the head of the Iranian central bank a ham sandwich and a beer.

The federal government also staged a panel discussion to convince international investors that contrary to what the *Wall Street Journal* thinks, the Foreign Investment Review Agency (FIRA) and the National Energy Policy are not the greatest threats to private property rights since the *Communist Manifesto* was published.

On the other hand, for the thousands of mostly male minor-level functionaries at the receiving end of these attentions, the event provided an opportunity to mix business with whatever small pleasure someone from Paris or Singapore could derive from a visit to Toronto. They could get away from their wives for a week, empty their expense accounts and ogle at Federal Reserve Bank chairman Paul Volcker as he swept imperiously through the throng. Or spread the latest gossip about David Rockefeller and preen themselves in public before a popeyed and largely uncomprehending press.

Typically, the Toronto newspapers were full of chatter about the spending habits of the delegates, the sin of drinking past the official 1:00 A.M. closing, and how well the bankers knotted their ties. The gloom that the professional incompetence of the press engendered was partly relieved by one enterprising reporter who had enough imagination to go looking for a hooker who would tell him "what these guys are really like". The mood was relieved too by the presence of a contingent of National Democratic Party head Lyndon Larouche's minions, representing the view that the IMF meetings were but the latest development in a conspiracy led by the British Royal Family and embracing David Rockefeller, the environmentalist movement and the KGB to undermine technical progress and destroy the industrial power of the U.S.A.

Also in the category of entertainment was the annual Per Jacobsson Lecture, this year delivered by the effervescent Gerald Bouey, Governor of the Bank of Canada. He is best known as the man who has piously exhorted Canadians since 1975 on the evils of overoptimistic market expectations and on the effects of inflation in eroding the moral foundations of Judaeo-Christian civilization. Indeed, in its energetic drive to defeat inflation, the Bank of Canada managed to reduce it from an annual rate of about 6.9 per cent in 1975-76 to about 11.5 per cent in 1981-82, while at the same time losing track of the money supply altogether.

The Governor finally stood before the lecture audience to declare that monetary targeting in Canada had not been successful — that an anti-inflationary climate will generate cutbacks in production, business failures and increases in unemployment rather than better cost and price performance.

Despite this confession and the devastating state to which monetary policy as practised by his bank has brought to the Canadian economy, Bouey wound up his extraordinarily illogical dissertation to the assembled money lenders with the rallying cry, "We must be determined not to temporize with inflation." It was like an Alcoholics Anonymous appeal to an audience knowingly served triple martinis as a starter.

All this was for public consumption. In private, matters were much more serious as talk in corridors and private parties turned to multi-billion dollar disasters and how to unload them onto the taxpaying public. It turned as well to the topic of mutual accommodation. For one of the little publicized features of the annual IMF meetings is its role as an adjunct of the Eurocurrency inter-bank market.

Bank loans, to final customers and to other banks, are rationed not just by price, but also by a queueing process with second loans becoming increasingly important when, as in recent times, the volume of lending is declining in the face of deteriorating corporate and country balance sheets. The IMF meetings provide an opportunity for the bankers to size each other up and shift places in the queue.

This is not to suggest that visitors and guests completely ignored the formal program of speeches by the ministers of finance of the participating countries. Many were indeed present as the honourable politicians droned on and on from the podium, reading speeches that were already printed and distributed and which (with the exception of the Iranian delegate's) were virtually devoid of interest, content or both. But attendance tended to be in inverse relationship to the existence of more entertaining pursuits elsewhere. Those who were present spent most of their time reading newspapers, doing crossword puzzles or hobnobbing with old friends.

Meanwhile on the street outside, a populist gut impulse to dislike bankers manifested itself in a number of ways. Taxi drivers complained of 25 cent tips; merchants accused bankers of being tightwads; and demonstrations by political powerhouses such as the Social Creditors ("bankers are crooks") and the Communist Party of Canada (Marxist-Leninist) militants ("bankers are imperialist blood-suckers") rocked the foundations of the Canadian political system.

More to the point, the official opening of the IMF meetings coincided with Labour Day, and the organizers of the annual parade marched their ranks down University Avenue and turned right onto Queen Street. Apart from the obvious political symbolism in the choice of directions for the turn, the organizers, in truly Canadian fashion, missed the opportunity for some great street theatre, since a left turn on Queen would have marched them in front of the Sheraton Centre and paraded them past the assembled bankers.

Can one imagine the French, Italian or Spanish labour movement, or dozens of others, missing or deliberately avoiding such an opportunity? But then no self-respecting European or Latin American labour movement would be parading at the beginning of September instead of on May Day, and none outside the Soviet Bloc would have permitted the parade, as it was, to be escorted by military bands. Perhaps it was intended as a none-too-subtle message to the Third World delegates inside — for where the IMF goes, military regimes and the shackling of free labour movements all too often follow.

PART ONE
After Bretton Woods: Global Jeopardy

The Rise and Decline of the IMF

Gerald K. Helleiner

Gerald Helleiner is a professor of economics at the University of Toronto and chairman of the Commonwealth Advisory Group. In 1981-82 he was a member of the Tanzanian Advisory Group, which attempted to develop alternative approaches to the IMF's structural adjustment program. He has published numerous studies on economic development and international trade, most recently as author of International Economic Disorder: Essays in North-South Relations *(1981) and editor of* For Good or Evil: Economic Theory and North-South Relations *(1983).*

Let me begin by talking about the origins of the present international economic order, such as it is, and the adaptations made over the course of the sixties and seventies, concluding with the raging debates now underway in downtown Toronto, and the prospects for the international financial system — with the IMF playing a role perhaps not as central as some think in the outcome.

The present economic order stems from the chaos not simply of the Second World War but also of the great depression. The purposes of the original founders of the three key institu-

tions* which have to this day governed the international economy were to prevent a relapse into massive unemployment,
international chaos, international bullying, the spheres of
influence, competitive search for markets and competitive
devaluation and protectionism — everyone trying to export
one's own unemployment to one's neighbour — culminating in
the war itself. It was a determination to try to prevent that kind
of series of events from ever coming again that led men of that
time — men of unusual vision and commitment — to sit down
and, with extremely noble purposes, even before the war was
over try to put together the elements of a system that might last
and protect at least for some years the world economy from
those sorts of disasters — disasters, I need hardly add, that as
always hit the weakest the hardest.

The original notion was that the World bank was to deal
with development finance, that is, to provide long-term
project-oriented money for the building of dams and utilities.
The IMF was to provide temporary finance — temporary credit,
short-term liquidity — meant to prevent nations from taking
certain actions in response to temporary diffculties, actions
that would be unnecessary and harmful to themselves and the
rest of the world.

It's true that at the time these institutions were created, the
developing countries were scarcely there in any significant
way: Their interests were not considered. Most probably it
wasn't the case that the great powers were actively malevolent
to the interests of the developing countries; they just didn't see
them as particularly important.

From the first the developing countries paid back their
debts fairly quickly. In fact, the results are such that when you
study the numbers you can see periods such as 1978 and 1979
when all the members of the IMF were collectively repaying
more than they were getting from the IMF. That's perfectly normal in a system which is designed to provide temporary assistance for temporary problems.

* The International Monetary Fund (IMF); International Bank for
Reconstruction and Development (World Bank); and General Agreement on Tariffs and Trade (GATT).

As events emerged in the 1960s and the developing countries in particular came on the scene, there were a number of adaptations made in the functioning of the IMF, some of them designed specifically to address the specific problems of poorer countries. The poorer countries always said those adaptations were inadequate, but at least they were more than they had before.

The most important change was probably in the introduction of a Compensatory Financing Facility, which provided virtually automatic — or at the least, low conditionality — short-term finance in circumstances where a country's export earnings could be demonstrated to be below its trend of export earnings. This change was certainly inadequate, a lot of things were wrong with it, but still it was an attempt to do something for primary producing countries that had suffered the biggest ups and downs in prices received for their exports.

In the late 1960s, under the pressure of a deteriorating monetary system based on the dollar, the IMF even set out to create a new form of international money, a new international reserve asset. This was to assist countries that try to protect themselves against temporary problems by holding reserves. This means holding foreign exchange, that is, hard currency, other people's money: usually dollars in the post-Second-World-War period, pounds in the earlier years. (Nowadays it's still mainly dollars but increasingly the Deutschmark, Swiss franc and other convertible currencies. They hold gold as well, the price of which sometimes bounces around like crazy from one day to the next.) And in addition to these reserves, a country in temporary difficulties can go for credit to friends, allies, friendly central banks and, following the agreement in 1944, the IMF.

In addition to these sources of reserves, by the stroke of a pen the IMF created a new asset called Special Drawing Rights (SDRs) which it made available to all its members according to their quota-based borrowing rights in the IMF system. These new quota-based rights were distributed on the same basis as voting rights, which were themselves based on power and economic strength. This meant that the poor countries got a little less than 30 per cent of these new paper assets. They simply gave these SDRs to all the member countries, providing thereby automatic, unconditional borrowing rights at low interest rates, to be used when necessary to overcome temporary difficulties. The plan was that these would ultimately replace the dollar. It's quite expressly stated in the second amendment to the articles of agreement of the IMF, which followed the Jamaica agreement in 1974, that it is the aspiration of all the members that the SDR would become the principal reserve asset of the international monetary system, that it would replace gold and the dollar. This was a very farsighted and even visionary step.

The move towards "long-term adjustment"

In the 1970s and 1980s it has become more and more difficult to tell what's a short-term problem and what's a long-term problem, to distinguish a permanent problem calling for major adjustment and long-term financing from a situation where short-term funding should come in to tide countries over for a temporary period. The recessions are bigger and longer, the world has stopped growing at a rapid rate as it did for the previous 25 years, there were two massive oil price increases as well, plus massive terms-of-trade deteriorations especially in the poorest countries. Given these situations and the problems they create, it wasn't evident that those countries could fully repair themselves. So the question became: Is this a long-term problem, appropriate for the World Bank and donors? Or is it a short-term problem appropriate for the IMF?

Indeed, whenever there was a permanent deterioration in the external environment — like the one the poor countries saw in the 1970s — it would be nice if everyone chipped in and said "Oh! Fine, this is a difficult problem and we're going to help you out. Short or long, it's not your fault. We'll push in the resources and help you." But that is not in fact the way the world works. Instead, if the situation is seen as a permanent state of deterioration, the *necessary* reaction of those who are subject to it is to adjust to it. You may adjust in many ways but if you have collapsing prices for what you sell and rising prices for what you buy, the most obvious thing you must ultimately do is to sell more and buy less, cut back your imports one way or another, and expand exports one way or another to finance the remaining imports that you somehow can't escape and must continue to have. As a short-term solution, during the time that it takes to adjust these permanent deteriorations you can deflate, you can cut the budget, you can devalue, you can cut back investment programs, you can reduce wages, you can cut consumption, you can do everything that it's necessary to do to reduce demand to get your imports down. If you don't have the time to adjust and nobody is offering you credit to allow you to adjust in an orderly, planned fashion, you *will* adjust — because you have no option — in a chaotic, disorderly, costly fashion. But by doing so, you don't in fact adjust at all, because one of the elements of adjustment is to keep investment going; you can't adjust if in the process you are stopping investment.

Now the only way in which you are likely to adjust to a major, permanent change is through the provision of the necessary investment, probably requiring some external financing, to allow you to do it in an orderly and planned fashion. The IMF, then, has seen itself traditionally as providing short-run credit to countries in temporary difficulties, to prevent them from cutting their imports when they don't really have to.

In the 1970s, however, some of the problems facing the IMF's members are major changes which appear to be of the permanent type, or at least much longer-term than anything the IMF has felt it necessary to respond to in the past. The IMF has been trying to adjust to provide longer-term finance, to provide advice and requirements for investment programs and structural adjustment on the supply side, not simply demanding deflation which has been its traditional practice.

At the same time that the IMF has come to the realization that it must offer longer-term help, that it must help countries to adjust by providing credit for longer periods — by not simply discussing demand but also discussing investment programs for the supply side — at the same time that's been happening, the World Bank, the long-term people, have come to the same realization and said, "My gosh, they've got massive problems. They cannot deal with more projects of the kind that the Bank has been accustomed to funding because they haven't got the imports in the short run to pay for the spare parts required for the last project. They must have support — general structural adjustment support." So the Bank has been moving into so-called "structural adjustment lending", at the same time that the Fund has been moving into longer-term, more supply-oriented programs, and there is very little difference in fact between the programs of this kind at the Bank and the Fund today. They in fact co-operate now extremely closely, much more closely than ever before in the provision of advice and finance in respect to structural adjustment of this kind.

The role of the commercial banks

In the 1970s there was a major change in the international monetary scene which does not relate to the behaviour of the IMF or the Bank or their origins, their purposes; it's instead something that just grew. I speak not of the collapse of fixed exchange rates, which most people think of as the major monetary happening of the 1970s. The major change is the massive rise of the private commercial banking system in its Eurocurrency market form. The banks came to function in international lending essentially unregulated, unsupervised, outside the borders of their own countries, expanding their credit at a rate of over 20 per cent a year for the last ten years. Large parts of these loans were directed to the developing countries, the better off ones: Many of them used the opportunity to tap the private commercial banking system in the 1970s to *avoid* the IMF, which they preferred not to deal with because of the advice that they sometimes got and didn't particularly want from it. What happened in the 1970s was that the basic monetary function for which the IMF was created in the post-Second-World-War years was taken over by the international commercial banks.

As the IMF was shunted aside in this area of providing short-term balance of payments assistance, that is in the area of the provision of world liquidity, in favour of the commercial banks, still another set of actors became increasingly important and they are today enormously important. In downtown Toronto today they are probably more important than the IMF itself, and that is the major governments of the industrialized world. When some countries get into short-term balance of payments difficulties it is not the IMF that bails them out, it is not the commercial banks that bail them out, it's the governments of the Western world assisting those they particularly want to assist, for reasons that have to do either with strategic considerations or the survival and support of the entire international system.

When Hungary got into difficulty earlier this year because the banks were pulling out their money a little too fast, it was the governments of the Western world that stepped in, *fast*, to bail it out. Mexico is a major trouble spot, along with Argentina, Brazil and other countries to follow, but the IMF has neither the resources nor the speed to bail them out. They will be bailed out, as they are even now being bailed out, primarily by quick, short-run action coming from official institutions of the major Western powers. Those institutions can act much faster, they can mobilize funds over the telephone without long political hassles, without having to make voting arrangements, and they do so on a much less formal and multilateral basis. So what has happened is that this carefully constructed system for the provision of inter-governmental credit to tide all the members of the system over temporary problems, has been replaced increasingly in recent years by a system which is private and, when governmental, bilateral. It's been many, many years — decades — since we've been prepared within nations to tolerate the risks and the inequities associated with the total privatization of credit in monetary systems. But that's what we have increasingly got at the international level. The inequities are clear enough: Private banks do not lend to people who are not considered credit-worthy, so Mr. Jamal (finance minister of Tanzania) and all his friends in the poorest parts of the world get no credit from the commercial banks, nor *will* they get any. In fact, there are a lot of countries on the borderline which had been getting some money from the banks, which are now being shut out because of the banks' increasing nervousness about their exposure in these countries. So there will be in the 1980s fewer countries getting commercial bank credit for their balance of payments problems than there were in the 1970s.

This system is grossly inequitable in its distribution, and the credit it provides developing countries is concentrated in some relatively well-off ones. It's risky because banks behave like a herd of elephants: When times are good, in they go and the psychology is one of support, the credit goes pouring in. But when things turn a little shaky, out they go just as fast, and the highest penalty is paid by the bank that's the last to go. The object of a banker is not to promote socially-responsible behaviour, in spite of what is being advocated for them downtown this week, where the managing director of the IMF is asking the banks to be responsible. The Bank for International Settlements, the central bank for the central bankers, in its annual report this year, said, in effect, "Bankers, for heaven's sake be responsible. Don't pull your money out in lurches this way. It's dangerous." But it's not the job of a bank to be socially responsible; it's the job of a bank to protect its stockholders and its depositors. Some of them may panic — they get nervous, they move their funds out, so do others, and one thing leads to another and everyone contracts credit — it may be even worse of course if depositors run for their money as they did in the 1930s — and the penalty is paid not just by the developing countries that have been borrowing, it will be paid by all of us.

When banks cut back their credit they cut back on every form of credit. If the crunch comes it will be the investment program of the small businessmen and the mortgages and whatnot here in Canada that are cut just as much as overseas lending. It happened in the 1930s and it could happen again. That's the major link between the international meeting going on downtown and our domestic economy now: If our financial system falls apart *we* will pay as much as the Argentinians and the Mexicans and the rest. We will recover faster, probably, they won't get back into the credit markets for 45 years or so, they didn't last time — but it would be foolhardy to think that we have somehow overcome the history of the last couple of hundred years in which there have been repeated financial hiccups of this kind, and I can assure you there is now exteme nervousness about these risks.

So while the IMF was to provide these short-term forms of assistance, what has actually emerged is that the private banks and Western governments do that job. The way in which international credit for this purpose has been expanded bears no relation to the way in which it was originally planned to occur. There have been major gains for those who happen to produce gold — South Africa and the U.S.S.R. — and major gains for those who provide the money that other people hold in reserve — basically the United States. The commercial banks, above all, have increasingly been "residualizing" what was the original multilateral scheme.

IMF: cutbacks in a period of crisis

The poorest countries have no gold, they have very little foreign exchange in reserve, they have no informal credit arrangements with major governments in the Western world. They won't quickly be bailed out because they're not strategic and they don't really matter to anybody. They have principally today the IMF to rely on. There's no one else. There's one other possibility: They may not pay their bills and a lot of them haven't been doing that — arrears have been building up on import payments, in some cases two and a half years long already — but the IMF is their lender of first resort, they haven't got any options.

When it comes to getting credit from the IMF, it can come in either a low or a high conditional form. Some of the credit that comes through the IMF system is virtually automatic — the creation of SDRs was of that kind, the first "tranche" of borrowings from the IMF are of that kind, the compensatory financing facility I mentioned, to tide countries over primary export fluctuations, is of that kind. But the rest are highly conditional upon programs which the IMF itself approves and it is the poorest countries therefore which are most rapidly thrown into the arms of the high conditionality facilities of the IMF. The poorest countries are the ones that have the most difficulty getting automatic finance because the automatic component of the IMF system, of the world system, which is available to the poorest, is very, very small *and falling*.

Since 1979 these poor countries have been hit by an absolutely brutal deterioration in the terms of trade — and the word "brutal" is actually used by the IMF in its reports. The IMF also says in its reports that the problems of the poor countries are not of their own making. The typical export of the least developed countries has dropped in value between 30 and 40 per cent in the last four or five years. There have been five successive years of terms-of-trade deterioration and the volume of their imports has been massively cut. In response to what are seen as "severe shocks" — the oil price increases, for instance — these countries have made far greater adjustments than any ever contemplated by developed countries. So when there is talk about the need to adjust, it rings a little hollow for countries that in 1981 had already cut their imports on average by 7 per cent, and that had cut them in the previous year as well. Some countries had already cut imports by over 20 per cent.

What's happened in the last two years? A decision was taken in the IMF to issue no more SDRs — which was supposed to be the principal reserve asset of the system — not gold, dollars, commercial banks. The last SDRs were issued on the first of January 1981. This week again, downtown (the IMF meeting of September 1982), the decision was taken that there would be no new ones.

These SDRs are the principal source of *unconditional* liquidity — they matter the most to the poorest because those countries have no alternatives. The Group of 24, the developing country caucus, has begged the IMF repeatedly to resume the creation of SDRs; they were to be the centre of the system: What happened to them?

The "orthodox" argument is that the creation of SDRs in the present world circumstances is likely to be inflationary. But the contribution of the SDRs to the expansion of world liquidity since they were created is roughly one per cent of the total expansion in world liquidity. It's absolutely absurd to suggest that the creation of SDRs now, even if they were three times larger than those created in the past, would have any effect on inflation whatsoever. So the argument now has become that to create SDRs would offer an inflationary *signal* to the world.

Second, in the last couple of years, the Trust Fund's activities have stopped. The Trust Fund was another source of either unconditional or low conditional credit for the poorest countries, and came out of the sale of some of the IMF's gold. The IMF sold off about a third of its gold at the time when they were arguing that the SDR was going to be the centre of the system. Consistent with this aspiration they decided they were going to give up this "barbarous relic", gold, and become more rational. So they sold gold and turned over a portion of the proceeds for use in the poorest countries. That "kitty" has dried up and I haven't heard anyone downtown this week discussing the uses of the remaining hundred million ounces of gold still owned by the IMF — at today's prices worth about $50 billion.

Thirdly, with the shock of 1979 onward — oil and global

recession, the worst since the 1930s — the conditionality associated with IMF programs has vastly turned around from that
which was present in the last recession of 1974-75. The last
time around the IMF organized itself so that two-thirds of the
credit it provided was virtually automatic, low conditionality.
This time around: only one-fifth.

Fourthly, since the Reagan administration was inaugurated
— I don't know whether this is a coincidence — there has been
a sharp cutback in IMF credit provisions to its members and a
noticeable change in the terms of lending. A recent paper from
the independent Institute for International Economics, a highly
prestigious "establishment" body in Washington whose key
people are at the meetings downtown this week, documents the
reduction in the number of credits from two-and-a-half a month
to one a month since the middle of 1981, the shorter length of
IMF programs since about October 1981, and the increased
toughness of all the programs.

In 1982, and here's a fact concealed in the IMF annual report
— certainly not purposely, it just happens that way — there was
an incredible cutback in the credit the IMF offers to its members. The annual report goes up to April 30th, the end of the
financial year. There are later figures available, they're no secret, they just aren't in the annual report. To carry the numbers
through to the end of June and compare the first six months of
1982 to the first six months of the previous year, there's been a
cut in new IMF commitments to its members, new lending commitments, to one-fifth of what they were in 1981: That's gross,
that's new commitments. But they have also cancelled enormous amounts, $2.5 billion worth, so that in fact allowing for
the cancellations, the IMF in the first six months of 1982 was
taking out more money than it was putting in. How can this be?
Is the world recovering from a recession? Are we trying to
tighten things? Is 1982 a year in which the body we set up for
contracyclical purposes and stabilization should cut back on
credits? It's perverse, and this independent report says it's perverse. Of course it's perverse — unless it's overridden by an
overwhelming determination to beat down inflation and that
must be the rationale. Which must lead you to ask, at whose
cost?

The U.S. vs. credit expansion: attack on the poor

The remaining main issue at the moment — beside the fact that the developing countries want SDRs, they want easier conditions, they want a resumption of lending, they want a higher proportion of low conditionality credit — is quota size itself. The obvious means of expanding liquidity for the system, and that to which all the members have agreed in principle, is just to expand borrowing rights or quotas. When quotas rise by multilateral agreement, borrowing rights rise and the automatic access rises, because these are linked to the size of the quota. The developing countries have therefore predictably been calling for a substantial increase in the size of the quotas. There appears to have been agreement at these 1982 meetings that there will be a "substantial" increase but what substantial means remains to be fought out, essentially between the United States and the rest. The United States insists that there is not a great need for expanded liquidity because the commercial banks can basically handle the international liquidity system. Commercial banks, however, do not help the poor.

Those who oppose larger credit expansion again say that it will be inflationary. And again, if you tell them that it has never been inflationary, that the IMF is not at the centre of the international financial system, the banks now are, they say alright, but credit expansion will set off inflationary *signals*.

The danger is that the clock is being so rapidly rolled back. The IMF has been massively weakened relative to the private banks, who are both inequitable and jerky in their behaviour. The United States is consciously promoting an IMF which serves primarily as a policeman and lender of last resort in support of an international system which is run basically on private banking and strategic principles. It argues now for a small quota increase, coupled with special bailout arrangements for abnormal circumstances or crises. This would have the effect of bailing out banks while minimizing the credit available on low conditionality terms for the poorest. I should add that meanwhile in the General Agreement on Tariffs and Trade the U.S. is being consistent; it's pushing for freer access on the part of its bankers and investors to all the members of the GATT on the grounds that this would be a liberalization of trade in services.

The United States today is consistent, whatever else they are. They make no apologies for their stance: Free markets, foreign investment are best for everybody; the poor basically should just pull themselves together. Their cutting of the IDA budget is consistent with that: The massive 35 per cent cut last year in loans to the poorest is a result. And they're not particularly enthusiastic about multilateral government institutions, but if there are to be governmental institutions at the international level better they be with immediate allies, rich and poor, but reliable.

I believe the U.S. is now isolated in its extremism. Even Mrs. Thatcher's government appears genuinely horrified, certainly about U.S. behaviour with respect to IDA and to a substantial degree with respect to its behaviour around the size of the quota increase. The British don't want a quota increase as large as the one the developing countries want, but they sure want it bigger than the U.S. has in mind. The U.S. is isolated now, as it has been in the Law of the Sea, the World Health Organization on infant formula, East-West trade and all of that.

But let me assure you, however bad this sounds, and however modest the reforms that I am suggesting sound to you, these will not deal in any case with the longer-run needs of the developing countries, with major reforms of the kind that have been discussed in the United Nations and other fora for years and years. The role of the IMF in the monetary system, in the building of a new order, a *real* new order dealing with trade, commodity markets, rules for transnationals and the whole range of things, is not that great. If anyone is running the system now it is again — as it was in the thirties — the banks and powerful governments. The risks are of the same kinds of inequities, chaos, bullying that we had in the thirties.

The Global Impact of the World Bank

R. Cranford Pratt

Cranford Pratt is a professor of political science at the University of Toronto. He also worked for a number of years in Tanzania, including a stint as a member of the Tanzanian Advisory Group from 1981 to 1982. He is author of The Critical Phase in Tanzania 1945-68 *(1976) and, with Bismarck Mwansasu, of* Towards Socialism in Tanzania *(1979).*

A few years ago the image of the world as a global village was widely popular. It is an evocative image, but it's also enormously misleading. We can claim to be a global village only in the sense that the industrialized countries are able to reach out globally to find the resources they need and sell the products they manufacture. However, our world has neither the institutions of self-rule nor the sense of community and mutual responsibility that the image of a global village suggests. Our world, dominated as it is by the nation-state system, with that system in turn dominated by the rich and powerful within it, has developed neither the will nor the institutions to ensure that global economic independence operates with tolerable fairness.

We have witnessed over the last 20 years a monumental failure of both international morality and of nation-states to co-operate effectively for common humane objectives. Let me first underline the dimensions of this failure. For the first time in history it is now within humankind's technological capacity to eliminate absolute poverty by the turn of the century, and this is possible through a global effort that would not be at all overwhelming. But, not only are we very far indeed from that objective, we are in fact not even moving towards it.

The World Bank recently estimated that by the year 2000 there would still be at least 600 million persons around the world living in conditions of absolute poverty. There will be growth over the next 20 years but the Bank expects so little of it to find its way to the non-oil-producing developing countries that their per capita income will hardly increase at all. This is the global context in which the World Bank operates.

The ideology of resource transfers

The World Bank is undoubtedly the most important institution that the international system has been able to create to ameliorate this massive poverty and to promote substantial development in poorer countries. We must first explain this rather ironic fact because, as we know, the World Bank was not created with the problems of the Third World in mind and has always been dominated by the Western powers. The explanation lies in two primary and two reinforcing factors. The first primary factor has been the dominant ideological influence in most Western governments — what can be labelled as international liberal capitalism or international Keynesianism. Central to this ideology or world view is the conviction that economic development in Third World countries is in the economic interests of the already-developed nations. Thus, just as it was seen to be in the American interest in 1945 that Europe should recover after the war, so it was also seen to be in the interest of the industrialized countries generally that development should be promoted in the Third World.

International Keynesianism in the last several decades has been a very powerful and influential ideology. Its most recent and authoritative exposition came in the report of the Brandt Commission. The influence of its ideas leads some commentators to a deep cynicism. Certainly its influence has meant that a major reason for Western international aid programs has been the perception that those programs are in the enlightened self-interest of Western capitalism. If it is an unsullied, high idealism that you are after, you will find little to reassure you in the realm of international economic relations.

However, it is at least arguable that while global solidarity could be a more attractive basis for major resource transfers to the poor countries, a sense that such transfers are in the enlightened self-interest of the powerful may be a more certain basis for such transfers than ever altruism could provide.

The second basic explanation for the emergence of the World Bank as the major international development agency is the cold war. Development assistance was seen by many in the West as an important check on the spread of communism. It is, in effect, a dovish expression of the anti-communist concern to contain the Soviet Union. Together with international Keynesianism, the ideology of the cold war goes a long way towards explaining how it happened that the Bank evolved into an international development agency.

These are neither lofty nor moral reasons to support resource transfers to poor countries. Nevertheless, it was certainly in the interest of the Third World that these attitudes should dominate Western decision-making circles, rather than the attitudes which were their main contender — namely the twin conviction that Third World development threatens the prosperity of the rich countries and that communism is best contained by military alliances with uncompromisingly anti-communist generals.

Two additional factors reinforced the impact of these two primary factors. The first was the growth within the Third World of articulate pressure for greater international development assistance. In response to that pressure an expanding aid program became a standard feature of the relationship between the Western industrial countries and the Third World. The second reinforcing factor has been the Bank's own effort to augment its role. The World Bank is staffed by able men and women. They are confident in themselves to the point of arrogance. They have, as a result, sought to expand the responsibilities and power of the Bank.

These then are the four explanations I offer for the transformation of the Bank into a major international development agency — international Keynesianism, a dovish approach to containment, Third World diplomatic pressure and self-promotion by the Bank itself. Needless to say, in response to such a varied set of influences, there are many ambiguities in the policies and institutions that have resulted.

The role of IDA

One sees ambiguity, for example, in the International Development Association (IDA), the concessional finance wing of the Bank. All four of the factors I have mentioned were present at the time IDA was established. By the late 1950s there was strong pressure from India in particular for a new United Nations capital assistance program. This proposal was initially rejected by the rich countries and by the Bank. As the pressures nevertheless increased, the rich countries, not wishing to deliver a total rebuff to the poor countries, proposed a compromise: that there should be such a program but it be located within the Bank, where those who had opposed such a new program could at least control it.

The staff of the Bank, having initially tried to discourage the idea of international capital assistance at concessional rates when the idea was linked to the creation of a new institution, quickly accommodated themselves to the idea once it would instead mean an increase in their own operation.

IDA, in the manner both of its creation and its operation, provides an extraordinary illustration of the morally ambiguous character of even quite positive inter-state initiatives. IDA's funds are contributed to it by the richer countries from their aid budgets. IDA loans these funds to the poorest countries for projects agreed upon by the country concerned and IDA. The loans are interest-free, save for a nominal service charge, and typically are for repayment in 50 years' time. It is small wonder that, as we shall see, Amir Jamal (Finance Minister of Tanzania) speaks so positively of IDA.

There has been since 1960 a number of developments relating to IDA, which are widely regarded, and correctly so, as progressive advances. The kinds of projects eligible for IDA credit have widened from narrowly-defined infrastructural projects to include rural development projects, educational projects and social welfare projects. The sums dispersed have also increased significantly. The professional staff became in the mid-1970s some of the most intellectually venturesome people among those working on development issues. For example, they pioneered the demonstration of the real economic work of education and welfare expenditures and actively promoted the concept of a basic needs strategy for development.

Nor was all of this mere intellectual speculation. The Bank announced that it would concentrate IDA activity on developing the productive capacity of the poorest sectors of the poorest countries and quite quickly this decision had its impact on the country-by-country distribution of IDA credits.

Loans and strategic interests

One final development that at least initially seemed a positive one was the recent introduction of structural adjustment loans. These seemed an imaginative innovation, because many countries were facing the necessity to make significant structural adjustments in their economies in order to overcome severe and persistent foreign exchange deficits. These kinds of major adjustments are painful and cannot be accomplished without real social cost. An effective program of structural adjustment loans therefore would meet a very real need.

The ambiguities, however, continued even as the Bank, through IDA, became a major aid agency. For one thing, the poor countries were never able to secure any significant change in the distribution of votes within the Bank's ruling structures. The rich countries would not countenance any sharing. They even blocked the proposed global negotiations to be held at the General Assembly of the United Nations, because they did not want any issue within the jurisdiction of the IMF and the Bank to be discussed in a forum they did not control.

These same considerations explain as well their total rejection of the Brandt Commission's recommendation of a new World Development Fund that would not be dependent for its funds on annual or triennial votes in the legislatures of the rich countries, and which would be governed by a board made up of a significant representation from poor countries. International ability to co-operate for humane objectives is still stuck at that early point at which the rich countries will participate only in activities and structures they can control.

A second ground for unease, a second evidence of ambiguity within the Bank, is the recurrent evidence of undue U.S. influence in the country allocation of Bank loans. Hard facts are hard to come by on this sort of issue. Nevertheless, there are strong *prima facie* grounds to suspect that the Bank has been recurrently influenced by U.S. geopolitical considerations. For example, major loans were made to Egypt shortly after it broke with the Soviet Union. The Bank did not extend any loans to Allende's socialist Chile while nevertheless hastening to support Chile after General Pinochet's military dictatorship came to power. The United States struggled hard to get Bank credits for South Vietnam and then struggled again to block any credits to Vietnam after the end of the war there. It is also suggestive that the two largest structural adjustment loans have been to Turkey and Korea and that those countries had received by mid-1982 nearly 60 per cent of the total committed in the 15 structural adjustment loans to date. A U.S. Treasury study early in 1982 reviewed some 80 issues in which the United States had sought to influence policy decisions of the Bank. It reported that 85 per cent of these attempts had been successful.

A third source of Third World anxiety can be summed up in the two words *conditionality* and *leverage*. The Bank has always attached conditions to its loans and credits, over and above the obligation to repay and cover interest charges. Initially these conditions related directly to the projects that were being financed by the loans or credits. Gradually, however, the Bank has sought on the basis of its loans to secure leverage on a far wider range of economic policies. Moreover, it has organized Western bilateral agencies in a common front to support these conditions.

Anxieties of these sorts explain the unease of many Third World countries about the World Bank. They explain also the preference of the Brandt Commission for a new World Development Fund rather than an expansion of the activities of the Bank. Nevertheless it is also true that no Third World leader while in power has felt the Bank so discredited that it should be scrapped. The poorest countries had in fact nowhere else to go for substantial aid of this sort. There was no chance that the OPEC countries would finance an alternative agency and very little chance that even a close alliance with the Soviet Union would bring substantial aid.

The Third World wanted important improvements in the World Bank but it was not unrepentantly hostile. In this judgement they were surely right. As of June 30, 1981, 79 countries had received IDA credits. More revealing still, 87 per cent of the value of those credits was to countries with a per capita income of less than $420 a year. This is a vastly better record than the record of bilateral aid from the countries of the Organization for Economic Co-operation and Development (OECD). Six countries had received IDA credits totalling more than $600 million. The list does not suggest an overwhelming Western geopolitical or ideological influence. These six countries, in declining order of the size of their credits, were India, Bangladesh, Pakistan, Egypt, Indonesia and Tanzania. The next two largest recipients were Sri Lanka and the Sudan. It may not be an ideal list but it is better, I'm sure, than the country distribution of most bilateral agencies. To give an extreme contrast, the two largest recipients of U.S. non-military bilateral aid were Israel and Egypt.

The "new realism" and the retreat of Keynesianism

This whole story has a final and still incomplete twist to it. Much that I have so far identified as the positive side in the ambiguous progress of the Bank has been severely undermined in the last few years. Three closely related developments have caused this. First, the Western consensus in support of international Keynesianism collapsed. It is true that great efforts can be mobilized by the rich countries to save Mexico, Brazil and other major international borrowers from default. That effort certainly illustrates interdependence and the operation of enlightened self-interest. The consequences for Western banks and for the international monetary system would be severe if not disastrous were a major debtor to default.

But we see no such effort being mobilized for the poorest countries even though, unlike Mexico, they have very little responsibility for the intensity of their present difficulties. The truth is, I think, that it is in fact no longer an accepted component of the dominant ideology in many circles in the Western world, and particularly in the United States, that an enlightened view of Western capitalist interests requires a serious assault on the poverty of the Third World. Instead, the more prevalent judgement is that the absence of development in the poorest countries neither threatens the West nor would its elimination seem to offer much advantage.

This is the new realism. The truth would seem to be that without some compelling commitment to international justice, international Keynesianism quickly fades away when industrial societies face economic crises of their own. It is also the case that in these years of crisis, the Third World itself has proven less able to mobilize diplomatic pressure upon the rich. Each poor country is so absorbed in its immediate needs that the Third World fails to use effectively even the few instruments of pressure that it has at its disposal.

Finally, and simultaneously with all of this, in anti-communist circles what I have clumsily called the dovish containment view is in full retreat. The United States and its closest allies no longer act on the assumption that a vigorous aid program is an effective instrument for containing communism. Instead, priority clearly goes to the full military backing of strong anti-communist regimes whatever their records on either development or human rights.

These three factors — the weakening of international Keynesianism, the diplomatic disarray of the Third World and the return of a militant anti-communism — have led the new right in the United States to call for a virtual abandonment of IDA. Milton Friedman, for example, has declared: "The biggest question facing the World Bank is how to dissolve and get out of business." The general line is that the World Bank is financing socialism through IDA and is aiding governments rather than free enterprise. These arguments have received a sympathetic hearing within the American government. The United States reneged on a firm commitment to the sixth IDA triennium, from 1980 to 1983, and there is every likelihood of further severe cuts, if not worse, when the needs of the next triennium are discussed.*

* See also the Introduction, p. 13

But most disturbing of all in recent years has been that the decay in the concern to promote development in the poorest countries has extensively spread within the World Bank itself. The U.S. Treasury paper of March 1982 mentioned earlier was intended to check a total abandonment of IDA by the U.S. Congress. This defence of the Bank by the U.S. Treasury is extremely revealing and very disheartening. That the Treasury does not argue the case on the grounds of either morality or equity is not surprising. Also missing totally was the language of international Keynesianism. The paper takes on the new right's criticisms of the Bank. It seeks to reply to charges that the Bank is unresponsive to U.S. strategic interests, that it is insufficiently active in promoting the full sway of market forces and private enterprise. It does this by arguing that these criticisms are untrue. It suggests, as I have already mentioned, that the United States was successful in 85 per cent of its efforts to influence Bank policy. It argues as well that the Bank's use of conditionality promotes an adherence to the market and a checking of state intervention. It says that because of the leverage which the United States thereby acquired, a U.S. contribution to the Bank, to IDA, has far more policy impact on Third World countries than a bilateral effort by the U.S. using similar funds.

We should, however, not read too much into this U.S. Treasury report. It was very much an American defence of the Bank and aimed at right-wing American congressional critics. It is primarily useful as evidence of how far American attitudes have shifted. Nevertheless it is surely significant that they can find evidence to defend the Bank in those terms.

We can also find evidence of such a shift in the Bank's position. Let us list a few of these. First, the concern for meeting basic needs has receded markedly as an influence on World Bank policies. Look for example at the conditions attached to the new structural adjustment loans. No effort is being made to ensure that the structural adjustment that the Bank supports will, as far as possible, not affect adversely the poorest in these societies. The idea of basic needs is no longer — if ever it was — an important input into Bank policy.

Secondly, the Bank continues to be susceptible to U.S. pressure. For example, at the 1982 Cancun, Mexico, conference, 21 of the 22 participating heads of government asked the Bank to launch an Energy Affiliate. The United States opposed the idea and the Bank has not come forward with any further initiative on that. With the U.S. increasingly blunt in pursuit of its own economic and strategic interests and the promotion of its particular ideological position, we must anticipate that the Bank will be under increasing pressure in its allocation of loans and credits to different countries. There is evidence that this pressure has its results. The Bank continues to loan money to regimes such as Bolivia, which is dominated by a military leadership deeply involved in the cocaine trade, and to Guatemala and El Salvador despite their horrific records of human rights violations.

A third example of the disturbing trend of opinion is that the Bank is again defining its role increasingly as supporting and reinforcing the loan operations of the private banks. It seems likely that it will introduce a new affiliate to provide investment insurance for foreign firms investing in the Third World. It is vigorously promoting co-financing arrangements between itself and private banks. Its president constantly seeks to reassure the United States that it recognizes the primary importance of the private sector, international business and the market.

Arrogance and the magic of the market

It is legitimate to fear that as these attitudes have their impact on policy, the poorest countries will further suffer. Those who do loan money and are guided by the market, that is to say the private banks, certainly shy away from the Third World. Less than 3 per cent of private bank loans to Third World governments over the last 10 years went to the poorest 38 countries. Mahbub ul Haq, until recently a senior official in the Bank, said on his resignation, "The bilateral pressures on the Bank could greatly compromise the international character of the institution. To suggest that the Bank is not an international Robin Hood or a United Way, as Mr. A.W. Clausen of the Bank suggested recently in Tokyo, is to address strawmen. The role of IDA is to protect the developing countries against the market, especially those who do not have much of a chance to get capital directly from it."

There is a further important aspect to the shift that has been occurring in the attitude and operations of the World Bank these last several years. The Bank has become increasingly arrogant and ideological in its approach to development issues in the Third World. The Economist's recent phrase for the phenomenon I'm talking about was "overwhelming, organic and overt". Increasingly the Bank operates on the assumption that it already knows the policies it wishes to insist upon before it enters negotiations with individual Third World countries. These policies are deduced from the particular economic theories that now dominate its counsels. When an IMF mission comes to a country to negotiate a stand-by credit, its negotiators actually arrive with a prepared text for the letter they wish the finance minister of that country to send to the IMF.

Though perhaps not always quite so obviously, Bank officials have no doubt about the policy changes they wish to require of a country. Drag Avramovic, who should know because he was a vice-president of the Bank, said that Bank officials not only suffer from a messianic complex but also that every few years they change their gods. The present god they worship is export promotion and the form of service they require of Third World countries is a set of policy changes which would bring into play "the magic of the markets". Especially with its structural adjustment loans, the Bank is in a very strong position to secure an influence that is, to use The Economist's phrase, "overwhelming".

Finally, as if to confirm this trend, the Bank is increasingly insisting, with reference to structural adjustment loans, that the petitioning countries seeking these loans must first sign a stand-by agreement with the IMF. Thus the Bank is lining itself up behind the particular package of policies that is the earmark of the IMF. It is thereby greatly increasing the leverage that the IMF has over economic policy matters in many Third World countries.

It is important to realize that these two major institutions are together insisting upon policies that do not at all represent a professional consensus. They are insisting upon policies which do not primarily emerge out of a detailed study of the specific needs of the individual countries with which they are negotiating. They take little or no account of other national objectives that the governments unavoidably and desirably must pursue. They are inadequately concerned about the socio-political consequences of what they recommend. They do not reflect upon the fact that quite possibly only an authoritarian government could contain the urban discontent that is likely to result from the implementation of policies they insist upon. In their judgements they fail to acknowledge sufficiently that the poorest countries bear little responsibility for the severity of the crisis to which they must adjust.

In summary, the Bank has become increasingly arrogant and ideological. At a time when imaginative innovations are desperately needed and when long-discussed reforms might well have been advanced, the Third World instead is caught in a losing effort to save what little has been achieved through IDA, and to minimize the impact of destructive U.S. pressures upon the Bank.

Our obligation, it seems to me, has these components: first, to keep alive the awareness that many needs long championed and reforms long identified must continue to be advocated even though they have disappeared from the agenda at this time; second, to do what we can to minimize the damage that is now being threatened, particularly through American pressure. This means above all to support a strongly-financed IDA and a revised and expanded non-punitive structural adjustment loan program with loans of longer duration and not requiring ideological conformity from their recipients. Third, to insist that Bank conditionality not be used to curb governments whose egalitarian or socialist policies offend either the American right or the Bank itself, and to oppose every tendency to use the Bank to protect or to advance American or any other special economic, ideological or strategic interests.

This is a very modest set of immediate objectives. Given the dimensions of the problems the Third World faces, it is very much a minimum. Despite what else the Bank might and should do, because of the dominant views in Washington, London, Bonn and Tokyo, the immediate objective must be to achieve such reforms as these in order to preserve the World Bank — and IDA in particular — from further erosion of the capacity and willingness to be a substantial and effective international agency assisting the development of the poorest countries.

Power and the Third World Struggle for Equilibrium

Amir Jamal

Amir Jamal has held a cabinet post in the Tanzanian government since independence, most recently as a minister without portfolio responsible for international economic affairs. He was a member of the Brandt Commission on North-South Relations and has also served as Tanzanian governor to the IMF. With his 1983 election to the chair of the Group of 77 he assumed a leading role in negotiations between the Third World and the international financial institutions.

On the face of it, it may seem strange that nearly four decades after the end of the Second World War, out of whose ashes arose the Bretton Woods institutions of the IMF and the World Bank, buttressed by the interim General Agreement on Tariff and Trade, there should exist a need to educate public opinion in industrialized societies about the IMF and the World Bank.

But then perhaps it is not such a strange thing either. Perhaps it is indicative of the considerable distance existing between, on the one hand, these two institutions ostensibly under the direction of their respective boards of directors, and on the other hand the multitude of societies in whose names governments appointed the directors to supervise the running of these global institutions which, one way or another, affect the lives of so many people.

I hope that there will be general agreement that these institutions were primarily established to revive and safeguard the economies of the already industrialized societies, which were most adversely affected by the world war. At that particular time in history, a Keynesian school of economic management of society was almost bound to manifest itself.

The purpose was to provide a secure framework of agreed rules of exchange within which to ensure the reconstruction of war-torn Europe and the economic growth of the already industrialized countries, as well as to ensure that never again would there be the recurrence of the scramble for markets and for natural resources on the basis of everyone for themselves, thus planting new seeds of future international conflict.

Euphoria as well as fatigue at the end of the war ensured accommodation between those with power based on technology, and a heterogeneous group of less endowed societies in search of collective security and measurable economic growth. Thus was established the United Nations Organization, placing its trust and hope in the power and wisdom of the five permanent members of the United Nations Security Council. The same power-oriented values prevailed in the structuring of the IMF and the World Bank, but without the participation of the Soviet Union and with the intervening alienation of the People's Republic of China, which ended only recently. And the same dominant forces prevented the adoption in 1948 of the Havana Charter which would have set up the International Trade Organization, which in turn was intended to regulate trade relations among states and explicitly include provisions relating to the special needs of the underdeveloped countries. As for commodities, the struggle for a just price continues.

Power and the post-war period

I think it is important that within an inevitably brief but decisive period in the world's history, those who arrived there first and were preoccupied with the prevailing values of trade and exchange placed themselves in a strong position for controlling the course of these institutions. Predictably, the Marxist response to this state of affairs resulted in the Soviet Union staying aside from the process, although over the years the categorical imperative of technology and the specialization of production have brought about further accommodation between some Marxist governments and these institutions.

Developing countries protest that at the time these institutions were established, they themselves were under colonial, imperialist or feudal regimes and in conditions of acute and chronic underdevelopment, and therefore their particular needs became predicated on charity rather than justice. In response to this, they are told that on achieving political independence almost all countries have acceded to membership of the two institutions, as well as in most cases subscribing to the General Agreement on Tariff and Trade. The argument is that they have thus willingly compromised their position themselves from the very inception of their political independence.

We need to understand the historical process that has cumulatively built up the existing, almost universal membership of these two institutions. In the first place, membership in the post-war period comprises countries that have emerged from colonial rule. They had to start *ipso facto*, to deal with inherited structures of production, trade and exchange, even as they looked for ways and means of giving themselves new direction and purpose. These structures were already part of a global network that had the IMF as its central point of reference. It was not possible for these countries to bypass the IMF and GATT without creating enormous, almost insurmountable, obstacles in their paths. Quite apart from everything else, the most critical of needs — that of education — could only begin to be met by the accelerated use of the inherited capacity, both physical and intellectual — no matter if it meant the accentuation of the already existing polarization of urban and rural communities.

The inception of the International Development Association in 1960, as an affiliate of the World Bank with a common board of directors supervising its activities, needs to be seen for all it is worth. It was certainly a most constructive development of mobilizing and harnessing resources of the industrialized countries for combating underdevelopment in the world. Here was a concrete recognition that the reconstruction and development of Europe was now to give place to the needs of the larger world community for developing a basic physical and social infrastructure, without which no meaningful economic activity could take place. And of course the access to the natural resources and markets of the underdeveloped called for a certain magnitude of investment of available resources.

At the same time, no newly independent developing country could have recourse to these much-needed resources without first acceding to the membership of the IMF. That few of them understood, let alone appreciated, the premises of "market forces" on which these institutions were founded was neither here nor there. Each successive accession of these countries on independence day consolidated the doctrine of primogeniture, as epitomized by the power structures that sustained the two institutions, which in return were determined to derive sustenance from them in order to maintain the status quo.

The newcomers of the world, as empirical evidence so amply illustrates, had little choice but to accept the scheme of things that history had pre-empted for them.

The burden of adjustment: borne by the poor

It is now becoming increasingly clear that more and more of the millions who populate the developing countries want to know the value of membership of these institutions and what it is likely to mean in the years ahead.

It is the case that the industrialized market-oriented countries increased their material prosperity significantly in the post-war years of fixed exchange-rate regimes ordained by the IMF. The capital formation that had taken place within their respective boundaries enabled them to increase economic interdependence in a variety of ways. Most significantly this was achieved through the emergence of transnational corporations, weaving a fabric round the globe by drawing sustenance from the premises of the Bretton Woods' institutions. These corporations eventually reached a decisive stage in international economic structuring when in the interest of expansion and extension they could actually ignore and bypass these institutions when it suited them to do so.

At the same time the institutions continued to enforce compliance of the doctrine of free trade from others too weak and
too needy to be able to protest, even if such compliance precipitated social upheaval in the form of street riots and like erup-
tions.

I do not wish to be misunderstood here. Certainly the International Development Association has made a real contribution towards assisting developing countries to build up their
economic and social infrastructure. It has succeeded in demonstrating that, like the undernourished person who develops
more appetite by the day as he is helped to find more nourish-
ment, development itself creates more appetite for further
development. The 20 years of IDA's assistance to the poor represents the best in international affairs so far, demonstrating that
humanity is indeed civilized.

Precisely because of this achievement the institutional
impact on international relationships threatens to be of a negative and perhaps disruptive nature: A pincer movement may
now be unfolding itself, so that what has been achieved since
IDA was founded is in danger of being undone. But much
worse, the clock may be turned back on what has been all too
rare a salutary chapter in the conduct of human affairs.

One prong of the pincer is the act of depriving IDA of additional resources, which are now needed on a greater scale than
ever before. This is being done on the plea that the resources
being made available to the poor are not producing desired
results. It is extraordinary that this should be stated as a cause,
when both the IMF and the World Bank have been at pains in
commending the LDC's economic growth-rate in the period
1960-75.

The other prong is the sharp worsening of the terms of trade
of primary products and of protectionism against processed
and manufactured goods from the developing countries. Those
countries are simultaneously subjected by the IMF to insistent
pressure to make rapid adjustment to such a formidably
oppressive environment.

The cumulative effect of prolonged failure on the part of the
industrialized countries to make adjustments when it was
absolutely necessary that they should do so has been the
unleashing of inflation on the developing countries without

providing them with any compensation in the form of improved terms of trade. The oil-price shock has been delivered twice over to these poor countries, first by the steep rise in cost of direct supply, and then by the sharp increase in the cost of imports of essential manufactured and capital goods, whose production costs had already risen due to inflation in the industrialized countries and were further inflated by the increased cost of energy.

The poor developing countries were not responsible for the deficit financing of the Vietnam war. They were not responsible for the economic policies of industrialized countries that led to price rises due to wage awards out of proportion to productivity increases. They were not responsible for causing oil producers to increase oil prices sharply. They do not determine the terms of trade which so unjustly afflict them. With such remorselessly formidable pressures on them, the fragile equilibrium of their own economies was bound to be pushed off course as they found themselves deprived of the necessary inputs for maintaining the steady momentum that in varying degrees they had achieved in the sixties and early seventies.

What option has been open to them but to be forced to inflate their economies as unit costs went up due to under-utilization of even their meagre capacities, as well as due to increasing shortage of essential items of development and consumption? The cumulative consequences of such an oppressive environment can hardly be adequately imagined. And then, to top it all, it is *they* who are expected to make the most painful adjustment by means of what is euphemistically called "trade and exchange rate policy". Of course the exchange rates were bound to be seriously thrown out of alignment. But I insist, through no fault of their own.

The role of the Bretton Woods institutions — the IMF, the World Bank and GATT — calls for serious scrutiny. The IMF has certainly not succeeded in disciplining the industrialized countries in time to nip the inflationary forces in the bud. The GATT seems to be powerless in arresting protectionism. The critical role of IDA has been diminished to a dangerous extent. And but for the clear stand taken by some Western countries, including Canada, which have made contributions to a special fund in order to mitigate the adverse consequences of the wholly negative U.S. position of abdicating its international responsibility, IDA would now be on its deathbed.

In the name of human decency...

The least that the industrialized countries ought to do, in the name of human decency, is to ensure that the global institutions under their control assist the poor countries in making adjustment. And this adjustment should be allowed to come at a pace and in a manner that takes into account the immense accumulated pressure under which poor countries are endeavouring to stay afloat — instead of demoralizing them with allegations that they are pursuing faulty economic policies.

Economic policies cannot be managed on quicksand. *A priori*, policies assume the existence of certain equilibrium, however fragile, at any given time. When the poor countries have been delivered a cumulative body-blow of such considerable magnitude as to put their economies in reverse gear — this is particularly true of many African countries — they should not be pushed into getting into still greater indebtedness through totally unrealistic adjustment policies.

Strong policies of adjustment are being demanded from low-income countries, despite the IMF's own judgement that, for the most part, their present plight is the result of factors outside their own control. Furthermore, commodity prices are now the lowest in 30 years, and developing countries are being asked to withhold stocks from the market. Is no one going to ask the IMF to make a significant adjustment in its own policies? Must adjustment always be made by the poor?

The prospects for the IMF to be able to meet the balance of payment needs of poor developing countries, especially those of sub-Saharan Africa, are indeed extremely dim. The present crisis is due to an accumulation of failures on the part of many developing countries, due to factors beyond their control, to meet in time the continuing need for liquidity. The fact of the matter is that the IMF does not have anywhere near the resources required to meet the needs of this crisis.

Extremely limited as the resources of the IMF seem to be, those resources appear to go to three groups of countries. There are those which have militarily strategic significance in the world power structure; those with very heavy debts that threaten the world's monetary system; and those which have the requisite managerial and infrastructural equipment and are capable of relatively short-term adjustment due to reasonably balanced internal and external linkages. This leaves many poor developing countries altogether on the margin.

The IMF, not having the resources to meet the needs of the times, asks for sharp, almost body-blow adjustment, which it must know will either be unacceptable, or if accepted, will lead to non-compliance of the performance criteria. This seems to be the only practical way of rationing out its residual resources. To make a virtue of its almost impossible demands on the poor economies out of such necessity is to contribute to the accentuation of the present ills to a point where the weakest link in the international chain that interlocks us all can no longer bear the stress and strain on it.

The limited resources of the IMF in comparison with the magnitude of the need of so many countries, big and small, for balance of payment support have to be seen in the context of the liquidity of the commercial banking system. The primary concern of the powers that be seems to be to ensure that the banking system is not destabilized. The economies of the poor countries, which by definition do not receive the resources of private banks over anything other than the very short-term, are supposed to be able to remain *illiquid* for an indefinite period of time, no matter what suffering this may cause to their people. The time-frame needed for effective adjustment on their part is in sharp conflict with the short-term nature of the private banks' framework of operation.

The diversion of resources within the short-term framework, aimed at providing a safety net for commercial banks, means depriving the poor countries of resources to facilitate the effective adjustment of their ill-equipped economies, which necessarily need a longer time framework.

The struggle to regain equilibrium
Those in positions of power and responsibility need to understand the nature of the crises we are all in now. The contortions being forced on the entire global financial system cannot continue indefinitely.

Creative minds are now immediately needed to work out the recycling of a significant magnitude of liquidity in the capital market by means of an interest-subsidy scheme. Today, the paradox of having on the one hand pockets of illiquidity which cannot afford to borrow commercially and, on the other, excess liquidity which cannot be recycled to already too-vulnerable debtors, is extremely frightening. Here is a classical situation where indeed there is a hairbreadth of difference between the sublime and the diabolical. It depends on the turn the financial managers collectively take or fail to take.

Nobody can deny the necessity of managing available resources wisely and equitably in the interest of the many and not just a few. The development of peasant societies, steadily being linked with the already industrialized and still-industrializing global infrastructure, is now an irreversible process. Developing countries, no more than the highly industrialized countries, cannot develop their respective state structures with their feet in the air and their heads on the ground. There is no way technology can spread from the hinterland to the ports, or from the village railway stops to the main railway terminals, from the village telephone booth to the central exchange, or from the village users of electricity to the economically selected generating centre. In short, a critical minimum quantum of urban-centred investment must continue to be made, with all its implications for workforce development and therefore education policies, as well as its implications for channelling available surpluses which inescapably must come for primary peasant production.

The balance between investment in urban-oriented centres and the villages must remain a matter of continuing preoccupation. This equilibrium has to be dynamic and needs to be sustained. The vagaries of weather, fluctuating prices in overseas markets, rising costs of essential imports: All these continuously and cumulatively press upon this tenuous equilibrium. The industrialized countries are rightly anxious about the high level of unemployment prevailing in their countries. Not many speak of growing unemployment in the urban centres of the poor, which lack any cushion whatsoever of social security schemes.

Are the industrialized countries convinced that it is in their interest to push poor countries to the wall? Is the IMF convinced that it has any chance of helping the poor countries to regain their equilibrium internally as well as externally with such shock treatment as it is prescribing to the group of countries least equipped to withstand it — after the shocks already given to them with such devastating cumulative effect?

Exchange-rate gyrations and highly costly and volatile interest-rate movements have been taking a continuous toll on the economies of the poor countries. The devastation of the Second World War led to the founding of institutions with the message "never again". And yet the poor developing countries' economies are now coming apart, one by one, while the industrialized countries themselves face most uncertain and perhaps deeply unsettling prospects ahead of them.

Is this what human ingenuity and resourcefulness are capable of? Is this not the moment when the industrialized and the poor developing countries, the not-so-industrialized, and the not-so-poor, all close their ranks, and through global negotiations begin to reconstruct and reform global institutions in the interest of humankind? While preparations for such negotiations are being made and negotiations get underway, should not those immediately responsible for the Bretton Woods institutions deal with the immediate challenge in a manner such as I have endeavoured to indicate, so as to give hope and confidence to the historically disenfranchised societies of the world? Which other institutions are there to discharge this responsibility?

The IMF, World Bank and GATT have become organically ensconced in the world's body politic. They are there, monumentally all-pervasive. They have accumulated massive information and immense technical capabilities. And yet, in varying degrees, by omission and by commission, their global impact is not only that of consolidating the historically inherited asymmetry in the community of nations but also of creating despair and despondency when the need is to give hope and self-confidence.

It is the case that these institutions can only be what those who wield power over them wish them to be, or through short-sightedness, default and lack of imagination render them to become — man-made dinosaurs. And yet this tragic state of affairs is surely totally avoidable. It does not have to be a global Greek tragedy inexorably unfolding itself. Human ingenuity in the environment prevailing at the time created these institutions. It was the exercise of power and wisdom by those who arrived there first, primarily to secure their own perceived interest. But others have now come and are part of the same globe.

It is neither wise nor intelligent to keep on insisting that simply because some arrived first, that they alone have the right to determine how global equilibrium should be maintained. Prosperity, and prospects for increasing prosperity, took firm roots in industrialized societies when equitable taxation was securely built into the economic and social management of nations. Without it, the democratic values so much cherished by the industrialized countries could not have been sustained over the decades.

The values of equity and democracy need to be built into the structures of the Bretton Woods institutions. These institutions can be restructured and given a truly global mandate for achieving global equilibrium by ensuring prosperity for many instead of a few in the course of the next 50 years. Their impact can indeed transcend the most sanguine expectations of the original founders.

But this will be achieved only if statesmanship and courage can be combined by those in power so as to endow these institutions with basic human values. The institutions need an automatic flow of resources to finance the channelling of available liquidity in the market to the most needy, for example through an interest-subsidy policy. They need the competence to deal with the real issues facing developing societies as much as those confronting the industrialized nations, and the power to discipline both the surplus and deficit countries in proportion to their respective economic strength.

To achieve this, the firm establishment of an international unit of reserve, under the control of a restructured and reformed international monetary institution, is an absolutely urgent necessity. Only when irrevocable commitments are made towards these ends will the international community turn the corner in the direction of economic progress in harmony with itself.

The international community is at the crossroads, and so are its institutions. The global impact of these institutions is not in question; it is very much being felt already. The question is about the nature and character of that impact.

Researching the World Bank

Cheryl Payer

*Cheryl Payer is a political economist who has
taught at North West University, the University of Hawaii
and the New School of Social Research (New York). She is
the author of two important books on the key international
financial institutions:* The Debt Trap: The IMF and the Third
World *(1975) and* The World Bank: A Critical Analysis
(1982).

I don't suppose I have to justify to this audience the reason why I felt it was important to do a book on the World Bank. It is the Mount Everest of development lending institutions; aside from the huge amounts of money it lends — in fiscal year 1982 they committed something like $13.6 billion for various development projects in the Third World — it has abrogated to itself a position as the institution co-ordinating many other sources of aid and loan money, including a number of bilateral aid programs. It plays a key role in chairing the consultative groups of aid consortia, which include bilateral donors. It participates in co-financing with commercial banks and tries to play a role in deciding where and how the commercial banks direct their lending. In the field of technical expertise it has co-operative relationships with such specialized agencies as the Food and Agriculture Organization of the UN, UNESCO, World Health Organization and so forth, in which the Bank decides policy and these organizations provide technical experts to implement those policies.

I think the reason that the Bank has achieved such a hegemonic position is not so much because they have any wisdom superior to other people working in this field but simply because of the huge amount of money they have for financing their programs, to purchase talent and so forth.

Now, I have in the past written a book on the International Monetary Fund and thus when Robert McNamara began talking about how the Bank was working to alleviate poverty in the Third World, I was rather suspicious because I knew the Bank was very closely related to the IMF and that it has the same governing structures, with the same governments controlling roughly the same amounts of voting power. I also knew that the IMF policies were very socially regressive, very damaging to the interests of poor people and therefore there was a sort of cognitive dissonance when I heard all this publicity to the effect that the World Bank was really helping poor people — just as an astronomer might notice that a planet was in a certain orbit that would not have been predicted according to the gravitational pull of all the other known planets, and he would suspect that there was something going on that we didn't yet know about. I felt there was a need to investigate what the World Bank was really doing in its project lending, including the so-called poverty-oriented projects. I therefore felt there was a need for a study of World Bank project lending. The problem was how to do it?

The search for sources

If you rely simply on the policy statements that come out of Washington I think you get a very limited picture, which would be more or less defined by what the Bank wants you to know about what they're doing. Some people have done a very good job of describing and criticizing Bank policies on this basis but I felt a hunger to know what was going on out in the field.

My first attempts were not very satisfactory. I wrote two drafts of an article I'd been asked to do on the Bank and agribusiness and neither draft was satisfactory to me or to the people who had asked for the article. I made a real methodological breakthrough when a visitor informed me that there were in fact lists of all the loans that the Bank had made from its founding in 1946 on up to the present. In fact, the loan agreements for each of these loans were published and available in the UN depository library. I began to look up these lists and project agreements and writing a book began to seem a real possibility to me because here were thousands of different projects which I could now identify by name.

Although there were so many projects it was impossible for one person to make a study of all of them, if one could form a cognitive map of the more important projects or series of projects in various borrowing countries, if one could find out just what the Bank was doing with all these billions of dollars for building structures and financing projects, one could then go on to evaluate these activities given one's own values about what humane development should be. This was my methodology.

I didn't think that doing an insider report with interviews in Washington of Bank personnel was very feasible for me; in the first place I had a rather high profile as a critic of the IMF and I didn't think that they would be very friendly to me as a critic. Even if they were friendly I think there is a real danger that one can be very subtly co-opted in the course of interviews inside an institution; one gets so excited about having insider information that one begins to accept the assumptions and the parameters of the people one is interviewing. Although I did do some interviews in Washington I didn't have any "deep throat" inside the Bank. I was also aware that if employees of the Bank were noticed talking to a critic, they could be in jeopardy of losing their jobs, so I didn't think for moral and practical reasons this was a very good way to set about my research.

So basically I've done a library study, using reports published by the World Bank on its policies. Project appraisal reports of individual projects the Bank has done are not published and technically speaking I'm not supposed to have access to them but there are a lot of them floating around and I was able to obtain enough to get a picture of what the typical Bank project in any given sector is like. I used publications such as their popularly written *Finance and Development* magazine and a newspaper called *Report*, which carries articles on specific projects and types of projects.

Perhaps more important than these, I collected as many independent accounts as I could of various Bank projects from people who had been consultants for the Bank in the field and from scholars who had done field work on various projects or in areas where projects were located. There is a tremendous amount of material like this and if you have a sort of mental map of where the important projects are, then you can identify these materials even though they may not have World Bank in the title or may not even mention the World Bank. If you know that the Boké bauxite mine is a World Bank project, then any material you find about that project can be used in doing research of this type.

The selection of projects — since there were several thousand I could not cover them all — became a rather important question. I didn't have systematic means of selecting the projects that I wanted to study, but I did have a few principles. First of all, of course, there is the availability of material, and if a lot has been written about a project I would read it.

This, however, introduces a certain bias towards projects that are notorious failures — which are often the projects that are most written about. I did not want to criticize the World Bank just because it makes mistakes — any institution that is trying to achieve something is going to make mistakes — and unless one can prove that these mistakes are systematically biased in one direction, this is not a very useful way to proceed. I think arguments can be made along these lines but I chose to concentrate on what I felt were typical projects, successful projects, very big projects or projects in a sector where there had been a whole series of Bank loans (which would imply that the Bank was more or less satisfied with developments in that sector).

I organized my chapters in the book by sectors, using particular projects as illustrations of what the Bank is doing in a particular sector. In looking at the Bank's literature, I used the second policy papers as a very important statement, approved by the executive board, of what the Bank thinks it is doing, I used project appraisals, as I have mentioned, and I used independent sources to find out how a project actually works, how it is perceived by the people who are affected by it. In this way I tried to build a picture of an ideal type of Bank project in each sector, and how it actually works.

Projects and policies: aid to the private sector

I've been able to identify at least four levels on which World Bank lending affects what is going on inside any particular country. Going from the most specific to the most general, the first level is that of the individual project which involves building or construction — the way the face of the earth is changed by a road or dam, a factory or mine. In some cases the project involves training personnel or administrative reorganization, which overlaps with the second level identified.

This second level of influence is that of policies for a particular sector. When the Bank makes a loan for a mine in a given country it is likely also to demand some say in how the mining laws are changed and how mining corporations are to be taxed in that country. Few people are aware of this, but it's a way the Bank can influence what's going on in the country — not only by financing a particular project but also by affecting the way all other activity in that sector is carried on.

The third level — moving to a higher level of generality — is the effect on macroeconomic conditions, and this is where the Bank's role overlaps with that of the IMF in trying to affect the overall direction in which a country is going. The Bank is getting into this more and more with its structural adjustment loans, introduced in 1980.

And the final level, the most general, is when the Bank influences the direction of development in countries simply by deciding whether it is going to support or to discipline a particular government.

I think most of you are probably familiar with the activities of the Bank in the last two most general levels, of macroeconomic policy determination and support for governments which its most powerful controlling members like. It's not supporting other governments which these controlling members dislike. This fact has been covered by many people, including my book on the IMF, Theresa Hayter's book on the World Bank*

* Teresa Hayter, *Aid as Imperialism*, Penguin, 1971.

and other studies. Although this level is very important, I decided that my new book would concentrate on what the Bank is doing in particular projects and in particular sectors.

I think that Bank projects can be classified in two categories. The Bank tends to call these, on the one hand, industry-oriented projects and, on the other, people-oriented projects. In the first category would be infrastructural projects such as roads, dams, ports, airports, telecommunications and so forth, the traditional areas of Bank lending that are still a large part of their total project lending. The Bank has never abandoned these sectors, it has only added to them so that proportionately their importance is somewhat less than it used to be. So infrastructure is one example of this. Lending to industry is another, mining is a third, and recently we've seen the addition of lending for oil and gas development and exploration. Now when the Bank calls these industry-oriented projects, I think that we can generally conclude that these projects represent, more or less, aid to the private sector and particularly aid to the foreign private investment in a particular country. If there is one overarching theme in my book, it is that the World Bank is a huge public subsidy to private profit. I've been able to trace this theme in most if not all of the sectors I have studied, including the so-called people-oriented sectors. I'll get to that in a minute, but in the four sectors I've just named — infrastructure, industry, mining, and oil and gas — one can often clearly identify large corporate beneficiaries of this lending. This is most clear in mining, where I can name a few because mining projects are very large and very important: There is Miferma in Mauritania, an iron mine owned by and producing for a consortium of European steel companies; there is the Boké bauxite mine in Guinea, similarly owned by a consortium of aluminum companies from Europe and North America — including Canada. There is the Selebe-Pikwe copper and nickel mine in Botswana, owned by Amax and Charter Consolidated of South Africa. There is the Hannah Mining Company, which owns iron and bauxite mines in Brazil as well as a couple of mines in other countries in Latin America. Falconbridge in the Dominican Republic and Inco in Guatemala have received assistance from the World Bank or its subsidiary, the International Finance Corporation.

Guaranteeing investment

Although one can identify specific corporations that have benefited from such mining projects, there are also several other
sectoral issues that I found to be extremely important when I
looked at the mining sector. For example, there is a tremendous
political risk involved for a corporation from Canada or the
United States investing in a mining project in a Third World
country these days. They have to put a lot of money into the
project, it will take five or six years until they begin to realize
profits, and there is a very real danger that sometime in this
five- or six-year period, or after the mine is producing, the
country will say, "Well thank you very much, we're going to
nationalize you and we're going to realize the profits." One can
even perhaps sympathize a little with the foreign corporation
in this circumstance, it's running a very real risk.

The World Bank's participation in these projects is important not just because it sometimes lends money to the government of the country so that the government will build some
necessary infrastructure and thereby economically subsidize
the project. I think what is really more important to the corporations is the fact that the World Bank's participation in the
project, even in a minor way, is a sort of political insurance to
them. If the World Bank is involved in this project, the government simply can't get away with nationalizing the mine,
because the World Bank with its tremendous amount of loans
will immediately apply sanctions to that country.

There are specific provisions written into some of these
mining agreements which state that the government cannot
renegotiate the contract with the private corporation. This is
one very important role which the bank plays in guaranteeing
the investment of private foreign coporations in the mining sector of a particular country.

There are other issues, for example whether certain areas of
land in a country are going to be opened up to foreign exploration and exploitation of the mineral rights, and the Bank often
insists that the mining laws in that country be changed so that
they are more favourable to foreign investment. The Bank has
made some loans to the nationalized coppermines of Pinochet's
Chile as well as to other nationalized coppermines in countries

such as Zaire and Peru. This may look like a nice socialist policy but I believe that its real significance is as a way to keep future mining projects in those countries available for exploitation by foreign corporations and that the Bank is using its leverage, its influence, to do this.

The World Bank is also intervening on the issue of tax policy for mining. The countries prefer to impose royalties because this is a very easy way to collect taxes, you can actually measure how much of the mineral is being carted out of the country and you can compute your royalty on that and you know how much money you're supposed to get in taxes. The mining corporations, with the World Bank exerting its influence on their behalf, are effecting a change from royalties to corporate-style income tax.

Now, in this case the companies hold most of the cards because they're the ones who know how to use creative accounting to minimize their tax liability. I think that the switch to income taxes is really to the benefit of the mining corporations rather than the country collecting the taxes. It's difficult to evaluate this issue because at present we're in a very depressed period for the world mining industry, so there is not a great deal of competition for going into new areas and companies are not willing to bid very high against each other to get in and build a mine in any particular Third World country, especially given the political risk on top of the economic risk. So in these depressed conditions Third World countries don't have a whole lot of leverage on the issue of taxation and where any new investment is taking place at all it's more or less taking place on corporate terms.

But I would like to emphasize that my research shows the World Bank solidly behind the corporations in this respect. They're not advising the countries on how to maximize their tax revenue and certainly not on how to maximize the revenue per unit of resources shipped out of the country, but quite the opposite. They're saying that if you want to maximize your revenue you've got to give the corporation the best deal possible so they'll invest more in your mining sector and take more resources out of the country. Maybe the total will add up to something but they're not encouraging them to maximize returns on units of production.

Building energy dependence

I've talked a lot about mining because I think it is a very good example of what is happening. The oil and gas lending is another interesting example because it's a relatively new innovation in sector lending. In fact, it represents a reversal of policy. Before the 1973 oil crisis the Bank had consistently refused to do any lending for oil or gas exploration or production, using the argument that private capital was available for this whenever it was economically feasible and therefore the Bank was not going to interfere with this. Basically the oil companies had told the Bank to keep off their turf and the Bank was obeying them.

It was not so easy to maintain this line after the 1973 rise in oil and gas prices and in fact, I think the officials of the World Bank became very concerned that the cost of importing oil and gas was putting a very severe burden on the financial system of their borrowing countries and thereby perhaps endangering the Bank's own financial security, because these countries would simply not be able to manage their debts. Therefore there was a review of this previous refusal to lend for oil and gas exploration and eventually the Bank changed its policy in this respect, first agreeing to lend for production of proven oil and gas fields.

They did this and not much happened because production was not really the key issue here. Once a country has discovered and proven its oil fields, it's easy to get finance for it and the Bank didn't make a great deal of difference one way or the other when it agreed to lend for production.

Therefore, about a year and a half later there was another reconsideration and the World Bank agreed to lend for oil and gas exploration, which was a real breakthrough for the Bank because previously they had always insisted that their loans be for economically viable projects — and there is just no way that you can guarantee that oil and gas exploration are going to be profitable. They were venturing into a risk field in a way they had previously refused to do. The Bank was only supposed to lend for safe projects but in order to make any dent in the energy situation they had to agree to change this.

Now, I think that some people in the Bank were sincerely concerned about energy independence for the countries they were lending to, but either because of their own political predilections or because they were still under the control of governments such as the United States and the other wealthy countries, they had to maximize the opportunity for private sector participation. So you find that Bank loans for oil and gas exploration are kind of a Trojan Horse for the private sector. Usually when the Bank sends consultants on energy policy to any given country these consultants advise them how they can make their territories more attractive for exploration by the private corporations.

There is more ambiguity in this area, I think, than I've found in most other Bank lending because at least one of the private oil corporations, Exxon, has been quite hostile to any Bank initiative in this field at all. The other companies have generally welcomed the Bank's presence in oil and gas lending. Just as the mining corporations tend to feel the Bank is guaranteeing their security in Third World countries, so the oil and gas corporations do not see the Bank as a competitor but as an ally more or less guaranteeing that they will have access to these fields.

I might add that throughout all the years when the Bank was refusing to lend for oil and gas exploration it was nevertheless in many important areas systematically insisting on a kind of development which increased the dependence of these borrowers on imported oil and gas. For example in the transportation sector there has been a very strong bias towards building highways instead of railroads in the Bank's borrowing countries, which has tied these countries into the whole automobile/truck complex and therefore maximized needs for imported fuels. You could find the same thing in the field of power generation where the Bank has financed a lot of hydroelectric projects, but beginning in the 1960s there was a fairly strong bias in favour of thermal plants — which use imported oils as fuels — rather than hydro projects. The Bank claimed that hydro projects were too capital-intensive, but of course once you've built a thermal plant it is perpetually dependent on fossil fuels to run it.

Again, we can go to the sector of agriculture and note that a high proportion of Bank lending for agriculture, including the small farmer projects, is simply money for the application of fertilizers, pesticides and farm machinery, all of which utilize either fossil fuels for energy or oil and gas for the production of fertilizer. So there is a very interesting case to be made that the World Bank has actually been responsible for a great deal of the energy-import dependence of its borrowing countries.

People projects and supply-side policies

The second major category of projects is called the People-Oriented Projects, which have been heavily publicized by the Bank's public relations as evidence of what the Bank is doing for poor people. When you examine closely how the Bank justifies these claims, you find that most of it boils down to a sort of Reaganomics "trickle-down" theory. I would like to underline this point. I think that the Bank is quite correct when it brags now under the Reagan administration that it has been encouraging so-called supply-side policies for a long time in its borrowing countries. I would agree, it has been doing just that. For example, the Bank argues that if you have unrealistic minimum-wage laws, a lot of people are not going to be employed, so let's get rid of the minimum wage laws and let the employers pay as little as they want. This is an exact point of similarity between the Bank's arguments and the Reagan administration policies.

There is another and I think very sinister aspect to the so-called People-Oriented Projects of the Bank. Quite often these projects seem to be aimed at people who are not fully integrated into the market economy; that is, they are not delivering their surplus to the market, to the cities, to international trade. They are still growing and eating their own food, making much of what they need. The Bank's idea of how these people need to be developed is to tie them into the market and make them labour for the market, either on their own lands or on settlement projects designed by the Bank — by making sure that they have to purchase inputs like fertilizers, pesticides and machinery at a price determined by the World Bank and the project authority.

They have to grow certain crops in a certain way and they have to deliver their harvest to the project authority, which then makes the calculations: We've supplied you with such and such inputs, we're charging you so much for them, we're going to pay you so much for your crop, we're going to deduct the first category from the second and this is what you get in the end. I think a lot of evidence is accumulating that people may be worse off in real terms after they get this kind of "aid" than they were before they were so heavily tied to the market.

I would like to point out that these small farmers are not allowed to make their own cost-benefit evaluation of whether they really need these inputs, whether they're going to get enough increased production out of them to justify this sort of expenditure, whether the risk of using Green Revolution seeds which are much more vulnerable to crop diseases is really justified by the prospects they have of increasing their earnings. When the Bank lends to large farmers, the ones with several thousands of acres, it's not so authoritarian. It allows the larger farmers to make more decisions, because after all they're already producing for the market, they are the type of people the bank understands, whereas the small farmers are labelled "backward" and opposed to technology and so forth. In fact, the small farmers really don't see any percentage for themselves in adopting these programs, but they can be forced to do so one way or another by the World Bank.

I think use of land is the most important issue but I've also devoted chapters of my book to water resources and to tree farming and forestry because these are two other very important resources for the livelihood of people living in the rural areas of the Third World. Many people are dependent on the common resources of water and forest for their living. In many of the projects I've studied the Bank has actually been appropriating these resources for the benefit of corporations and urban elites and using the poor people (if they use them at all) as sort of hired labourers on their own land, as tree farmers for example, growing wood for paper mills.

Doing away with the World Bank

I would like to conclude by saying that my research has opened up many troubling questions, not just about the World Bank as one very powerful institution but about our whole idea of what constitutes economic development. As I did the research for this book I realized that this sort of thing has happened not just in the Third World but also in my own country, in Canada, almost anyplace you look. A big dam is built and they need a reservoir for it and people who have lived and farmed in that reservoir are kicked out, with sometimes very laughable compensation. In the case of World Bank projects in the Third World, the compensation is actually derisory; poor people's land and houses are not considered worth anything in monetary terms and that's just about what they get.

One question I usually get asked when I give talks of this type is, "Well if you don't like the World Bank, what would you put in its place?" My answer to this is, if the Bank is really doing as much damage as I think it is, why would we need to put anything in its place, why would anybody even ask this question? If the Bank is so much in love with market forces why doesn't it just get out of the Third World altogether and see how things would arrange themselves without its money? I think that the world might in fact be a better place if only because some people would have more breathing space to fight for their own land, to change the policies of their own country. I think these arguments which accuse me of being anti-progress, antidevelopment, are actually themselves the argument of the forces that don't want any change. I see prospects for progressive change that the World Bank is actually blocking. I think that the Bank has been working so hard to advocate its model of development because there are in fact other ways of doing the same things. If we cannot imagine other paths of economic development that do not hurt the poorest people, the ones we are using to justify the whole project of aid and economic development, if anything that is done is going to hurt these people more, then maybe we just shouldn't do it at all. I'm willing to say that. I certainly don't think that there are no other solutions, I think there is a great deal that can be done for progressive change. But if the change is not going to be more progressive, I do oppose it. Let's not say that we have to do something if that something is going to hurt people.

The World Debt Crisis:
A Scenario

R.T. Naylor

Thomas Naylor teaches economics and Canadian economic history at McGill University. He is the author of The History of Canadian Business: 1867-1914 *(1975) and continues to write on Canadian banking and international finance. A former economic consultant to UNIDO, he was also a witness before the UN General Committee on the Inalienable Rights of the Palestinian People.*

The 1982 annual meeting of the boards of governors of the IMF and World Bank group took place in an unusually sombre atmosphere. Numerous panic scenarios were debated in private and in public. In fact, one of the principal tasks facing the IMF officials was specifically that of calming the frayed nerves of banks and their sovereign borrowers.

IMF Managing Director, Jacques de Larosière, insisted that the system was stable, that the international financial community led by the IMF could handle any crisis — while the Americans (who would have to foot the largest part of the bill for any big bailout operation) claimed that solvency, like prosperity, was just around the corner.

Such soothing words must be judged against the record of recent history. Since the cash-flow crisis of 1976, there have been increasingly numerous and increasingly loud warnings about the inherent follies of the international financial merry-go-round that has been conducted since 1973. But as late as 1980 the official response had been one of searching for ways to increase the volume of borrowing and to ease the terms of access of borrowing countries to international money markets.

Then, at the 1981 IMF annual meetings in Washington, the Reagan administration, under the combined influence of hard-core monetarism and the voodoo economics of the supply-side school, decided it was time to turn off the tap, at least with respect to official and paragovernmental sources of liquidity. The result was to compound a private sector problem — the incipient transnational bank debt crisis — by a public sector problem, by casting doubt on the volume and terms of public sector funds that would be available to bail out the most impecunious debtors and, therefore, the transnational banks.

The roots of the sovereign debt crisis now unfolding can be found in 1973 when the United States, in an effort to shore up a besieged dollar and re-establish its pre-eminence in international economic relations, decided to replace a defunct gold standard with an oil standard. That year the U.S. government connived with the Seven Sisters — the giant oil corporations — and OPEC to quadruple oil prices, an event which had a number of beneficial implications for the U.S. balance of payments.

Profits per barrel reportedly rose 50 per cent, resulting in a considerable increase in the return flow of invisible earnings to the U.S. In terms of commodity exports, there were two appreciable gains. An energy cost differential that had long favoured Western European and Japanese industry over American was eliminated. And an enormous market was created, especially in Iran, for the American arms industry then languishing in its post-Vietnam doldrums.

On capital account, the obvious advantage lay in the fact that major OPEC countries held their foreign exchange reserves in the form of American treasury bills — in effect, the petroleum price increases were an underhanded tax on American and European consumers of oil, the proceeds of which went to help finance the American off-budget deficit and therefore to strengthen the administration and bureaucracy against Congress.

In addition to these highly visible gains there was another of even greater significance to the United States. This was the ability of the U.S. to continue running an overall balance of payments deficit while at the same time creating an increased demand for U.S. dollars, thereby discouraging a return flow of accumulated overseas dollar claims.

Since most of the world's oil trade (and that of many other commodities) was denominated in dollars, the quadrupling of oil prices immediately drove up the demand for American dollar balances. The advantage was reinforced in the politico-financial manoeuverings that followed. In 1974, Saudi Arabia, which traditionally denominated a quarter of its oil sales in sterling, announced that subsequently only dollars would be accepted, thus ringing the death knell for any residual hopes that the British government and banks might have to re-establishing sterling as an international reserve currency.

In 1975 OPEC as a whole agreed formally to denominate all of its oil trade in dollars. The dollar-oil standard was further entrenched with a secret Washington-Riyadh agreement to create special Treasury instruments for Saudi investments, and by the collaboration of Henry Kissinger with the Shah of Iran to sabotage a Saudi-led effort to reduce the price of oil.

In 1977, as a protective measure, the U.S. Congress gave the President the power to place a freeze on the assets of sovereign depositors — a device subsequently used against Iran to defend the Chase-Manhattan Bank a few years later.

However, the oil price escalation also revolutionized the world of private international finance. Until 1973, developing countries requiring foreign exchange in excess of current receipts usually obtained it by attracting foreign direct investment, by soliciting official development assistance or, as a last resort, by borrowing from the IMF — whose terms and conditions for lending most countries tried to avoid.

The recycling — and rescheduling — of debt

In 1973, the sum of world current and capital accounts doubled. Furthermore, "stagflation" became generalized in the industrialized countries. As a result, direct foreign investment and official development aid both shrank, while domestic investment in the industrialized countries also diminished sharply. Liquidity, from the decline in domestic investment and the temporary deposit of OPEC funds, piled up in Western banks, just at the point when direct foreign investment and official development aid were falling and developing-country financing needs escalated. "Recycling" became the watchword. And the now well-known and well documented explosion of both the unregulated Eurocurrency market and country debt followed.

The new recycling mechanism worked fairly efficiently in the early to mid-1970s. The major borrowers continued to sustain fairly steady real economic growth; primary-product prices, the ultimate collateral behind most sovereign borrowing by the developing countries, climbed sharply until late 1975; real interest rates were low, as nominal rate increases lagged behind inflation and debts were negotiated on a medium-term fixed-rate basis.

Warnings about the inherent precariousness of the rapidly escalating debt-loads were ignored. The IMF, whose resources were dwarfed by the new scale of international financial requirements, was largely shunted aside, even as policeman of the system, in the scramble by the banks to unload deposit money onto sovereign borrowers. A mini-crisis in 1976 did little to check the enthusiasm. But in 1979-80, a number of events coincided to dangerously expose the "system", if it could be graced with the term.

A new round of oil-price increases suddenly, but temporarily, topped up the supply of liquidity to the transnational banks, at the same time driving up the demand for balance of payments financing. By itself, the oil-price hike would have created little difficulty. However, underlying economic circumstances were quite different from 1973-74 when the "recycling" mechanism had first swung into action. Hence, as financial conditions deteriorated, it became increasingly difficult for the debtors to carry the rapidly escalating load.

Most of the problem stemmed from central banks in the industrialized countries taking so seriously the 19th-century nonsense recently rediscovered by academic aggrandizement:

that in order to control inflation it sufficed to control the rate of growth of the supply of money.

The proposition assumes, among other things, that the velocity of circulation of "money" is stable, and that precisely what functions as "money" can be defined and controlled in quantity. That such a notion could seriously be accepted when electronic fund-transfer credit instruments were proliferating is only comprehensible if one pauses to look briefly at the institution of academic tenure. This involves a state guarantee of an inflated salary for life to those who agree not to disturb the social order by the exercise of native intelligence or even common sense.

As central bankers adopted increasingly restrictive growth-rate targets for their favourite monetary aggregate, interest rates began to climb steeply and fluctuate wildly. Along with high and volatile interest rates came a shortening of the term of lending and the evolution of floating rate instruments. On top of these financial disasters came recession in the industrialized countries, shortly turning into bona fide depression, squeezing international primary-produce prices and developing-country export volumes, and raising the spectre of a resurgence of protectionism.

Thus for the developing countries (and Eastern Bloc) borrowers, 1979 was a watershed point. Real borrowing costs rose sharply; commodity prices plummeted; and trade deficits soared. But the debt-load continued to increase as bankers, flush with liquidity, hustled their loans to virtually any and all borrowers.

Hence, at precisely the time when national monetary authorities in the major industrial countries were busy "fighting inflation" by wrecking domestic capital markets and appreciating their currencies through competitive interest-rate hikes, the banks began pumping short-term, floating-rate credit into the international financial systems. The result was to create an awesome problem of bunched obligations as the maturing of medium-term debt from the early 1970s coincided with the need for annual roll-overs of short-term debt acquired after 1979 at escalating rates of interest.

The bankers were, of course, simply obeying the herd instinct for which they have become notorious. After all, transnational banks are corporate bureaucracies, and obey the same rules of behaviour as other corporate bureaucracies. The primary rule for such bureaucracies is to make decisions that will maximize the rate of growth of assets. This involves a competitive scramble to hustle loans, resulting in the periodic flooding of countries with liquidity they do not need — followed by panic withdrawals when they do need it.

The system is completely irrational. It is preposterous in principle and dangerous in practice to mix private and public functions in this way. The provision of international legal tender should be closely regulated by the public sector. Sovereign lending by private banks politicizes the process of providing legal tender, adding enormous potential political problems on top of sufficiently awesome financial and economic ones.

For one thing, there is the problem of the socially irrational criteria by which liquidity is provided — the fundamental guiding principle of which is the herd instinct of international bankers. For another, there is the fraudulent character of the analyses those bankers pretend to carry out to justify decisions already taken. Here enters the farce of "country risk analysis" — plugging worthless numbers into silly equations and using the meaningless "results" as a cover for overexposed corporate posteriors.

Analysts who endorsed many of the country loans, to the extent they thought about it at all, blithely assumed that the unique experience of the industrialized countries in the postwar period, until 1973, was valid for all times and places. They assumed that private or public consumption expenditures (as distinct from capital project spending by either the private or public sector) could lead the growth process in the absence of specific and highly favourable supply-side conditions.

Given the practical absence of growth generated by much of the expenditure of borrowed money, given the mounting real burden of the debts, the result would be that repayment of sovereign debt often could be assured only by massive confiscation of private wealth in some of the debtor countries. And given their social make-up one can be sure that in most cases the already destitute would suffer most — with potentially explosive political consequences.

The year 1981 saw the financial chickens come home to roost in Washington, begging for a public sector bailout facility via the IMF or beyond. It was a year when panic over potential defaults focused initially on the Eastern Bloc, but also coincided with one last major surge of lending to the LDCs, especially in Latin America, thus assuring that once the Polish situation was stabilized, even more awesome problems would appear elsewhere.

Over the entire period from 1957 to 1979 there were 14 sovereign reschedulings, embracing loans totalling $16.7 billion. In 1980-81 there were 20 cases involving 17 countries, and a total of $15.3 billion. Estimates of the total LDC debt that was due, and had to be repaid or rolled over or rescheduled in 1982, ran as high as $175 billion. And the outlook for 1983 and 1984 was even bleaker.

As rescheduling became increasingly necessary, on political if not financial grounds, the queue in front of the Paris Club promised to reach halfway around the world. On top of continued grim forecasts about world trade and commodity prices, the fall in world oil prices was squeezing the deposit base of the transnational banks at precisely the time when so much of their assets were in the form of endangered sovereign loans.

And talk became quite open about a debtors' cartel to bargain coltectively about terms of renewal. Indeed, whispers about potential repudiation became a chorus of shouts by the summer of 1982. It was against such a happy background that the bankers and their friends gathered in Toronto in September, 1982, for the 37th Annual IMF-World Bank meetings.

The changing role of the IMF

The first blow to the IMF's well-established system came with the creation of the two-tiered gold market in 1968 — which restricted convertibility of the dollar to official uses. Then in 1971 came complete suspension by the U.S. of gold convertibility — combined with a formal devaluation. This destroyed the basic, hitherto prevailing notion of a system of exchange rates fixed in terms of dollars — which in turn were linked to gold.

Then came 1973 and organized bedlam. All currencies floated; some were valued against dollars; some in other foreign currencies; some were valued in Special Drawing Rights; some were fixed in value in terms of a complex set of economic indicators. Furthermore, foreign exchange reserve reporting became distorted: Some countries valued their gold reserves at the old official prices, some at the new market prices, some wherever they wanted.

With world inflation and commodity price changes causing a sudden increase in the volume of deficits to be financed, the IMF resources — based on its quotas, supplemented by a small issue of SDRs — were too small for it to have a major influence in the international monetary field except for marginal countries unable to tap the transnational banks. And the banks themselves, flush with cash, paid little attention to the IMF's advice about credit-worthiness or borrowers' policy mixes.

The importance of the IMF underwent a resurgence after 1976 — when a cash-flow crisis of LDC debtors caused a brief panic among bankers, and when the bankers' own efforts to impose "conditionality" and an IMF-type package on a sovereign debtor, namely Peru, were a complete failure.

There were two reasons for the newly enhanced importance of the IMF. One was that it could devise and administer policy packages to help assure the repayment of private loans; the second that its own disbursements provided "seed money" for private consortium loans. As a closer co-operation with the transnational banks evolved, and as the scale of international financial flows increased, IMF resources also grew. Apart from the periodic increase of quotas, the IMF also created a number of special financial facilities to increase country access to its resources. During the late 1970s, the IMF's attitude toward country policy also mellowed, with loans and credits being also extended for longer periods.

In 1979, to finance further oil price increases the IMF allowed drawings up to 450 per cent of quota for periods of three years, with due regard to the structural and supply-side rather than simply the demand-side nature of developing-country problems. And with the progress of the SDR as both a unit of account and a means of financing transactions, it looked as if the IMF was beginning to evolve into something approximating a world central bank.

This was a development encouraged by the transnational banks, heavily involved in sovereign loans and balance of payments financing. They increasingly regarded the IMF as a lender of last resort to bail out ailing countries with heavy sovereign debts — with credits often going directly and immediately to repaying arrears due to private banks. By 1980 there was open talk among bankers, led by the then Bank of America chief, A.W. Clausen, about formalizing the arrangement.

With this evolution came the ever more vociferous demands of Third World countries for a New International Economic Order. The demands began in the mid-1970s and reached their peak in the form of a set of proposals for reform of the international monetary system proffered by the Brandt Commission.

The Brandt report called for a movement away from a dollar-based financial system. It called for an upgrading of the role of the SDR, with a substantial increase in SDR allocations and a link between new SDRs created by the IMF and a massive transfer of resources to the LDCs. In private, Willy Brandt, supported by former World Bank chief Robert McNamara, also called for the creation of a genuine World Central Bank to remove from the U.S. the power to create and distribute liquidity. Such an institution was to be politically under the control of the majority of member governments, instead of subject to the staggered voting system which gives the U.S. a veto over crucial IMF decisions.

In a similar vein the Prime Minister and finance minister of New Zealand, Robert Muldoon, before the 1982 IMF meetings, tried to win approval from the Commonwealth finance ministers for a new Bretton Woods conference. The great majority backed his call, but the opposition of Britain, Canada, Australia and Jamaica (under its new conservative administration) prevented such a proposal being made as a unanimous Commonwealth demand.

Reaganism: The U.S. "gets tough"

There were calls too from developing country representatives for other measures to meet the debt crisis. Mexico proposed a new IMF facility to aid countries whose balance of payments problem was due to debt-service costs. Amir Jamal, the Tanzanian minister of finance, raised the possibility of an interest-rate subsidization scheme. But obviously none of these plans had any chance of success without the agreement of the party that would have to pay most heavily for them, and which held a veto over any such decisions. This was particularly true given the hardline approach of the Reagan administration, which had come to power with a commitment to reverse many of the "soft" policy trends of the late 1970s.

The Reagan administration demanded monetary restraint, both domestically and internationally, and less government intervention. This translated into a posture of confining the growth of the IMF.

Any increase in world liquidity, the U.S. felt, would lead to financial laxity on the part of debtors and generate inflation. It insisted on giving priority to adjustment, to domestic economic and financial housecleaning, and avoiding measures that interfered with the "magic of the market". This stance was partly determined by ideological conviction. But it was also hardball politics.

The impact of Reaganism was quickly felt at the 1981 IMF-World Bank meetings in Washington where the U.S. blocked further SDR allocations, demanded a tightening of conditionality, denounced plans for a World Bank Energy Affiliate, and threatened cuts in its subscription to IDA, the World Bank's "soft loan" window.

In fact, SDR allocations were held down to levels previously agreed on — despite Third World protests — and the IMF was refused permission to borrow on the open market to supplement its scarce resources. The IMF then had to borrow massively from Saudi Arabia to meet its responsibilities in 1982. Conditionality was tightened under the table by stricter interpretations of the terms and conditions attached to loans. Furthermore, many IMF credits were shifted from a three-year term to one year. And payments on nearly a third of the credits already negotiated were suspended in 1982 for failure by the countries concerned to achieve their performance objectives.

At the 1982 meetings the United States arrived with a view to maintaining its tough stance of the year before — despite the fact that the debt crisis and global recession had reached alarming dimensions. Demands for new SDR allocations were swept aside and the U.S. announced its commitment to block any substantial increase in quotas. It also continued to oppose private sector borrowings by the IMF — despite demands by some bankers that the route be opened. And it put its voice on record as opposing further borrowings from Saudi Arabia.

(This was an act of unenlightened self-interest. After Iran's experience of having its assets frozen, Saudi Arabia began attempting to protect its resources by substituting IMF loans as an alternative to U.S. Treasury bills, and hence the U.S. had both a political and financial reason for taking the stance.)

While the Mexican crisis and the combined demands of all other member states forced the U.S. to moderate its stance on quotas — with a 50 per cent increase, somewhat below what the IMF itself felt to be a necessary minimum, as the likely outcome — it remained adamant on the other issues, forcing the international community and the banks to look elsewhere than to the established IMF facilities for any massive bailout mechanism that might become necessary.

The U.S. position was to point to declining interest rates (for which it claimed credit), noting that each one percentage point drop in LIBOR (London inter-bank rate) took some $15 billion off sovereign-country debt-service charges. It also expounded its sunny prognoses of an early return to economic recovery and therefore increased export earnings for the developing country debtors.

Finally, on the financial front the U.S. proposed a safety net against potential crises. This would be a superfund made up of pledges from industrial countries who would agree to make funds jointly available in the event of a liquidity crisis. It would be a similar approach to that extended to Britain in the 1976 bailout under the General Agreements to Borrow.

Of course, the trick with the Emergency Fund proposal was the safeguards it provided the U.S. to ensure a maximum American control over the extension of credits and the assurance that such credits as were extended carried near-commercial rates of interest. IMF loans financed via quota increases were subject to the general review of the IMF Board of Directors over which the U.S. had no veto, while quota increases were inevitably bound up with the tricky question of the distribution of voting rights — something the U.S., with its over-representation in relation to its economic weight in the modern world — had no desire to broach. And while regular IMF credits carry concessionary rates of interest, those accorded under the General Agreements to Borrow bear near-market rates.

Furthermore, the U.S. pressured for the IMF in general to step up its surveillance functions, and it was during the 1982 IMF-World Bank meeting that the Group of Seven held its first meeting to co-ordinate economic policy under the auspices of the IMF, as agreed at Versailles in June, 1981.

The Saudi connection

The plans for increasing IMF resources via special facilities could take time to approve and implement. In the interim, the U.S. relaxed its opposition to further reliance on Saudi Arabia for additional funds. In the U.S. view, looking to Saudi Arabia would be preferable to open market borrowing, a new SDR issue, or a substantial increase in quotas.

Reliance on Saudi Arabia for topping up the IMF's resources carries two difficulties. The first is that with falling oil revenues and enormous demands on Saudi funds, both for domestic investment and for inter-Arab loans and investments (including financing the Iraqi war effort in the Gulf), it is not clear how much longer Saudi Arabia can make good the shortfall of IMF resources.

The second is that Saudi Arabia and the other surplus Arab oil producers are increasingly likely to lose patience with the American practice of allowing the Zionist lobby in Congress to determine foreign policy directions.

Saudi Arabia and the United States came close to an open public break (albeit the relationship in private remained largely intact) during the ten-week siege of Beirut from June to August 1982, when Saudi Arabia threatened massive withdrawals of money from American banks if West Beirut was stormed. Granted the U.S. could easily have frozen Saudi Arabian assets; but the real issue was not the funds currently on deposit, so much as the stress on future political and financial relationships.

The biggest headache for the U.S. in its relations with Saudi Arabia at the IMF is the issue of the PLO's observer status, the history of which took a new twist in Toronto.

The issue opened up in the 1979 meetings when the Group of 77 (the Third World members, then numbering 119) voted, apparently unanimously, to extend observer status to the PLO for the next round of talks. There were ample precedents for this action: The PLO exercises a wide range of social and economic functions with respect to the millions of Palestinian refugees, and in many ways has the attributes of a national government — including the overwhelming endorsement of its citizens whenever this has been tested electorally or by poll.

The subsequent year (1980), with a presidential election at stake, saw a resolution initiated by the U.S. demanding that observers to the IMF meeting be limited to those who attended in 1979. The chairman of the meeting, Tanzanian finance minister Amir Jamal, reportedly threatened to resign, but a U.S. under-secretary of the Treasury called on Saudi Arabia for support, insisting that if the PLO were invited, Carter's chances of a re-election would be weakened. The Saudis, of course, bought the argument, hook, line and sinker. Jamal was hastily summoned to Riyadh and asked to relent.

In 1981 there were fresh manoeuverings. The Kuwait delegation was prepared to refuse all new loans if the PLO was not admitted, but the Saudis would not go along. A massive loan from Saudi Arabia to the IMF was secured and an arrangement established to defer the issue to Toronto when Kuwaiti finance minister Abdel-Latif El Hamad would be in the chair.

But once more the issue found a detour. The PLO delegate arrived at the Toronto meetings only to find that the Arab Governors in the Fund and World Bank had already resolved not to put the issue on the agenda. Instead, in April of 1982, Abdel-Latif El Hamad had referred the issue to the International Court at the Hague, and no further actions were contemplated until a ruling was received. Arab lobbying would now be focused on ensuring that the U.S. did not prevail on the court to delay its procedures.

One powerful instrument the Arab leaders have at their disposal, if they choose to use it, is the world's increasing dependence on their monetary reserves; both to keep the regular IMF facilities running and for the future success of any Emergency Fund.

The emergency fund plan

Since the United States seems adamant about the plan for an
Emergency Fund, and since some such scheme is certainly
going to play a major role in rescuing the international financial system from the follies of the 1970s, it is worthwhile to
examine in detail the nature and genesis of the plan — to the
extent that can be patched together from scraps of information.

The story seems to begin in Hungary in December 1981,
when transnational bank depositors began a run on the country's foreign exchange reserves. The run was partially due to
general jitters over COMECON (Council for Mutual Economic
Aid) lending in the wake of the Polish debacle, partly to the
need to finance OPEC withdrawals, and partly to a Reagan
administration program of economic sabotage aimed at the
Soviet Bloc as a whole. The outcome certainly hastened Hungary's admission to the IMF. But in the meantime, with its foreign exchange reserves depleted, and with IMF membership
still months away, Hungary asked the Bank for International
Settlements, the Basle-based central bankers' central bank, for a
lifeline.

The BIS arranged a credit facility from 13 of its member
banks — sometimes in the form of underwriting the BIS facility,
sometimes, as in the West German case, in the form of a
government-guaranteed direct central bank-to-central bank
loan. It was administratively ad hoc and messy, with very weak
precedents. And of course the BIS was not really placed in a
position where it could demand IMF-type conditionality. The
lessons were not unheeded.

Then came the Versailles summit in June 1982, which
reached certain decisions, the importance of which were not
well appreciated at the time — with the world's attention being
directed towards the carnage in Lebanon. The summit resolved
to strengthen the IMF's role in two crucial respects.

The Group of Seven agreed to regular policy co-ordination
discussions under IMF auspices, and therefore to a moral but-
tressing of its "surveillance" activities. And in response to
increasing symptoms of cut-and-run sentiment among the
banks, the conference called for a stronger role for the IMF in
co-ordinating the activities of the transnational banks in their
sovereign lending and recycling activities.

In fact, in June, after Versailles and the first meeting of the Ditchley group of international banks (to plan a "creditors'" cartel), the IMF and 30 transnational banks met to discuss the idea of the banks modelling their international lending on that of the IMF, with credit granted in distinct tranches and withheld if the country in question failed to meet appropriate performance criteria. IMF-supervised multibank lending would carry the conditionality clout that the banks alone had failed to achieve with Peru and other earlier cases; there was an expectation that Mexico would be the next test case.

The Mexican disaster was the final step on the way to the creation of the Emergency Fund. In mid-August, when it was evident that financial collapse was imminent in Mexico, U.S. Secretary of State George Schultz is reportedly pushed the idea of the BIS administering a bailout facility on very tough conditions.

When the Mexican crisis actually hit, the plans went into effect. The IMF buttonholed the private banks to keep them from running, maintaining the pressure for several weeks. And the BIS, assured that the private banks would agree in principle to rolling over the Mexican loans, collected a $1.85 billion facility through the Group of Ten plus Switzerland central banks.

The BIS facility had several unique features. It was the first time a developing country had benefited from this kind of collective central bank rescue operation. The central bank loans were all guaranteed by their home governments — the Hungarian operation had been quite inconsistent in this regard. And most importantly, it was the first time Western central banks had formally and publicly tied aid to a debtor country in trouble to an agreement for it to put its domestic financial policy under IMF supervision.

The next step was to use the model of the Mexican rescue as the basis for the creation of a formal Emergency Fund of $10 to $25 billion to run in tandem with the IMF; and that is what the Americans brought to the September 1982 Toronto meeting.

While the other industrial countries, and the developing ones in general, were initially antagonistic to the idea — and the developing group remained so — the industrial countries were gradually won over. The U.S. traded a relaxation on the

issue of how big a quota increase to allow against developing
G-10 consensus in favour of the Emergency Fund. Financing
was to be arranged by opening the General Arrangements to
Borrow (GAB) (the mechanism through with G-10 central banks
agreed to support each other in times of balance of payments
crisis) to non-G-10 countries.

Fears by the G-10 that their fallback funds would be drained
off, to Mexico for example, were alleviated by the promise of a
substantial hike in the total volume of funds earmarked for GAB
credits. And the issue was referred, along with the question of
the extent of the quota increases, to the April 1983 executive
board meetings (subsequently moved up to February, 1983
after the Brazilian financial crisis).*

The Emergency Fund and the quota issue were not the sole
bones of contention at the 1982 IMF-World Bank meetings. But,
as a result of the Mexican debacle and the associated threat of
Latin American sovereign borrowers dropping a collective debt
bomb, they certainly grabbed the bulk of the attention and
dominated the proceedings.

For a change, the World Bank avoided a major ideological
onslaught. This was in part because the changes demanded by
the U.S. administration were already being put into effect.
Under the new direction of A.W. Clausen, the Bank was rapidly
shedding the image Robert McNamara had given it, an image
that had allowed U.S. ideologues to attack it as an instrument
of international Keynesianism and for being in the business of
financing "socialism" throughout the world. (The fact that it
had never lost a penny on its loans and investments over 35
years of operation, and that it was constantly under attack from
the left for being a neo-imperialist institution went blithely
ignored in all the neoconservative-generated tumult.)

Clausen increased the degree of co-financing undertaken by
the World Bank in conjunction with private financial institutions, and proceeded to draft the principles of a World Bank-
administered multinational investment insurance agency. Furthermore, the report of a U.S. Treasury investigation into multilateral international development banks gave them the ultimate

* At those board meetings it was decided to increase quotas by 50 per
cent and to activate the Emergency Fund — although this decision
remained to be ratified by each member government.

accolade — of being good for U.S. business interests. (Whether or not they were of any real value to the developing countries does not seem to have been at issue.) However, the Congressional decision to pare back contributions to IDA threatened the immediate efficacy of the soft-loan window of the World Bank, and clouded its long-term prospects — an issue left largely unresolved in the patch-up job done at Toronto to keep IDA afloat.

Apart from the customary tirades from the countries that had been denied funds on overtly political grounds, and the usual posturing by delegates in preparation for the next round in April 1983, very little more of importance took place at the official meeting. Even on the pressing question of country debt, the issue of Mexico remained completely unresolved, although Argentina's deal with the United Kingdom for the unfreezing of its assets was drafted under IMF auspices and accepted by both parties shortly after the meetings.

International debt: outlook for the 1980s

The events in Toronto seemingly demonstrated: first, that everyone was finally prepared to admit there was a serious problem, albeit differing in their assessment of the magnitude; and, second, that there was some will to deal at least with the immediate symptom, if not the underlying causes.

The symptom is of course the cash-flow crisis now extant, and likely to persist for another two years, barring unforeseeable major changes in the underlying circumstances.

The cash-flow crisis on the surface results from a temporary confluence of circumstances — the coincidence of two years of unprecedented interest rates on short-term floating rate debt, the maturing of medium-term debt contracted in the 1970s, and the need to roll over the short-term debt contracted since 1979-80 — all against a background of falling commodity prices.

In the short run, cracks in the financial edifice can be covered over by bailout facilities, injections of cash from the BIS, an Emergency Fund, bilateral government-to-government or central bank-to-central bank loans, or IMF credits. These patch-works will enable the countries under financial siege to maintain some of their essential imports and, much more important, to continue to pay interest and therefore avoid the ignominy (to the country and to the banks) of default.

In the meantime, the principal can be rolled over or rescheduled, and any arrears of interest simply capitalized. On the surface these operations are not unwelcome to the bank lenders, for rescheduled loans often carry a higher interest rate than the original ones, and the results help brush up the appearance of the balance sheets. But in reality the problem is only deferred and compounded in the process.

In the medium term, the process of international lending must be rejuvenated in order to keep the banking system healthy.

At issue here is the degree to which the Euromoney market has ceased to be basically a recycling mechanism for petroliquidity. There always were sources of funds additional to the temporary surpluses of OPEC countries, but in recent years these have tended to dominate the market. Apart from the more exotic sources of funds, such as the laundering of the proceeds from heroin traffic, the secretion of all sorts of political flight capital and earnings from the private arms traffic, the principal accumulation of funds seems to have become based on the normal savings of the OECD countries.

OPEC deposits have recently fallen to a mere 10 to 12 per cent of all Eurodollar deposits. The combined OPEC surplus dropped from $120 billion in 1979-80 to $30 billion in 1980-81, and has since vanished completely in the face of declining sales volumes, falling prices and the coming on stream of new non-OPEC sources of oil.

The Secretariat of OPEC in Vienna has officially projected a combined current account deficit of about $9.5 billion for the OPEC group this year. Furthermore, falling OPEC surpluses do not translate themselves into equivalent falling deficits for non-oil LDCs. For every $1 billion decline in OPEC surpluses, only $140 million gets chopped off the deficits on the other end. Hence falling oil revenues squeeze the deposit base far more than they affect the demand for funds.

Granted that some OPEC countries may continue to have surplus earnings for some time, the Eurodollar market for years danced to the tune of the net OPEC injection; hence the refinancing of sovereign loans will increasingly have an impact directly on the savings and investment process within the OECD group. Furthermore, the net OPEC withdrawal is likely to escalate as the surplus countries divert more of their funds into reconstruction finance in the Persian Gulf.

The Iran-Iraq war led to a sharp reduction in oil output, but Saudi Arabia, Kuwait and the Emirates stepped up production to offset this. However, the impact of each dollar of OPEC revenue on the international financial system differs according to which country earns it. Iran and Iraq, even in normal times, had the capacity to absorb most of their revenues domestically; whereas Saudi Arabia, Kuwait and the Emirates generated surpluses for foreign investment. Hence their stepping-up oil production meant that in 1979-80 the flow of funds into the Euromoney market (and the accompanying orgy of sovereign lending) was greater than would otherwise have taken place.

However, increasing sums have been diverted into financing Iraq's war effort; a bribe of $75 billion has been offered Iran in exchange for a truce; and reconstruction of the two belligerents will substantially drain what used to be surplus earnings bound for Euromoney deposits, even without the additional complication of falling oil prices and falling OPEC oil export volumes. On top there will be the cost of rebuilding Lebanon — estimated at about $27 billion, most of which will have to come from the Gulf.

Moreover, even assuming the establishment of successful bailout facilities in the short run, and a new infusion of liquidity via the transnational banks in the medium term, in the long run there is still a fundamental problem that must be faced. Somehow or other the flow of payments for debt service charges from debtors in developing countries has to be increased or the volume of the debt (and therefore of debt service payments) reduced.

With the first option the chances of raising the export income of the LDCs to improve their capacity to service their debt in the long run do not seem very bright. Expectations currently are for a very weak recovery in the industrial countries. It might be a long time before a recovery translated itself — if it ever did — into a major hike in prices or quantities of exports of developing country commodities.

And the turnaround must be in basic commodities; for with

rising levels of structural unemployment that will persist even in the event of a substantial recovery, the rich countries are unlikely to tolerate substantially larger imports of developing-country light- and medium-manufactured goods. The current glut of key commodities darkens the prospect for a substantial improvement along these lines.

A second possiblity is that increases in exports could take place at continuing weak terms of trade and in a context of continued stagnation in the producing countries. This would require, in effect, massive virtual confiscation of private domestic wealth and its diversion into the external trade sector. Given the political realities, this would generally require military governments and would be conducted largely at the expense of the already poor.

Alternatively, individual debtor countries could repudiate selected parts of their debt.

But a more likely scenario is collective action to renegotiate and/or scale down debt. The debtors would bargain collectively with the banks, the BIS, the Paris Club and the IMF. Brazil has taken the lead in calling for an "OPEC of the indebted", and Argentinian diplomacy during the Falklands War reputedly included efforts to get Latin American debtors to take joint action against British creditors.

International debt renegotiations do have historical precedents, including the plans devised for scaling down the burden of German reparations in the 1920s and 1930s. But under existing circumstances, the scaling down of sovereign debt to private sector banks would likely require the home governments of these banks to agree to indemnify them against at least part of their loss.

In effect, the national central banks would move to monetize part of the bad debts sovereign borrowers have incurred with their banks. These moves might well be accompanied by widespread bank nationalizations to stave off panic and collapse. They would also set off an unseemly squabble among national central banks over responsibility for overseas branches and subsidiaries, much as the Banco Ambriosano affair did.

Any more optimistic long-term scenario is necessarily tinged with utopianism. It would require dealing with the core of the problem — the irrationality of turning the business of international means of payment over to private sector banks effectively beyond national or international regulation. Not only do such banks have an inherent propensity to competitively maximize their rate of growth of assets; but they also have a penchant for alternatively flooding borrowers with credit and then running for cover when the cream starts to turn sour. Furthermore, sovereign lending is necessarily a political operation: It is impossible for major lending institutions to avoid being dragged into the abyss of the national politics of scores of sovereign debtors. Any effort to attach policy conditions to loans necessarily involves meddling in national politics. Both the provision of international liquidity and the attaching of terms and conditions to loans are very much the responsibility of public sector institutions.

The challenge for tomorrow is not to scale down the IMF, or to replace it with an American-run emergency fund to prop up the tottering private transnational banks. Nor is it to return to an exclusive dollar standard, where the ebb and flow of international liquidity depends on spending decisions by the American administration aimed at addressing the U.S. balance of payments deficit. Even less useful would be a return to the gold standard, given the chaos with which that operation historically has been associated.

Rather, the challenge lies in one of two possible routes of development. One is to have national governments assert full control over banking and credit institutions on the French or more recently the Mexican model, along with some form of exchange controls when and if necessary. The second route would require the evolution of an institution along the lines demanded by Robert McNamara, a body that could conduct an international, managed money system above the demands of partisan and power politics.

That is what is needed — but don't hold your breath.

PART TWO

Politics
and
Human Rights

Financing Injustice: Canada's Role

James Morrell

James Morrell is the director of the Center for International Policy in Washington, which undertakes policy analysis on financial and human rights issues involving the Third World with the purpose of influencing the U.S. government and international financial institutions.

Canada doesn't have an aid program in El Salvador; you don't have a war going on in El Salvador. Nevertheless, some of your tax dollars are being inadvertently diverted to the war in El Salvador and used for assorted other purposes that you wouldn't necessarily approve. Every time the IMF or World Bank makes a loan to any country in the world, for every dollar that's lent out Canadians pay about three cents. For example, South Africa may soon get a loan from the IMF of up to $1 billion. You will be paying $30 million of it. There's discussion of $200 to $300 million going to fund the war in El Salvador for the next three years, also from the IMF. Of that, $6 to $9 million will come from your tax coffers. Guatemala has a shopping list of loans in the same range. By virtue of your contributions to the international banks, your money will go out to Guatemala.

Yet, in figuring out a way of counteracting this trend, Canada is really the key country. For the next couple of years I have almost given up hope on Washington. But along with the Western European nations, Canada comes close to forming a majority of votes in the major international financial institutions. The purpose of this conference is to draw these institutions out of the shadows and out from under the esoteric status they have enjoyed up to now, to make them a public issue. It certainly is your public money those institutions are spending when they send funds to South Africa, El Salvador and Guatemala.

Delivery Mechanism

How is your money delivered to these various destinations and others that I will mention? Briefly, the International Monetary Fund is basically a pool of currencies that all the member countries contribute to. The strong currencies, including Canada's, are used to make the loans to Third World countries or South Africa.

The World Bank and its sister agency, the International Development Association, are also sources of loans. The IDA is simply a collection of funds donated by the rich member countries and given out to Third World countries for 50 years at no interest. The ordinary capital facility of the World Bank works in a slightly more complicated way; the money is collected and pledged by the rich member countries — the United States, Canada and Western Europe. On the basis of those contributions and pledges the World Bank goes to Wall Street and other capital markets and raises money from private bankers. This money, along with repayments of previous loans, is used to make new loans. Here there is a point the World Bank likes to forget. Not a single penny could be raised on Wall Street or anywhere else if money from countries such as Canada had not first been pledged to the Bank as backing for its bond sales.

Canada's participation in the Inter-American Development Bank works the same way: It's simply a regional version of the World Bank operating in Latin America.

Human rights implications: Chile

Where does this money go and what are the human rights implications of it? The story begins with the case of Chile in

1970 to 1973. As you know, the perennial socialist candidate
Salvador Allende finally won an election in Chile in 1970. As
president, Allende nationalized the copper mines, thereby out-
raging their owners. Even before Allende could take office,
President Nixon called a meeting of his crisis committee and
ordered it to "make the economy scream".

"Not a nut or a bolt shall reach Chile," Nixon determined.
The World Bank, the IMF, the Inter-American Development
Bank all fell in line, in perfect lockstep, with his directive.
These ostensibly non-political, technical institutions became
tools of the get-Chile policy. Not a penny of World Bank loans
went to Chile under Allende, from 1970 to 1973, and only a
negligible amount of Inter-American Bank loans. The IMF
denied Chile a stand-by arrangement. This credit blockade had
a considerable effect in undermining confidence, leading to the
army coup and the terrorism that took place in Chile in 1973
through 1976 and which persists today.

The IMF and South Africa

In 1976, South Africa applied to the IMF for assistance, first for
$93 million, then after the Soweto riots and massacres had
further eroded confidence, for further helpings that brought the
total up to $464 million. Canada unfortunately supported this
loan, although the United States and Great Britain worked
hardest for it inside the IMF. A number of other countries in the
IMF seriously questioned whether South Africa really needed
this type of assistance. They noted, for example, that South
Africa had one of the largest gold stocks in the world and that
perhaps it ought to be assisting other countries — rather than
getting assistance itself. But having said that, they all went
along and supported the loan to South Africa.

All this, of course, was taking place behind closed doors. No
minutes were published and no explanations made to the public. Indeed, if you even raised the possibility of public accountability to IMF officials, they would find it completely foreign
and alien. In addition, a state department cable has recently
surfaced which says that South Africa may approach the IMF
for a large loan from both the compensatory financing and the
stand-by arrangement facilities, which we calculate could be
for as much as $1 billion. Apparently the South Africans are

sounding out the IMF on the possibility of such a loan. Of course this again is not going to be discussed publicly. The only public notice that will be given by the IMF will be a press announcement the day it gets the loan and that is all, no explanation.*

Central America loans

It's in Central America that you can see how the disregard of human rights standards has its effect most clearly. We've recently learned of a plan to assemble, over the next year, international credit for El Salvador on the order of $500 to $600 million dollars, some half of which would come from the IMF and the balance from the Inter-American Development Bank. At the same time as this is going on, the Bank and the Fund have more or less cut off Nicaragua from access to capital. In February 1982 the World Bank circulated an internal report in which it decided to cut off three of the six sectors of lending to Nicaragua.** One sector to be cut off is education. Here the Bank noted that Cuba and the Scandinavian countries are already helping out with education, so the Bank can back out. Rural roads were also cut off. The Bank said that the road system in Nicaragua was in good shape already. The third sector to be cut off is water supply and sanitation. The same report noted elsewhere that only 34 per cent of the people in Nicaragua even have access to clean piped water. But clearly the Bank felt no urgency in that sector either.

The other three lending sectors were to be delayed, not totally cut off. These were agriculture, energy and industry. Since February the World Bank has carried out this general program while denying it publicly. It has made no loans to Nicaragua.

As for the IMF, it has a very peculiar recent history in Nicaragua. Just nine weeks before the late and unlamented dictator Anastasio Somoza was overthrown, the IMF made available $66 million to him for what turned out to be his going-away present. The civil war was so close to a conclusion at that

* The loan, for $1.1 billion, was approved Nov. 3, 1982.

**Copies of this report are available from Jim Morrell, Centre for International Policy, 120 Maryland Ave. NE, Washington, D.C. 20002, U.S.A.

point that the incoming Sandinistas made representations to the IMF not to make this money available because they knew they would be the ones with the obligation to repay the debt. Otherwise, of course, *they* would be considered irresponsible members of the international community. The Fund made the loan anyhow, and sure enough, when the Sandinistas' financial people got to the capital, Managua, they found that Somoza had cleaned out the central bank. Since then, I hardly need say, relations between Nicaragua and the Fund have been very cool. Perhaps both sides are a little rigid, but the upshot is that in a period of acute balance of payments need, a member of the fund, Nicaragua, has not been able to receive one penny of assistance from the IMF.

Canada's crucial role

Canada has a swing-vote in all these controversial loan decisions. Take El Salvador, for example. The first of a series of loans came in 1981 from the International Monetary Fund. In making this loan the Fund clearly and flagrantly broke its own rules. All the directors representing Western Europe — England, France, West Germany, Scandinavia, Belgium, Holland, all except Italy — strenuously objected to this loan. In this case, unfortunately, Canada fell in behind the United States and with the support of Third World countries, whose position in the Fund is generally to call for easier loans and conditionality to any country, the loan was railroaded through. But it was a close call. It was the most hotly-disputed meeting of the executive board in the IMF history. It was so closely balanced that Canada had a key role. With its swing-vote, if it had pursued an energetic policy, Canada might have stopped the loan. In that case, it didn't.

In other cases, though, Canada has taken an independent stand. Until recently, Canada was consistently voting against loans to El Salvador through the Inter-American Development Bank on the common-sense grounds that normal development projects couldn't proceed in a country undergoing civil war like El Salvador's. However, I guess American pressure has been stepped up and that other priorities have come up, because this summer (1982) Canada did approve another $66 million loan from the Inter-American Bank to El Salvador. It's not the last chapter because the Inter-American Bank has another $130 million in loans to El Salvador on the planning board. One of them happens to be for rebuilding a bridge known as the Golden Bridge, which was blown up by the guerrillas in October 1981, and which happens to be one of the most strategic military targets in the country.

Now, what a development bank is doing rebuilding a strategic target, I don't know, but this is the type of question that could perhaps be raised by Canada and other countries that don't want to be part of the military operation there. And you know far better than I do how to make your voices heard by those who represent you, if indeed you do think there are people who represent you. Sometimes I wonder who represents us in the United States but here, that's your problem. There are many examples of citizen action that I have been told about. The Catholic religious conference in Ontario sent out action alerts to all its members, who sent in telegrams and letters about the Guatemala loan to the Canadian government. They didn't succeed in changing Canada's vote in that case, but it set an example of public awareness.

Greater public awareness is the theme from this soap box. Don't be deterred by the esoteric nature of these institutions; it's just money, it's just your taxpayers' money, it's another way of spending it. They like to hide behind a technical façade but a look at the minutes of the executive board meeting for the El Salvador loan, which I'm happy to share with anyone, shows clearly that by insisting on minimal human rights standards you can't politicize the IMF or World Bank. They are already politicized. The object now is to institute a basic humanitarian standard.

Sovereignty vs. Human Rights

A debate with Earl Drake, Maurice Dupras, John W. Foster and Jan Shinpoch

"... political rights through quiet diplomacy."

Earl Drake

Earl Drake began working for the Canadian Department of External Affairs in 1955. He has since been counsellor with the Permanent Mission of Canada to the OECD (1968-72), director of multilateral programming for CIDA (1972-75) and executive director for Canada at the World Bank (1975-82). Most recently he has served as Canadian ambassador to Indonesia.

For centuries the rights of humans in society have been protected in one way or another by national laws concerning the relationship between the government and the individual. What is new since World War II is the right or even duty of *other* governments, acting as part of the international community, to monitor the level of respect for national law. The idea that governments are somehow limited in their enjoyment of sovereignty by the rights of people to certain levels of civil and political freedom is not one we have inherited. The novel element in the field of human rights is the role assumed by the international community.

The United Nations charter established fundamental obligations of the UN and its member states to protect human rights. The Universal Declaration of Human Rights (UDHR) was adopted without opposition on December 10, 1948; it declared a common standard of achievement for all people, embracing economic, political and civil rights. It aspired to "the advent of a world in which human beings shall enjoy freedom of speech and belief and freedom from fear and want".

UDHR was conceived as the initial part of an international bill of rights. The Declaration would enunciate principles and subsequent covenants would form the binding portion. A covenant on civil and political rights and another on economic, social and cultural rights were adopted in 1966 and came into force in 1976. In the latter covenant, the "rights" have the character of "goals" which require positive action and are exceedingly difficult to measure — for example, the right to an adequate standard of living.

The civil and political covenant is a wholly different affair. The rights that it sets out to protect are all realizable, absolute and capable of legal definition. Article 4 provides that public emergency, even of a type that threatens the life of a nation, cannot permit derogation from certain rights. Among these are the rights to be free of arbitrary deprivation of life, of torture, and of slavery and servitude. They are about individuals per se whereas the concepts of economic and social justice are on a national scale.

Debate has arisen over the relationship of these twin covenants and the rights of the individual person versus people together as a political community. Since the UN General Assembly decided, "Civil and political freedoms and economic, social and cultural rights are interconnected and interdependent", the debate has centred on the question of whether the interdependency of rights can be used to weaken demands for compliance with civil and political rights. If the two sets of rights are accepted as interdependent in the strict sense, can countries plead that their inability to assume full economic and social rights justifies a lesser standard of adherence to civil and political rights? The debate has now gone beyond the philosophical and is becoming one of competition in claims between the rights of individuals and the rights of peoples.

While the UN has been lively in debating the issues, it has been passive about remedial action. The UN Commission on Human Rights has confined its action to two highly political areas: decolonization and apartheid. It has done nothing concrete about the 20,000 petitions it receives annually detailing violations of human rights, the Amnesty International report documenting torture in some 60 countries or the International Commission of Jurists' report of massive killings in Uganda.

The constitutions of the World Bank and other IFIs state that only economic and financial criteria can be applied to projects and only unconditional contributions can be accepted from governments. IFI managers discourage discussion of the human rights issue because it is politically divisive within their boards and because their staff has no legal authority or training to deal with the subject. They also worry because the issue distracts the congressmen and parliamentarians who formerly supported development assistance. Some of these legislators now try to ensure that aid will not go to repressive regimes and, thereby, imperil the passage of the aid program.

Government positions

Over the years Canada and most other governments have taken the traditional positions, which can be summarized as follows. The human rights issue should be pursued in the UN or through quiet diplomacy, and not in IFIs, whose constitutions require that all decisions be judged solely on economic and financial criteria. It should not affect development assistance programs; indeed it would be wrong to deny economic benefits to poor people because of the human rights violations of their governments. A typical statement on an agricultural project in Chile in 1976, made by the World Bank's Canadian Executive-Director for Canada, Ireland and the Caribbean, was:

The articles of agreement of the World Bank, as well as the custom and practice of this board, require us to judge all projects solely on economic, financial and developmental criteria and on the technical soundness. On these bases I have no option but to support these two projects. The President's reports elucidate why Chile is credit-worthy for lending. The projects show good economic and financial rates of return. In human terms the agricultural project is particularly attractive because it will improve the living conditions of some 50,000 small farmers and rural poor. Lest there be any misunderstanding of my position, may I say that all of the countries I represent have consistently and vigorously opposed violation of human rights in Chile and elsewhere. The countries of this constituency believe, however, that human rights issues should be pursued in the United Nations and not in the World Bank, which should concern itself exclusively with economic development.

Since that statement was made, the Canadian government has recognized that there could be exceptional circumstances, such as Uganda under Idi Amin, where the political and human rights considerations are of such an overriding importance that an exception would have to be made to our traditional policy. Such a course of action would, however, risk undermining the operations of the IFIs and great caution should be exercised before resorting to it.

The predominant view among developing countries was recently articulated by Jahangir Amuzegar, one of the executive directors in the IMF, as follows.

Reams of statistics from national and international sources show that nearly a billion human beings in the Third World lack literacy. To the extent that the basic needs of these vast masses of human beings are unmet, their "human rights" in a larger context are certainly not adequately safeguarded. If the leadership in these countries is to be pressured from outside, the pressure should be directed toward satisfying the people's basic economic needs rather than abstract political rights.

In Third World countries suffering from poverty, widespread illiteracy and a yawning gap in domestic distribution of incomes and wealth, a constitutionally guaranteed freedom of opposition and dissent may not be as significant as freedom from despair, disease and deprivation. The masses might indeed be much happier if they could put more into their mouths than empty words; if they were assured gainful employment instead of the right to march on the capital. The tradeoffs may be disheartening and objectionable to a Western purist, but they may be necessary or unavoidable for a majority of nation states.

U.S. policy, from Carter to Reagan

In direct contrast to the foregoing positions, the Carter administration and the U.S. Congress gave high priority to human rights objectives in the conduct of foreign policy with developing countries. One of the key elements in the Carter posi-

legal determination on whether civil and political rights have been transgressed. If the civil and political rights covenant is capable of legal definition, it should be possible to designate or devise an international body of competent professionals to make judgements, which could then be referred to a political body to decide on what sanctions were in order.

If this international machinery were ever put in place, there would be a case for amending the articles of the IFIs to permit consideration of any sanction recommended against a country because of a consistent pattern of gross violation of human rights. Such an amendment might recognize that although the IFIs themselves were not qualified to make judgements in the field, they could legally take into account the findings of a competent international juridical body. I would hope and expect that sanctions would be used only in the most abhorrent cases so that needy people in most countries would not be denied the benefits of economic developmental projects because of the sins of their rulers.

In summary, I sympathize with the concern to protect individuals from the abuse of civil rights. But I also believe that we should be careful not to hamper the IFIs from promoting the economic and social rights of whole communities.

"... management of the international economy is too important to be left to bankers and economists."

Maurice Dupras

Maurice Dupras, a Liberal Party Member of Parliament since 1970, has most recently served as Chairman of the Sub-Committee of the Standing Committee on External Affairs and National Defence in charge of examining Canada's relations with Latin America and the Caribbean.

I have returned recently from a 17-day trip to six countries in South America. I can assure you that the eyes and ears of many Latin American leaders are focused intently on the proceedings this week in Toronto. Few if any Latin American countries have escaped the effects of the severe international recession. Regardless of ideology, they face acute problems of adjustment in the next few years. Regardless of ideology, they are seeking ways of manoeuvering between the twin perils of international insolvency on one hand and domestic upheaval on the other.

The debates being waged in many of these countries resemble the great Canadian debate. Governments point to international economic forces as the main cause of their problems. Opposition critics blame domestic economic mismanagement. In either case, however, there is considerable interest in and appreciation of international economic forces and of the role played by International Financial Institutions. Rodrigo Botero, former finance minister of Colombia and a member of the Brandt Commission, presented a powerful argument to us that these institutions will have to play a much greater role in the 1980s than they did in the 1970s. There is some question as to whether the U.S. administration has been convinced of this.

It is my view that the IFIs, in particular the World Bank and the International Monetary Fund, will play a vital role in the world economy of the future. And, for that reason, the question before our panel — human rights and the IFIs — is an important one. It is really a sub-question of a larger issue: What are the politics of these institutions?

There are those who would like such questions to go away. They point to the constitutions of the IFIs as specifying that only economic and financial criteria can be applied to projects and, further, that only "unconditional contributions" can be accepted from governments. As my distinguished friend on this panel, Earl Drake, pointed out several years ago in his paper, "Human Needs and Human Rights: Towards a Canadian Approach", international financial managers dislike the human rights issue because it is politically divisive, their staffs have no legal authority or training to deal with it and, perhaps most disturbing of all, it distracts congressmen and parliamentarians who formerly have supported development assistance.

I admit that I am a parliamentarian who has been "distracted" by human rights issues from time to time. During the course of my work as chairman of the House of Commons Sub-Committee on Canada's Relations with Latin America and the Caribbean, my judgement about the problems and prospects of countries has been influenced by human rights consider-ations. I have been deeply moved by the courage of those who risk their lives in the struggle against repression. My percep-tions of Nicaragua, for example, have been affected by my knowledge of the grim terror suffered by its people under the Somoza regime.

My image of El Salvador was shaped in part by the words of the former President José Napoleón Duarte when he told us in February 1982:

There is a complete loss of values, morals and basics of society. This is the way I found the country when I came back from Venezuela. I saw a country where everybody hated everybody. I saw a country that had lost the capacity to understand. And it is still like that. Here, there is no justice. There is no legal basis.

I am personally convinced that such considerations cannot be completely isolated — shut off in a water-tight compartment — from judgements about the economic or financial prospects of a country or its government. My experience as a politician in a democratic society reinforces this conviction. Is there in our own national life such a thing as "pure economic policy", unaf-fected by political or moral considerations? I have yet to see such a policy. During my recent visit to Chile, I saw the twilight of the "Chicago Boys" — the American-trained econ-omists who had practised the fiction of pure economic advice. It appears, however, that this doctrine had heavy political and social costs, which were disguised for a time only by repres-sion.

Banking and political judgement

The fact is that politics, of one kind or another, are everywhere. Judgements about human welfare and human rights are lurking about and can be found if you look hard enough. The Interna-tional Financial Institutions have been no more successful than other powerful institutions at preserving their innocence from politics. To take only one example, the lending activities of the IFIs in Central America support El Salvador much more strongly than Nicaragua. Is this the result of economic and

financial analysis alone? There are some who will doubt it. I
do.

The parliamentary sub-committee recommended that pressures to exclude certain countries from lending because of
ideological considerations alone should be resisted by Canada.
This was not a technical or financial judgement alone. It was a
political judgement quite consciously opposed to certain other
political judgements.

It would, in my opinion, be a step forward to acknowledge
that the IFIs have been, or will remain, in part, political institutions. So long as the need remains greater than the resources
available to satisfy that need, decisions about who gets what
will reflect political judgement, among other things.

Having opened that door, however, we must now think very
carefully about what lies on the other side. It is one thing to say
that bank managers are subject to moral and political judgements: It is another thing to say that *they* should make those
judgements. Should a man's mortgage be renewed according to
whether or not he beats his wife? Should a country receive a
loan or IMF credit on the basis of whether or not it systematically tortures its citizens? These are not questions that can be
easily answered. The problematic nature of this issue is illustrated by the sub-title of our panel: "Questions for National
Policy".

A framework for policy

I am not about to answer these questions definitively. I would
suggest, however, that there are three requirements for a sane
handling of these issues: first, the strengthening of an international law of human rights; second, closer and more continuous involvement of political authorities in the decision-making
of the international financial institutions; and third, the education of public and political opinion, not least in Canada.

The strengthening of international law is essential if there is
to be any reliable framework for making and enforcing human
rights judgements. To revert to our example of a moment ago,
the Canadian bank manager is excused from making moral
judgement about his creditors by the fact that effective laws
and courts exist. Someone who frequently abuses the right of
others may reasonably be denied a loan on the basis that he is

serving five to ten years in jail. Unfortunately, there exists no means at present for putting repressive governments behind bars. At the same time, slow but steady progress has been made in developing codes of international conduct and instruments — weak though they may be — for passing judgement on violators of those codes. In my opinion, our efforts as a country should be concentrated on the further strengthening of this system of international human rights. It is neither reasonable nor, I think, desirable to expect a credit manager in the IMF to do this job for us.

Second, there should be closer and more continuous involvement by the political authorities of member countries in the decision-making of IFIs. I was first made aware of this need in the course of my work last year with the Parliamentary Task Force on North-South Relations. In studying IMF conditionality we were struck by the fact that terms of lending often had far-reaching political and social consequences for the borrowing country. While such costs can never be avoided, neither should they be ignored in designing credit packages. For this reason, the Task Force recommended that political authorities, in particular finance ministers, be more continuously involved in the activities of the Fund, to "help officials make their assessments of these difficult political and human questions". The same principle applies to human rights issues. If they are to reliably influence these institutions, it must be through some framework of policy established by political authorities.

The third and final requirement for approaching this issue intelligently is to vastly improve the understanding in member countries of both the International Financial Institutions and international human rights. This certainly applies to Canada and to Parliament, where examination of these issues has been sporadic and perfunctory. If war is too important to be left to generals, management of the international economy — and the fate of many developing countries — is too important to be left to bankers and economists, however knowledgeable they may be. The Sub-Committee on Latin America and the Caribbean has recommended one small step in this direction: the creation of a Canadian Parliamentary Human Rights Association.

With these remarks, I will listen with great interest to the debate which will swirl around the issues of human rights and the International Financial Institutions. In pushing open the door, I for one have no illusions that consensus and tranquillity will greet me on the other side.

". . . there is a human rights constituency in this land."

John W. Foster

John Foster has been chairman of the Inter-Church Committee on Human Rights in Latin America and a board member of the Task Force on Church and Corporate Responsibility, as well as a member of the Toronto-based Latin American Working Group. He is a staff associate with the Research and Coalitions office of the United Church of Canada.

This week in September reminds us of the bloody price that armed privilege can exact from those — like Chile's workers, peasants, academics, politicians and progressive Christians — who seek to build social justice in fact as well as in word. I personally cannot separate the debates regarding the reform of international corporate or financial institutions from the picture of the late President Salvador Allende addressing the United Nations General Assembly, or the next frame of the burning Moneda palace during the September 1973 coup.

During the months of destabilization, copper marketing problems and credit blockade that laid the foundations for the 1973 coup, some Canadians, spurred to action by missionaries resident in Chile, tried to alert the public to the part played by the multinationals, the banks and the international financial institutions in the strangulation of reform and reconstruction in Chile. We produced a little book called *Chile vs. the Corporations.**

* Development Education Centre and Latin American Working Group, *Chile vs. the Corporations*, Toronto, January 1973.

An important section of that pamphlet was a letter (Nov. 14, 1972) addressed to Prime Minister Trudeau by seven Quebecois missionaries in Chile, who were responding to a _Le Monde_ story about World Bank participation in an international credit blockade of Chile, and about the possibility of Canadian private bank co-operation in this blockade. They attacked the great transfer of resources, of copper and money, which was the linchpin of the dependency of countries like Chile, stating "The poor countries are the best bankers of the rich countries." They protested the blockade and appealed for positive action by the Prime Minister. The letter was filled with urgency, and very personal. The authors concluded: "Excuse the tone of this letter. It is meant to put forth some of the feeling today of the Chilean people, faced with a boycott of which it is the victim, and of which our government is one of the authors."

So, when we prepare the list of patrons for this blessed event — a conference on the Global Impact — we should not forget Henry Kissinger, the CIA and their colleagues in private and public life who provided that particularly bloody demonstration project in the use of international financial power to assist regressive political ends. They taught us the negative political uses of this power, yet their progeny are quick to accuse us of politicizing the discussion when we merely reverse the question, and ask whether or not the same power can be used to support positive ends.

I remember being in the gallery of the UNCTAD building in Santiago, Chile, in 1972, watching representatives from progressive governments in Chile, Argentina, Peru and many others develop the chapter and verse of the project for a New International Economic Order, including proposals for the reform and democratization of the major international financial institutions. While the reams of paper and miles of recording tape provoked by UNCTAD, NIEO, and successive dialogues, conferences and summits have piled up like the waves on the beach at Cancun, so also have the wrecked hopes, development plans and often, bodies, of those governments who have sought to break the hammer-lock of poverty in ways that put the majority first. The agenda of reform, in my view, has hardly progressed since UNCTAD 1972. Instead we have witnessed a program of political rollback brought to new levels of vulgarity

by the present U.S. administration, which has subsidized the
subversion of Nicaragua, and utilizes organizations like those
meeting this week in Toronto to boycott progressive governments and bail out the assassins — and I use the word
advisedly — who preside over the regime in El Salvador.

Chile winds

Canadian churches and religious orders responded immediately to the Chilean coup, forming a body which became the
Inter-Church Committee for Human Rights in Latin America.
Pressing the Canadian government initially not to recognize
the Pinochet junta, they went on to campaign against any Canadian foreign aid to the Chilean regime and for the immediate
reception of refugees, thousands of whom ultimately found a
home in Canada and added a wealth of insight and experience
to our social, political and religious life.

The churches also responded to the use of corporate power,
which they had seen engaged in opposing Allende and feared
would give succour to Pinochet. They had long challenged the
investment in apartheid by Canadian banks and corporations,
and turned to address Canadian copper companies seeking a
share of the inheritance of the Chilean people, and Canadian
banks proferring loans in consortia for Pinochet. Canadian government aid and export development agencies were also
approached. As experience deepened the role of international
financial institutions came to take on greater significance.

The churches organized a Taskforce on Corporate Responsibility as a means of developing their work with corporations,
banks and relevant government agencies. Citing their heritage
of God's working throughout the world for just relationships,
the churches recently restated the roots and foundation of their
work together as expressing God's concern for the justice and
well-being of all peoples as incarnated in the life of Jesus
Christ, his work among the poor and oppressed, his crucifixion
and resurrection.

A new debate

Concern for human rights is no longer stylish at the Department of State or on Capitol Hill. It is no longer something to be
considered or emulated by the Department of External Affairs

in Ottawa. Yet public interest has grown rather than retreated in the Reagan era. Outrage at Canada's sycophantic perambulation down the Reagan policy-path in Central America has been widespread and durable. When a Tory faction attempted to kill the Parliamentary Sub-Committee on Canada's Relations with the Caribbean and Latin America recently, it was reported that letters of protest to parliamentary offices rivalled the numbers of complaints about the last Liberal budget. There is a human rights constituency in this land.

The Sub-Committee itself is largely a response to public pressure on the Cabinet over Nicaragua and El Salvador. When Secretary of State for External Affairs Mark MacGuigan made his opening presentation to the Sub-Committee in 1981, he dealt almost exclusively with trade and investment, avoiding political analysis and human rights issues. Nevertheless, when the Sub-Committee made its first report in December of that year it placed human rights first among its five policy priorities. Despite challenges since, human rights remains a priority item. There is a human rights constituency in the Canadian parliament.

The Sub-Committee has admitted the importance of examining the use of certain elements of Canadian policy, including trade and development assistance, to further human rights objectives. We understand that they are about to renew their examination of this policy nexus.

They note, further, that they have received evidence that international financial institutions are being put under considerable pressure to exclude certain countries such as Grenada and Nicaragua from their lending because of ideological considerations. "Nicaragua," they note, "unlike El Salvador and Guatemala, has been unable to obtain funding for its rural development and water supply projects." The Sub-Committee seems disturbed by this evidence, and suggests that only "legitimate developmental criteria" should guide the lending of international financial institutions.

In highlighting this matter the Sub-Committee has done Canadians a valuable service, first in declaring that international human rights questions are a legitimate matter for review and study, and secondly by initiating its own review and critique. To note that the World Bank or regional banks are being used for political purposes, and to argue in favour of developmental criteria, is important; but it solves few questions. The Secretary of State for External Affairs constantly writes that the banks do nothing but operate by "economic and developmental" criteria. Which merely leads into the debate about whether human rights criteria, beginning with the right to life itself, are fundamental developmental criteria — a position being developed and argued by the churches — or whether the popular wisdom of the dominant economic forces in dominant voting states of a multilateral institution is the standard, and only standard, by which to review "economic and developmental" aspects of loan requests.

The Secretary of State for External Affairs has, in lengthy correspondence, chosen to regard questions of human rights as matters falling into ideological or political categories, which he views as separate from and incompatible with the operation of the international financial institutions and the behaviour of Canada's representatives therein. The churches have argued that if you remove broad human rights criteria from the word "developmental" there is little assurance that the development sought will have much beneficial effect on the majority poor.

Both Mr. MacGuigan and finance minister Allan MacEachen have stated their commitment to resist efforts "to introduce political considerations into the deliberations". In summarizing their disagreement with this position, in the case of rumoured applications by the Guatemalan dictatorship to the Inter-American Development Bank and the IMF, the churches stated:

These applications embody the very model of economic and political repression which today nails the Guatemalan people to the cross. In specific economic terms they relate to the land price and control pressures which are driving the peasant population to rebel. In general terms they are test cases of international *confidence* in Guatemala's military managers. To argue that decisions on such credits can be or should be made on purely technical grounds places 'business as usual' as the official motto guiding Canada's relations with dictatorships and makes official statements regarding human rights little more than hollow echoes.

But the churches have also questioned the technical assessments that are part of the operative assumptions expressed by Mr. MacEachen and Mr. MacGuigan. The case of IMF support for Bolivia provoked an extensive correspondence in 1981-82, in which Task Force representatives raised the issues of the economic priorities of the Bolivian junta, for example its dedication to new military equipment purchases, and its personal engagement in the cocaine trade. In reply to Task Force concern, Mr. MacGuigan admitted that the criminal activities of the cocaine trade were of "a different order" than political considerations, but that it was hard to know what to do about it, and after all this is "a less than perfect world".

The Task Force replied by drawing an ironic scenario that could result should IMF directors and member states ignore the cocaine connection:

Members of the Bolivian junta make enormous private gains in foreign exchange from the illicit cocaine trade which benefits them, but not the Bolivian people. Ignoring the criminal gains, the IMF may direct these same corrupt generals to implement an austerity program as a condition for the balance of payment stand-by credit requested. The conditions exacted by the IMF have the effect of causing unemployment for the miners, severe restrictions on public spending and an end to various state subsidies which help the population to survive. . . . The IMF, Canada participating, may compound the suffering of the Bolivian people by holding them to ransom to make the junta 'creditworthy' according to the rules of the IMF. The cocaine trade of the generals is not an added, unpleasant but minor feature of the Bolivian junta. . . . On the contrary, it is intimately connected with the 1980 coup d'etat as well as with the present need for the IMF credit.

Levels of concern

The churches, in summary, have raised concerns regarding the international financial institutions and Canada's role therein on several levels. There is the *overall concern* with the impact of IMF prescriptions on economies characterized by grotesque divergencies of wealth, and by repressive military rule. The Bolivian case is a classic example, as was Peru a few years ago. The monetarist, private-sector, elite-oriented nature of IMF requirements raises profound questions for those interested in a decent life for the majority poor.

We recognize that the overall reform and democratization of the system is a long-term affair. There are, however, things to be done in the meantime of a more defensive nature. The most important of these is the implementation of *fundamental human rights* criteria when financial transactions are considered by the Fund and the Bank. The case of Guatemala is a most urgent, current example. We understand that the Guatemalan dictatorship is considering a significant series of applications to various international institutions — of up to $200 million in quantity. The Inter-Church Committee on Human Rights in Latin America has been in constant receipt of reports of massacres, village-burnings and cruelty, which has brought the charge of genocide from human rights bodies against the Guatemalan regime. Mass murderers in our prisons are now sometimes paid large sums for their testimony or their memoirs. We cannot, however, believe that the Guatemalan regime and the military who keep them in power are in any long-term economic or moral sense of the word good credit risks.

There is also a more *particular concern* relating to the selectivity and political manipulation of the Fund and the World Bank and regional development banks. This question was raised ten years ago by the missionaries in Chile, and by the rapid provision of World Bank assistance to the Pinochet regime after the coup. It is today raised graphically by the treatment of Central American countries. The IMF is providing large resources to the Salvadorean regime, and the Inter-American Development Bank is moving in a parallel direction. No "developmental" rationale is credible as a foundation for these loans, and there are very serious technical grounds for opposing their implementation. From the point of view of the churches, the loans subsidize and support a regime led by the accused assassin of Archbishop Romero himself, and one which has maintained power through systematic massacres, mutilation and intimidation.

The juxtaposition of significant aid to this regime, intimately advised and protected by the Reagan administration, with the reluctance of the World and Inter-American Banks to assist the reform government in Nicaragua — which the Reagan administration has chosen to isolate and subvert — is graphic and profoundly disturbing. We agree with the Parliamentary Sub-Committee in considering this type of evidence worthy of the most serious review and question in Canada. We consider that Canadian representatives in the international financial institutions ought to be instructed to oppose such manipulation of these institutions.

Our concerns on these questions also affect *the private sector* in Canada. We have long argued that major overseas exposure by Canadian private banks has significant foreign policy implications and ought to be open to public monitoring and debate. When one of the major functions of the IMF is to act as a safety net against default of these very loans, and when that leads to grotesque alliances like that with the Bolivian juntas, we feel our case is demonstrated.

At the foundation of this whole argument is our desire for public information, public debate and effective parliamentary review.

A first step

Recognizing the gap between the concerns of the Parliamentary Sub-Committee and the human rights constituency on one hand and the practice of the cabinet on the other, the churches through the Taskforce are making a number of recommendations regarding initiatives that ought to be taken.

Parliament must develop continuing instruments that can consider the issues if human rights is to become and remain an active factor in the making and review of Canadian foreign policy. This implies initiation of *regular review* in Parliament of human rights situations and of the economic and political policy areas that represent Canada's ties and interests in those situations.

In its recent report the Parliamentary Sub-Committee supports this concern, stating its belief that "The power and influence of the Canadian state can and should be used, wherever possible, to move other states to protect their citizens and provide them with the opportunities and freedoms necessary for their development." They support annual reviews and suggest the need for parliamentary investigatory missions abroad. These objectives ought to be applauded, and we all recognize they will need engaged and active public support if they are to be accepted and implemented.

The Sub-Committee suggests that a Human Rights Association of Parliamentarians be set up to undertake these measures. Here we have a number of questions. It would seem optimum to insure a full-status annual review, with staff support, public hearings and official record, together with whatever clout or leverage official proceedings can elicit from the governmental departments involved. The churches have therefore recommended that the reviews be undertaken by the Parliamentary Standing Committee on External Affairs and National Defence or a specially-constituted sub-committee thereof.

Such a process could elicit from the Minister of External Affairs and other cabinet ministers and their staff, reports on situations, statements of the governments' assessment and factual information regarding the nature of Canadian interests. It could facilitate preparation of assessments and recommendations by public interest groups, including the trade unions, Amnesty International, Oxfam, journalists and the churches.

We wonder if a parliamentary association has that kind of scope, resources or clout. If not, we hope that the Sub-Committee will take its idea further and secure an annual review by a standing committee or a sub-committee thereof.

We are also concerned about reporting. Within the last two years government regard for human rights factors in foreign policy has increased. It is no longer simply an item typed at the last moment into the final paragraphs of the minister's speech. But much more needs to be done to bring official policy and behaviour out of the realm of rhetoric, the "mights" and the "shoulds". We have therefore recommended that the government, through the Department of External Affairs, be asked to prepare and present for parliamentary perusal its own assessment of priority human rights situations. We cannot help but believe that such a process would strengthen the commitment to human rights within the government, and also encourage the minister to greater depth and consistency in pursuing objectives in this field.

We submit that the hearings and review might establish some priority situations of gross violation of human rights. We recommend that the review include Canadian military sales, security assistance and sales of dual purpose material. It should include a review of the profile of Canadian aid, export credits and insurance facilities with reference to such situations of gross violation of human rights. It should also include review of Canadian participation in loan and credit decisions of international financial institutions receiving applications from human rights violator countries. We have also recommended, renewing a demand made for the past four years, that the private banks be required to disclose details on major international loans (over $1 million).

We look forward to the time when the Parliament of Canada will be willing to enact legislation governing the behaviour of the Canadian government, its agencies and representatives, with regard to international human rights concerns. For example, in the case of international financial institutions, we recommend that Parliament act to direct Canadian representatives in such institutions to:

- oppose loans and other financial and technical assistance to any country that persists in a systematic violation of human rights and fundamental freedoms;
- seek to channel funds to projects which address the basic human needs of the people;
- seek in international financial institutions changes in the articles of agreement to establish human rights standards to be considered in connection with all applications for assistance.

With regard to the private banks in Canada, we recommend that Parliament act in such a way as to facilitate the placing of a control or a prohibition on any Canadian private bank loan or credit to countries engaged in a pattern of gross violation of human rights.

The implications of this position include legislation amending the Export Development Act so that when decisions about trade support facilities for a given country are under consideration, human rights data and estimates of the effect or impact of the given proposal should be before the decision-making group at the Export Development Corporation. There should be further legislation to withhold facilities for trade support with countries that engage in a consistent pattern of gross violations of human rights.

Conclusion

There are those who would prefer to keep the discussion of

human rights within multilateral legal or defensive bodies like
the United Nations Commission on Human Rights or the Inter-
American Commission on Human Rights. There are others who
see the drive for inclusion of human rights concerns in international economic policy only as a "cost" factor, interfering with
freedom of trade and the freedom of traders and lenders. Still
others argue that none of these means is effective.

It should be clear from this brief survey, that the churches'
fundamental position is that both the word development and
the concept of human rights are intimately connected with the
wholeness of individuals and of societies, that we cannot talk
of one without the other. There is no development unless the
majority poor participate and some measure of equity is won by
and for them. Thus human rights criteria must inform the
judgements of international and national financial agencies.

While the question of cost or benefit in economic terms has
not been our chief concern, we fully support those who argue
that to see human rights and emancipation in this hemisphere
as a cost factor is not only socially but economically short
sighted. Surely a nation of healthy, literate and productive
farmers and workers is a better long-term friend and trading
partner for Canada than an impoverished society under the
heel of a Somoza, a Rios Montt or a D'Abuisson.

Finally, we believe there are effects — positive effects —
which undermine the stance of those who say nothing can be
done. The most telling testimony comes from those individuals
whose lives or health have been saved by effective international human rights policy. Even at a minimum, the temporary
application of Carter administration denials of Export-Import
Bank credits to Argentina in 1978 elicited a promise from the
Argentine junta that it would accept an on-site investigation by
the Inter-American Human Rights Commission. An Argentinian human rights advocate, Dr. Emilio Mignone, president of
the Permanent Assembly for Human Rights, evaluated the policy pressure put by the Carter administration, which was utiliz-
ing the sort of tools we are recommending: "I'm absolutely
convinced that if this policy hadn't existed, the situation would
have been much worse in Argentina. Instead of killing thousands, they would have killed thousands more, because they
would have done it with impunity."

We believe it is time for a fresh and independent Canadian policy regarding international human rights. We believe that that policy must include emphasis on the relationship between international financial institutions, their power and human rights. We believe that Latin America is an important — indeed an urgent — theatre for the development and testing of instrument and policy. And we believe that the time to begin is now.

". . . to give a loan is a political act."

Jan Shinpoch

Jan Shinpoch works in Washington as staff director of the Sub-Committee on International Development Institutions and Finance for the U.S. House of Representatives. Her special interests are issues concerning the multilateral development banks, human rights and development.

I work for the United States Congress, for the U.S. House of Representatives Banking Committee. I want to make that clear at the outset because the U.S. House of Representatives is still controlled by the Democrats. We are the opposition party. The Senate and the presidency are in Reagan's hands, but we still have the House and I want to disassociate myself at the outset from the present administration.

I want to go on and explain the U.S. system of participation in international financial institutions because it functions very differently from Canada, and I want to explain how my sub-committee works within that system.

First, like most Americans, I have a love/hate relationship with my country. I think that the United States does some marvellous things. For example, it contributes heavily to the international financial institutions, more heavily than any other country in the world. But, we do have this problem of fluctuating between one policy and another depending on what administration is in and how that government perceives pursuit of U.S. political goals.

We have been trying within Congress, within the House at least, to make a point to the Reagan administration through a series of hearings, consultations and press conferences and other sorts of nagging. The point is that U.S. geopolitical goals do exist and we do recognize that they exist in that the government of the U.S. does not exist to be altruistic. But these goals cannot be met efficiently through alliances with human rights violators. We continually throw out the example of the Shah of Iran, whom we gave all this money to and did all these nice things for — and where is he now, what's he doing for us? And the example of Argentina and the invasion of the Falkland Islands, where the Reagan administration went out quite deliberately to rehabilitate Argentina internationally, to make it look less of a human rights violator. President Reagan had the President of Argentina on the phone the night before the invasion begging him not to go ahead. But the Argentinian President just sort of rang off.

The rationale behind the *rapprochement* with Argentina was very much that this would enable us to have all sorts of influence, but we really got nowhere for all that had been done. The sub-committee tries to impress upon the administration the problems it is creating for itself and the difficulties, even in terms of "America firstness", that are entailed in trying to become buddies with all the human rights violators in the Western hemisphere and over most of the world.

Human rights: basic issues

I'd like to go over the Canadian/U.S. levels of influence in the international financial institutions and talk about the U.S. laws that exist, and give some information on the application of those laws and Congress' role in applying them. First though, I want to very briefly address seven specific questions that were raised in my invitation to speak.

I'm a little bit of a fanatic on this and I would like to get some of this out on the table. The first question is: Should we give weight to issues of human rights in our evaluations of multilateral development bank loans? And that is the basic question that we've all been trying to address. Of course those issues ought to weigh in loan evaluations, because if torture and death don't have weight in all evaluations of things that governments do with your money and my money, we're in a great deal of trouble. I can't think of anything else more important to consider than whether a country we're aiding is killing its people.

The second question is: Do human rights issues have a place in these decisions? From the multilateral development bank viewpoint, from the point of view of the people who administer the international financial institutions, they do not. The MDBs consider themselves to be making technical and economic judgements. From the point of view of the U.S. executive director, these considerations weigh when they can't be avoided. And from the point of view of the International Development Sub-Committee, for which I perform as staff director, they weigh absolutely and we take our position as being to remind the administration of just how much they do weigh, so that the administration will in turn be forced to go in reluctantly and remind the administrations of the MDBs that the U.S. is taking these rights into consideration.

The third question is: Should countries direct their executive directors to vote in particular ways? This issue is a little bit more difficult, because it is true that all the charters of the international financial institutions, which we join as a sort of party to a treaty, will not accept tied contributions. This came up a great deal in the United States, for example, right after we lost the war in Vietnam, when there was considerable discussion about how we really ought to have some sort of provision that none of our money could go to the Vietnamese. And it's true that it is a violation of the charters of the institutions for any country to deny funds to any member country.

This does not mean that we are not perfectly capable of directing an executive director to vote against loans to particular countries. It does mean that if our executive director votes against a loan and the loan passes anyway, we cannot wash our dollars out of the general account at the World Bank and say that our money can't be part of the package that goes to a country. But I think it's really important not to be confused on the point of the charters because the charters do not deny all expression of concern about political issues. The charters simply say you can't take your money and go home if you lose.

The fourth question is: Should the international financial institutions themselves have policies that require observance of certain human rights criteria? And I frankly don't know. It's very hard to say that a lot of these people who sit around at the banks with lined paper and pencils adding things up can make these sorts of judgements. We have to consider who runs these institutions. They are run by the votes of their member countries and some of their member countries may make judgements that you won't like. It's not as though management exists in isolation from the members who pay for and elect it. It's difficult, I think, to say whether the institutions ought to have those sorts of rules within their own charters.

The fifth question raised: Is this all imperialism? Are we being "big brother" or "smarter than you are", "holier than thou" with "better cultural values" when we tell people that they can't torture their own people? I don't think so. I think that it's imperialistic to consider that a nation might find it culturally inappropriate to stop killing its own people. I think we have to assume that it is safe to consider that all people in the world wish to be free from torture. All people in the world wish to be free from arbitrary arrest and free from extra-legal execution. I don't think it's a particularly Northern viewpoint to assume that people don't want to die in the street.

The second to last question is: Does consideration of these human rights issues politicize the banks? Now, this is a really fun question because it's really easy to play it either way. You can say, obviously it doesn't politicize the banks. To use the familiar example, if you have a wife-beater turn up and ask for a mortgage, you can think . . . well, I won't give it to him because sooner or later he's going to get caught and they'll throw him in jail and he won't be able to make the payments and therefore I'm making an economic decision not to give it to him. We can do that as well with the international financial institutions. And we can do it quite reasonably in a sense.

It's very logical to assume that a country where people are being tortured and killed at phenomenal rates is probably not terribly stable. That sort of thing can go on for a long time, but it seems reasonably logical to assume that if a country experiences tremendous repression, it should be considered, from the standpoint of political risk, to be not credit-worthy. And you can do that. But I don't find it a very attractive position to take.

The position I take is that yes, we are indeed politicizing the banks, but in this case it is worthwhile. We do not believe that you should turn around and politicize the banks at every opportunity. The extent to which the Reagan administration has attempted to do blatant political things with U.S. votes at the banks is very distressing. But, as civilized people, you have to get to a point where you say, enough is enough, to say: yes, I will try to play along with all the charters and yes, we will observe them and won't take our money and go home if we lose on a human rights violator — but we are not going to support money for torturers. We are not going to support sending the tax money of our people to countries where people are routinely repressed. And to politicize the banks to that extent strikes me as necessary, rather than as inappropriate.

The last question is: Are the banks politicized now? This is a very easy question. If it is a political act to deny a loan to a country because it is a human rights violator, then it must be a political act to give a loan to a country even though it is a human rights violator. It strikes me that it is no less political to withhold funds from Chile than it is political to give funds to Chile. And we were able to see very clearly during the heyday of Chilean human rights activism that when the United States' bilateral aid to Chile dropped dramatically, multilateral aid to Chile went up to compensate for it. There were distinct political actions going on to try to fill in the gap left by the United States and those actions succeeded to a large extent.

The institutionalization of policy

I want to go on now to talk a little bit about the mechanics. There are a number of international financial institutions; the most important are — for human rights considerations — the Inter-American Development Bank, the World Bank and, in a little different way, the IMF. The United States holds virtual veto power in most of the institutions. It takes a 75 to 85 per cent agreement to get most major loan approvals in the international financial institutions. For example, a 25 per cent vote is sufficient to veto a loan in the World Bank. There are three different loan windows in the World Bank: the Bank itself, the

IFC (International Financial Corporation), and IDA (International Development Association, the soft-loan window that you probably hear most about, which loans to low-income countries). In those institutions, the United States holds a share that ranges from 20.84 to 21.35 per cent, so basically we can do anything we want. We're very close to having the 25 per cent veto required. The Canadian share runs from 3.22 to 3.8 per cent, so it's a much smaller per cent of vote.

In the Inter-American Development Bank, which has always been very controversial because of the human rights violations in Latin America, the United States, in the Bank's charter, holds a veto. The Canadian share is 4.56 per cent as of 1981. In the other institutions, the African Development Bank and Asian Development Bank, the situation is similar except in both of those Japan has more votes than anybody. In the IMF, the United States holds about 19.5 per cent and Canada less than 5 per cent. But in the IMF, it really only takes 15 per cent to veto anything.

So, in all of the institutions, the United States has power and that's one of the reasons that I think the United States Congress in particular has felt it rewarding to work with this, because they can actually make things happen. They can block a loan; they can keep somebody from getting the cheque; and that's more rewarding than just making symbolic stands.

Congress passed, mainly in the 1970s, a series of laws that makes it possible for us to do this. Those were almost all Harkin amendments, as in Tom Harkin, the Congressman from Iowa who tended to either offer them, or draft them for other people who were going to offer them. They include the Foreign Assistance Act, Section 116, which prohibits U.S. assistance to countries that are gross and consistent violators of internationally-recognized human rights. Section 502b of the same act prohibits security assistance, meaning military funds or what we call "economic security funds", which basically are funds that we send a country to plug into its budget so that it can then free up its own money to spend on arms. We sort of take over their road-building for them so that they can take their road-building money and buy machine guns.

The third law is Section 701 of the International Financial Institutions Act which is the act that our sub-committee administers and which prohibits U.S. aid through multilateral institutions to gross and consistent violators of internationally-recognized human rights. It does not cover the International Monetary Fund. The World Bank, Asian Bank, Inter-American Bank and African Bank are all considered development institutions, but the International Monetary Fund is considered a financial institution. We don't have jurisdiction over it.

The narrow arm of the law

I keep using the phrase "gross and consistent violators of internationally-recognized human rights" — there ought to be some kind of great acronym for that — because everything we do is rooted in international law. We just didn't invent standards of human rights. Those standards are laid out in a variety of different international compacts, mostly through the United Nations, and ratified by many of the member countries of these financial institutions, though certainly not all. The language of the statutes in all three of the laws I have referred to specifically refers to internationally-recognized rights. That does a couple of things for Americans and it could do a few things for Canadians, I think.

For us, it defines what we're talking about. We are not talking about the entire gamut of rights to which people are legitimately entitled. We are not talking about nutrition. We are not even talking about freedom of the press. We are talking about the right to be free from arbitrary arrest, which is referred to in the laws as detention without charge, the right to be free from torture and the right to be free from extra-legal execution. It's a very narrow law. It does not get into all sorts of fine points about whether or not somebody's election was valid. It gets into the very basic questions of whether governments are dragging people off the streets and killing them. And we try to stick fairly closely to those definitions.

I think this would be important in Canada because you lack specific statutory language in all cases and it seems as though it might be useful for you to try to refer to international law in the absence of any kind of statutory language of your own. To the extent that Canada has ratified various international human rights covenants, it ought to be standing up for those same international human rights in international forums. That's just an idea from the outside and I certainly wouldn't want to tell you your business, but it's something you might want to think about.

Congress does not have any right, of course, to demand things of the Banks directly. We can only demand things of the U.S. Treasury and State Departments, which are supposed to handle what we do at the banks. Treasury turns over loan documents; we go over loans and try to make some kind of recommendation. This becomes important because we have what I think is a very sensible loophole in our law, which says that we may not vote for assistance to a human rights violator unless the assistance is to cover basic human needs. So we're saying, "If people have stuck with Idi Amin, the least you can do is give them fertilizer." And we don't want to try to deprive hungry people of food.

But the fact is, a great many loans that go through the international financial institutions do not feed people, do not clothe people and do not teach people to read. They do these very nice things like build hydro-electric projects or build road networks; things that are perfectly legitimate development activities, but which tend to benefit the government and not necessarily the people in the short term. As I've said, the United States does indeed hold geopolitical goals uppermost — and in the long run these goals cannot be effectively realized through alliances with human rights violators.

PART THREE

Mortgaged Sovereignty: Third World Case Studies

The Philippines: The Failure of Bank Strategy

Elaine Elinson

*Elaine Elinson is an American journalist who has
specialized in Asian issues and events. In 1970-71 she was
publicist for the anti-war performances staged by Jane
Fonda, Donald Sutherland and Holly Near to mobilize GI
resistance to the war in Southeast Asia. She has served as
the national co-ordinator for the Philippine Solidarity
Network in the United States and is co-author with Walden
Bello and David Kinley of* Development Debacle: The World
Bank in the Philippines *(1982).*

Two weeks ago, on the eve of President Ferdinand Marcos' first
official visit to the United States in 16 years, the Philippine
strongman unleashed a violent wave of repression in his country. The crackdown, the worst since the declaration of martial
law in 1972, included the creation of a secret 1,000-member
police force whose first act was to ride through the streets of
Manila at midnight with sub-machine guns, killing 32 people.
This was followed by the callup of one and a quarter million
army reservists. The main target of it all was the militant independent trade union movement, particularly the *Kilusan Mayo
Uno* (the KMU or May 1st Labour Federation). The first to be

arrested was Felixberto Olalia, the 79-year-old president of the KMU. Marcos charged Olalia with three counts of "sabotaging the economy", charges the regime claimed were substantiated by public speeches Olalia had made throughout the year and particularly on May 1st. A few days later, Crispin Beltran, the vice-president of the KMU, was also arrested. A week later, 25 more labour leaders were picked up. According to the government, an additional 35 were being sought.

Why the brutal crackdown on labour at this time, and what does it have to do with the World Bank? Actually, the two are very closely linked. For the economic development strategy that the World Bank has imposed on the Philippines requires a labour force suppressed by strike bans and other constraints, and an authoritarian regime to keep it in place.

This may sound like a strong accusation to those who consider the Bank to be a neutral disburser of funds for development, to those who think of the institution as a liberal alternative to the domination of the Third World by private U.S. financiers and corporations. However, if we examine the internal assessments of the World Bank itself, it becomes clear that these formulations are at best naïve and at worst a complete inversion of the truth.

In our book *Development Debacle: The World Bank in the Philippines*, we combed through 6,000 confidential World Bank and IMF documents leaked to us by sources within the two giant institutions. Among these revealing documents were the *Poverty Report*, the result of a special Bank-sponsored mission to the Philippines in 1979; the annual World Bank country program papers for the Philippines; and, most importantly, the explosive Ascher Memorandum originally released in 1981.

The Ascher Memorandum, written by a political risk analyst at Johns Hopkins University, was commissioned by the Bank to determine what *political* forces were at play in the Philippines and to see how these would affect the Bank's economic policies. In fact, the question that the Ascher Memorandum attempted to answer was: If the political situation in the Philippines was to change significantly, what would then happen to the Bank? The Ascher memo assessed the current political risks for the Marcos regime as being so high that its publication threw the Bank, the regime and the U.S. government into a tailspin.

What the document reveals is that the primary role of the Bank is to thoroughly integrate the Philippines into the world capitalist system dominated by the United States and, subsequently, to increase the impoverishment of the Filipino people and preclude any possibility of meaningful development in that country. In our own study, we also assert that this role is not the result of bureaucratic bumbling or misguided development efforts. But rather, it is a conscious effort on the part of Bank directors, one that can be seen throughout the McNamara so-called "basic needs" period right up until today, where the Bank and the IMF have virtually taken full control of the Phillipines' national economic planning.

Finally, we assert that in acting in the interests of the United States — which as people know controls 20 per cent of the funds of the Bank and therefore has a block-vote that actually determines how the funds will be spent — and against the interests of the majority of Filipinos, the Bank's strategy has a thoroughly repressive character. Though the Bank's hands may not carry the M-16s into the village massacres in Samara, though they may not attach the electric currents in the torture rooms of military jails which hold slum dwellers who have opposed relocation projects, though they may not directly wield the truncheons that break up strikes in the export processing zones — their hands are not entirely clean of these vicious deeds because the Bank relies on and bolsters the very repressive regime which makes the implementation of its policies possible.

A World Bank model for development

It is important to note that a study of the complex workings of the World Bank in the Philippines has importance far beyond the borders of that country. The Philippines was selected by the Bank as a "country of concentration" in the early 1970s; that is, as a testing ground for Bank projects, programs and policies. Today, the Philippines model, despite its acknowledged failure (manifested by the severe economic crisis the country faces as a result of these policies), is actually being promoted throughout the Third World by the Bank. That model provides the basis for the formulation that the Bank has proposed for Indonesia and India. It is the idea behind the Caribbean Basin plan initiative and is even being proposed for the People's Republic of China.

Therefore, the World Bank strategy in the Philippines is important for us to understand as a model of the conscious effort to secure U.S. economic, political and strategic goals throughout the developing world — by using the multilateral lending institutions.

Now, just a word about the interconnection of the World Bank and the IMF, because I am going to focus on the Bank. The two institutions have separately-defined realms in the Philippines; that is, the Bank is supposed to focus on development per se and the IMF on finance, particularly the Philippines' external financial relations. However, the two institutions actually work together very closely. This closeness is formalized through what is called the "Joint Consultative Group", an IMF-Bank team (chaired by a Bank officer) set up in 1969 to oversee the entire Philippines economy. Also sitting in the Joint Consultative Group are representatives from the main lending countries to the Philippines, primarily the United States as well as from Great Britain, France, Belgium and others. Through the Joint Consultative Group, the Bank and the IMF implement their joint strategy.

Development and counter-insurgency

The World Bank's experience in the Philippines has been compared to the U.S. military odyssey in Vietnam. The image is apt: The economic build-up in the Philippines and the military build-up in Vietnam were both massive capital-intensive fixes applied to societies rent by deep-seated social conflicts. Like Robert McNamara's military adventure in Vietnam, his later development experiment in the Philippines exhibited the same pattern: early superficial success followed by protracted stalemate and spectacular collapse. Its dramatic entry was provoked by an ingrained crisis of the post-war social order, characterized by an elite democratic state presiding over a stagnant underdeveloped economy.

The World Bank effort in the Philippines had two fundamental objectives. The first was to stabilize the deteriorating political situation through development projects following the basic needs policy of McNamara. The second and more important was to more thoroughly integrate the Philippines economy into the international capitalist order dominated by the United States. Rural and urban development projects that were part of McNamara's basic needs formula, supposedly aimed at bettering the condition of the world's poor, were actually aimed at diffusing discontent among the rural poor and the growing urban underclass. That aim formed the core of the Bank's program of *political stabilization*. The *tighter integration into the international capitalist economy* was to be accomplished by a strategy of creating a favourable climate for foreign imports; "liberalization" of the economy; and fostering export-oriented industrialization geared towards satisfying the demand of markets in the U.S., Japan and Western Europe rather than the domestic market.

This ambitious plan could not be accomplished without an appropriate political framework. That is, without a state dedicated to repressing those sectors which stood to lose the most from the more intensified subjugation of the economy to U.S. corporate and financial interests.

The declaration of martial law on September 22, 1972, was a vital first step in establishing the necessary political superstructure. Authoritarian rule and the drive of Ferdinand Marcos and his faction to monopolize political power within the Filipino elite united the interests of U.S. business in "rationalizing" the economy to serve U.S. needs more effectively.

The role of the Bank in refashioning the Philippine economy stemmed partly from the crisis of U.S. foreign policy after its defeat in Vietnam. Popular disillusionment with U.S. foreign policy translated most concretely into the growing unpopularity of bilateral aid to repressive allies like Marcos. During the period of the Carter human rights doctrine, Congress did indeed cut off some aid to Marcos because of his notorious reputation as a human rights violator. Thus, the World Bank and the IMF emerged as alternative conduits of U.S. aid and influence to authoritarian regimes allied to the U.S.

The declaration of martial law came in response to a growing economic and political crisis. There was unrest in the coun-

tryside, there were massive strikes in cities, there was mobilization in all sectors against the growing repressiveness of the
regime. When martial law was declared, Congress was dis-
banded, the free press was entirely shut down and only
Marcos-controlled newspapers were allowed to continue pub-
lishing. Thousands of people were rounded up, interrogated
and imprisoned; some are still being held without charges.
There was a complete ban on strikes, demonstrations and any
kind of assembly. As the Ascher Memorandum reports, "Martial Law was declared at a time of deteriorating law and order,
increasing polarization between opposing political tendencies
and an increasingly violent confrontation between the government and its mass opponents in the streets." Ascher also dis-
tinctly adds that martial law ended this confrontation to the
government's advantage.

The hard line was to the advantage of both the government
and the Bank, because after martial law was declared in 1972,
the financial build-up was impressive. Between 1950 and 1972,
over more than twenty years, the Philippines had received a
meager $300 million in Bank assistance. By contrast, between
1973 and 1981, more than $2.6 billion was funnelled into 61
projects. Prior to martial law, the Philippines ranked 30th
among recipients of Bank loans; today it ranks eighth among
113 Third World countries.

But the significance of the Bank's post-martial law relationship to the Philippines did not so much lie in the actual value
of its loans as in the central position that it was able to carve out
for itself in national policy-making. The Bank's confidential
1976 country program paper proposed a framework for future
development which the Philippine government accepted as the
basis for future economic planning. The Bank strategy was
trumpeted as a broad-front development effort with several
components:

1) massive lending for rural development to raise agricultural
production by improving the productivity of small holders;

2) industrialization efforts emphasizing the manufacture of
labour-intensive exports with the strong participation of foreign capital;

3) a continuing drive to open up the economy by abolishing
protective tariff and foreign exchange restrictions;

4) massive spending on infrastructure and energy to lay the underpinning for agricultural and industrial advance.

Let's look at some of the projects that the Bank undertook, first under its basic needs policy and then the export-oriented industrialization, and see what the impact really was.

Containment in the countryside

Rural development was the name of the package that was supposed to help people in the countryside and build up agriculture production. One of its categories involved the bolstering of Marcos' land reform program through advice and credit. Another was a massive credit system called "Masagana 99" for which the Bank loaned money. The rest of the package was made up of sectoral projects in forestry, pesticides, fertilizers — the "Green Revolution" miracle for the Philippine countryside.

But the actual impact of the rural development package was the greater impoverishment of people in the countryside. Indeed, the Bank itself cites figures showing that since 1972 the average income of peasants and agricultural labourers in the countryside has decreased by 53 per cent. The massive land-reform program touted as "the democratization of large land holdings in the countryside" was extremely limited from the start. The eligibility to acquire land through redistribution was restricted to farmers who held over seven hectares. In the Philippines, where the average landholding was only 1.5 hectares, this limit already precluded most landholders.

Secondly, the land-reform program did not *distribute* land, it only distributed Certificates of Land Transfer, which entitled people to buy land. The Bank then financed credits for beneficiaries who held Certificates of Land Transfer. At the same time the conditions on which one was able to receive a Certificate of Land Transfer became so tight that by 1980, out of a target population of 300,000 people who were to receive the certificates, only 1,500 peasants had been given them.

Similarly, under Masagana 99 — the major credit program — credit was stipulated for only certain purchases: fertilizers, pesticides and tractors. Therefore, only those who had landholdings large enough to use tractors or to maintain an extended cycle of using fertilizers and pesticides benefited from the Masagana 99 credit program.

The rural development package actually created a small stratum of "kulaks" or rich peasants. They in turn became landlords themselves and hired others who, because they could not keep up with the new credit program, lost their land, and became landless farmworkers. According to Bank figures, 200,000 people were displaced from the land, from their small holdings, by the land-reform and credit programs. Some of these displaced peasants became agricultural labourers in the export agriculture sector or were driven into the city to work in the industrial sector.

Though the centrepiece of the Bank's rural development package was the goal of raising productivity in the countryside, in fact productivity was raised only in the export sector and not in the domestic food-consumption sector. According to a Bank specialist, "The underlying political rationale behind the Bank's poverty focus in the countryside is the pursuit of *political stability* through what might be called defensive modernization. This strategy rests on the assumption that reform can forestall or pre-empt the accumulation of social and political pressures if people are given a stake in the system. *Reform thus prevents the occurrence of full-fledged revolution.*" (Emphasis added.)

The stakes are high, and the areas of implementation reveal this quite starkly. Recently, on August 31 (1982), a new loan for $30 million in rural development funds was allocated for the areas surrounding the U.S. bases in the Philippines. These are the linchpin for U.S. military strategy in Asia and the Middle East. Major funds for rural development are being funnelled into four specific geographic areas designated for "Integrated Area Development" — areas that are the regions of greatest strength for the revolutionary New People's Army and the Moro National Liberation Front. Integrated area development means building roads, ports and other transport systems which, according to Bank and other government documents, facilitate Philippine military access in a specific area. Counterinsurgency is the aim and the result of the rural development strategy.

Pacification in the cities
On a smaller scale, the same aim of political pacification holds

true for the urban development program as well. The crisis in the countryside caused urban areas to become swollen with displaced peasants who had no place to live and no place to work. As a result, massive slums grew up around the major cities, the most infamous one being Manila's Tondo, considered the largest slum in all of Asia. The Bank program of urban upgrading was aimed at quieting discontent among the slumdwellers who were protesting against miserable conditions in Tondo and other urban areas. The program was also touted as an alternative to "First Lady" Imelda Marcos' plan for beautification of the urban areas: Her plan consists mostly of putting up high white fences around the slums to hide them from the tourists and the conventioneers she tries to attract to the Philippines with her extravagant convention centres, concert halls and film festivals.

Although Imelda Marcos put up fences and, in fact, brutally forced the relocation of slumdwellers, the Bank's velvet-glove techniques had rather similar results. The Bank called for the *gradual* relocation of the slumdwellers: The Bank developed sites outside of the main area of Manila and provided subsidies for residents to move into the sites. But when 2,000 families were forced to move out of the Tondo area, and into the relocated sites, they found that despite the Bank subsidies they could not afford the sites that were offered.

Hidden deep inside Bank documents on the urban upgrading, it is revealed that the poorest 10 per cent of the urban slumdwellers would never be able to afford the Bank-proposed rents for the new sites. An independent study by the German government stated that only the upper 40 per cent of the original Tondo residents would be able to afford the rent at the new sites. What happened was that the Bank removed people from their homes, but then provided new sites only for the upper strata. This resulted in massive protests by the slumdwellers, who were very well organized. At one open protest meeting, the Philippine military arrested over 7,000 of them.

A popular leader of the residents, a 40-year-old Tondo mother, was imprisoned for protesting the relocation and tortured with electric shock and water. Because she was a well-known leader and international opinion could be mobilized against her imprisonment and torture, the Marcos regime made a show of putting her military torturers on trial. As expected, the torturers were cleared of all charges and the tribunal implied that the woman had actually inflicted the torture wounds upon herself.

One of the most strikingly frank assessments of Bank programs comes from an officer in the Bank's urban division, who says:

It is simply difficult to demand rent from people who are not used to paying rent for their sites. When the Bank comes in with a slum improvement and resettlement program, what you get is a thank you effect. But it will be difficult to convince them to pay for water services and other improvements because they have other priorities. They would rather spend on food than rent. *In Tondo and in other places we've constantly come up against the reality that poor people and the Bank have different priorities.* (Emphasis added.)

Perhaps the key reason the World Bank sanctioned the imposition of martial law in 1972 was the unprecedented opportunity it offered for fundamental changes in Philippine trade and industrial policies along lines prescribed by the Bank. Martial law, in the view of one secret Bank assessment, "provided the government with almost absolute power in the field of economic management", and thus would clear away economic obstacles to the implementation of a new strategy hailed by the Bank as "the second phase of Philippine industrialization".

Prodded by the Bank, the IMF and international business interests, the martial law regime gradually instituted a new set of fiscal, trade and financial reform measures aimed at fostering the growth of "export-led industrialization" (EOI). The new formula represented a dramatic departure from the program of import-substitution industrialization (ISI) promoted by the government during the post-war period. It redirected the focus of Philippine industrial production away from a limited domestic market towards a seemingly limitless global market.

The Bank's EOI prescription was hardly unique to the Philippines. Indeed, its application in the Philippines and other Third World countries in the 1970s was most often justified by its earlier "successes" in South Korea, Brazil and Taiwan. But the much-heralded success of EOI in the Philippines was to be completely undermined by several flaws in the economic and political assumptions built into the plans of its promoters. By the time the Marcos regime established the foundation of the Philippines' "export platform", the global economic conditions essential to its success had ceased to exist.

Export-oriented industrialization was enshrined as a doctrine by World Bank president Robert McNamara in the early 1970s: "Special efforts must be made in many countries to turn their manufacturing enterprises away from the relatively small markets associated with import substitution toward the much larger opportunities flowing from export promotion."

This rapid shift of the economy in the Philippines was accomplished through a carrot-and-stick approach. The carrot of massive profits was offered to foreign firms and those members of the Filipino elite (mostly Marcos' cronies) who were close enough to the centre of power to benefit from the new strategy: The stick was for those who stood only to lose from the new strategy: local Philippine businessmen whose fortune lay in the domestic sector and, most importantly, Filipino workers who were to be sacrificed on the altar of foreign investment.

The unrestrained hand of martial law government accelerated the implementation of this strategy. A series of laws facilitated the "liberalization" of the economy for the service of foreign corporations and financial institutions. The Investment Incentives Act and Export Incentives Act were pushed through the Philippine Congress in an attempt to "rationalize" the economy. Under these Acts, export manufacturers were given special tax exemptions and other benefits underwritten by the Philippine government (and generally subsidized by World Bank loans). The impact of these incentives on the promotion of export manufacturing was significant — but foreign investors were still not satisfied.

The World Bank concurred. "Ideally," Bank advisors told the government, "all manufactured export industries should be on a free trade regime to the maximum extent feasible. This involves duty free importation of raw materials and components and *provision of additional assistance where necessary.*" (Emphasis added.)

The "additional assistance" came with the establishment of Export Processing Zones. Based on a Taiwan model, the first such Zone was established just outside of Manila in Bataan shortly after the declaration of martial law. Firms which exported 70 per cent of their products were rewarded for locating in the Zone with the following benefits:

- permission for 100 per cent foreign ownership;
- permission to establish a lower minimum wage than in the rest of the country;
- tax exemption privileges;
- low rents for land and water;
- government financing of infrastructure (from Bank loans) and factories;
- accelerated depreciation of fixed assets;
- legislation prohibiting strikes and all other forms of industrial action in the Zones.

By the late 1970s additional EPZs had been established in Mactan and Baguio, and 12 more had been planned around the country. Big name electronic firms such as Texas Instruments, Fairchild and Motorola flocked to the EPZs, attracted by the incentives which were virtual giveaways. By the 1980s, the government had expanded these areas with a series of "bonded villages" (where the same conditions apply) throughout the archipelago.

Keeping wages low

Cheap, repressed labour was the key incentive promoted by the World Bank and the Marcos regime for foreign manufacturers to relocate in the Philippines. As a Bank document noted, "The comparative advantage of the Philippines lies in the utilization of a skilled, low-wage labor."

Wage restraint came mainly in the form of a presidential decree which banned all strikes in "vital industries" — including *all* export industries. The strike ban was complemented by tight restriction on labour organizing and by a government-authored Labour Code which allowed, among other restraints, for the blacklisting of any workers involved in organizing activities.

By banning strikes and free unions, as the World Bank prescribes, the Marcos government succeeded in depressing wages to one of the lowest levels in all of Asia — 49 cents per hour, compared to $1.41 in Hong Kong, 95 cents in Singapore and 85 cents in Taiwan.

The failure of export-led growth

The export-oriented industrialization, erected as World Bank doctrine in the early 1970s, became an attractive ideological weapon to disarm Third World elites as multilateral agencies and multinational corporations went about the task of battering down tariff walls and aborting incipient nationalist restrictions on foreign investment in countries like the Philippines.

EOI, however, was a panacea that lost its promise very soon after it began to be applied in the Philippines. Expected to bring in significant foreign exchange earnings, EOI actually encouraged a hemorrhage of foreign exchange for the expensive infrastructure needs and raw material export goods and capital goods input of labour-intensive export industries. Expected to foster rapid industrialization, EOI actually created enclaves on profitable foreign-owned industries that had no interest in stimulating "backward linkages". Expected to bring in huge doses of foreign capital, EOI attracted relatively little.

The major factor that torpedoed EOI was the disappearance of two key assumptions on which the strategy had been based: cheap labour and expanding Western markets. While still cheap in the late 1970s, Philippine labour, organized by militant underground anti-imperialist unions, was no longer docile. It was only a matter of time before wage levels would rise to the point where fly-by-night foreign investors would feel tempted to leave for more profitable climes. The World Bank was, in fact, already creating new low-wage nirvanas in places such as the People's Republic of China and Indonesia.

Equally devastating was the deepening stagnation of the advanced capitalist economies and the subsequent rising protectionism against light manufactured imports from the Third World in those markets.

With the prerequisites for EOI vanishing, the World Bank and the IMF were left with an industrial strategy that was purely negative, purely repressive: the dismantling of protectionism, the destruction of the national capitalist class and the total denationalization of Philippine industry.

Saving the Philippines for the U.S.

Again came the carrot-and-stick. A huge "Structural Adjustment Loan" was granted to the Philippines to bail out the debt-ridden regime in 1981 — but only after even harsher conditions were placed on local industrialists and smaller banking establishments. These conditions, reluctantly accepted by the Marcos regime, drove many local capitalists completely out of business and forced others into becoming junior partners of foreign capital. Hundreds of Philippine-owned businesses went bankrupt: Some 300,000 workers lost their jobs in 1981 alone.

The political crisis that could have been precipitated by this disenfranchisement of a previously pampered elite was averted by perhaps the most stringent condition of all: the replacement of the Philippine Cabinet with one dominated by World Bank-trained technocrats, led by Prime Minister Cesar Virata, formerly the Philippine representative to the Bank. The installation of the "World Bank Cabinet" was necessary for the Bank and IMF to insure that their policies would be implemented without potential political obstruction.

But the question of the militant labour movement has been a harder one to resolve. Silenced by a decade of martial law, Philippine workers are now highly organized and are striking back at repressive conditions. The Kilusan Mayo Uno, which was established only in 1980, now boasts over half a million members and is part of a progressive labour federation with close to two million members, many of whom work in the Export Processing Zones. Despite a ban on strikes in the Zones, the KMU organized a general strike in the Bataan Export Processing Zone in 1982: Over 70 per cent of the workers participated.

Couple this new trend with the stagnating growth rate of the Philippines — in 1982 the IMF estimated the Philippine growth rate of only 2.5 per cent as the lowest in all of Asia — with its consequence of massive unemployment, and the combination is explosive for the regime and for the Bank. Now we see why the labour movement — the trade unions which fight for decent wages and which defy strike bans even in the sacrosanct export processing zones — is a real threat. The labour movement is actually the key which could blow the lid off the whole "development" strategy.

It is perhaps ironic that the current crackdown on the labour movement — interpreted by many as simply another example of the repressive nature of the local Philippine regime — comes only a few months after a U.S. statement on the role of the World Bank and IMF. In a U.S. Treasury Department report commissioned by President Reagan in 1982 to determine the usefulness of the multilateral lending institutions, the international dimension of the strategy becomes unequivocably clear:

The multilateral lending institutions have been most effective in furthering our global economic and financial objectives, and thereby also serving our longterm political/strategic objectives. Neither bilateral assistance, nor private flows, if available, are as effective in influencing less developed countries' economic performances as the World Bank. . . .

The Philippines: Collision Course

Sister Mary Soledad Perpinan

Sister Soledad Perpinan is a Filipina who belongs to the Sisters of the Good Shepherd and lives in Manila. She is editor and founder of both the magazine IBON *and the quarterly* BALAI *Asian Journal; and co-ordinator and founding member of the Third World Movement Against the Exploitation of Women as well as editor of its* Action Bulletin.

The Philippines (RP) is a unique example of a most co-operative neocolony that has willingly gone all the way, bowing and bending to the dictates of the International Monetary Fund and the World Bank. The record of the past 20 years is a striking testimony to such subservience. We have not only opened our economy to the foreign market, devalued our peso and sold human labour at the cheapest price. We have also mortgaged our patrimony through such outstanding achievements as being the first in Asia ever to avail ourselves of the IMF's Extended Fund Facility for three consecutive years, and one of the first — and of the few in the world — to submit to the programs of structural adjustment and Apex loans. We're the sanguine neocolony that is no longer accountable to its people but to the World Bank and IMF.

If the powers that be have pawned my country time and time again for bigger and bigger stakes, are my people any happier, any better for it? How are the rural and urban poor, the wage-earners and national entrepreneurs? How have we prospered as a people? Have our rights been respected? Or is the truth a sad and painful story of degradation, dehumanization, denial of our basic rights, not just as individual human beings but as a people? What has happened to our collective inherent rights to life and decent living, to our patrimony and national sovereignty?

In the 1980s the Philippines is at a fascinating conjuncture where the International Monetary Fund and the World Bank have come to a remarkable overlap, an intermeshed kind of role, with one reinforcing the other.

While the IMF and World Bank have always been two sides of one coin, so to speak, the Fund had taken the upper hand, dominating the macroeconomy of the country while the Bank was relegated to the background, funding development projects here and there — until two years ago, when it also assumed macroeconomic control.

Three dates in our history — 1962, 1970 and 1976 — cover developments showing how the IMF manifested an ogre's head in the Philippine experience. A fourth date — 1980 — marks the entry of the World Bank as an equally monstrous figure ready to gulp in the industrial structure and financial system of the whole economy.

The IMF takes the lead

1962: The year when the Philippine government finally succumbed to the stringent dictates of the Fund — the lifting of foreign exchange and import restrictions and the devaluation of the peso. To support the decontrol program U.S.$300 million was granted as the first significant IMF loan to the Philippines. In his state of the nation message that year President Diosdado Macapagal put this on record:

I am glad to announce that the special Presidential Mission to the U.S. . . . has secured financial support . . . in the amount of $300 million. . . . We can count on further support from both international and

U.S. entities including the U.S. Treasury once our decontrol program is underway.

Ironically, about the same amount was repatriated by American firms in the country as a result of the decontrol program. The sum had been accumulated during the period of controls but could not be remitted because of exchange restrictions.

The Philippines, a member of the IMF-World Bank group since 1945, was not granted any assistance even when it was in dire straits in 1949, suffering from an exchange crisis principally propelled by high-dollar expenditures of U.S. firms in the country. The reason was simply because the thrust of the twin financial institutions, in line with the Marshall Plan of the United States, was towards helping war-devastated European countries stabilize their economies in order to once again become profitable trading partners of American transnational corporations. As for the Philippine balance of payments problem, the monetary bosses recommended control of foreign exchange and imports.

The carrot of a stabilization loan remained dangling before RP eyes in the 1950s because the then Central Bank Governor Miguel Cuaderno refused to liberalize the economy and devaluate the peso. Conscious of U.S. interference in this matter, Cuaderno wrote in 1964: "I thought it was not good policy for an international organization such as the International Monetary Fund to allow itself to be influenced by any member country."

Seeking other means, Cuaderno skillfully weathered the crisis and the Philippines fared relatively well with a proliferation of light and semi-heavy industries during the control period.

But import-substitution, although a mere packaging and assembly type of industrialization, did not please an influential segment of American big business. Moreover, it still created a dependence on the importation of raw materials that could not be easily secured due to the dollar shortage.

In 1962 the orchestration of a number of groups, with the American Chamber of Commerce in the forefront, finally pushed the administration of the newly-elected President

Macapagal to end the 12-year control program and open the
floodgates for unrestricted outflow of dollars and entry of
imported goods. That same year saw the axe fall on the peso; it
was devalued by almost 100 per cent. With $1 equivalent to
P3.90, more exports from the Philippines could be purchased
by the United States and other dollar-rich countries. Because
the peso could buy less, imports became more expensive, to the
detriment of local entrepreneurs who required equipment and
materials from abroad. The rest of the Filipinos suffered from
the resulting inflation.

From 1962 onward, the International Monetary Fund super-
vised the major planning of the Philippine economy. One loan
led to another and, in order to restructure its mounting debts,
the Philippines was bound by stand-by agreements and a
yearly evaluation of how it accomplished each program and
met the requirements. The irony is that this kind of arrangement, instead of improving the RP economy, became the very
source of the problem.

Without ever getting out of the rut of debts, the Philippines
found itself with empty coffers at the end of the 1960s, especially after overspending in the presidential campaign for a
second term. This led the Marcos presidential campaign to seek
a $37 million IMF loan at very detrimental terms: the floating of
the peso and its drastic devaluation.

1970: Free trade in the Philippines was further entrenched
with the establishment of the floating rate. Without any fixed
rate of exchange, it was a free-for-all foreign exchange system.
Private transactions without government intervention determined the exchange rates. This resulted in a complete "free
trade" in goods and services, which brought the Americans an
enormous accession of political and economic power.

For the Filipinos, it meant depreciating the value of the
peso by over 60 per cent, from P3.90 to P5.50 a dollar. Prices
skyrocketed and the Philippines had the distinction of having
the third highest inflation rate in the world. The Filipino
became the most price-burdened Asian in 1970, according to an
IMF report. The domestic inflation rate rose from 1.3 per cent in
1969 to 14.8 per cent in 1970. The growth rate was depressed
and the national entrepreneurs suffered bankruptcy.

In the meantime, the IMF installed itself in the Philippine Central Bank and created a joint Central Bank-IMF Commission that had a direct hand in the foreign management policies of the government. The Fund representative had access to the most confidential reports and a big say in the running of things.

About this time the consultative group of aid-giving nations and agencies was formed to monitor the external position of the economy and co-ordinate foreign assistance to the government. At the helm was the IMF-World Bank group.

Intervention in Philippine affairs had a broad scope. The arena covered the structure and functioning of money and capital markets, the generation of domestic savings, the financial implications of development programs and external debt management. While both the Bank and the Fund shared these concerns, the delineation of responsibilities, according to a key confidential IMF memo, was: "The Bank is recognized as having primary responsibility for the composition and appropriateness of developing programs and project evaluation, including development priorities"; and the IMF "is recognized as having primary responsibility for exchange rates and restrictive systems, for adjustment of temporary balance-of-payments disequilibria, and for evaluating and assisting members to work out stabilization programs as a sound basis for economic advance".

A specific criticism that the Fund levelled at the Philippines in 1970 was its "investment inefficiency" due to the "highly protected" character of Philippine industry. The IMF-World Bank conglomerate was keen on knocking down the nationalist ferment brewing in Congress and boiling in the streets of Manila.

The stroke came when martial law was declared in 1972. Congress was abolished and activists and oppositionists were hounded and incarcerated. This paved the way for the lifting of protective barriers, for a series of incentives for foreign investors, for the strategy on export-oriented industrialization. Concretely, the Bataan Export Processing Zone, designed to be the foreign investors' "paradise", finally materialized. Presidential decrees enacted financial reforms allowing foreign equity to participate in various credit institutions: loan and savings associations, pawnshops, investment and financial houses.

As a reward, a massive financial commitment followed. Now a "country of concentration", the Philippines received more than other countries of similar size and income. According to the 1980 World Bank report, it rose from 30th place to 8th among 113 Third World countries.

From July 1973 on, Bank lending amounted to $165.1 million for that fiscal year, a fivefold increase from the $30 million per year in the previous five years. According to World Bank statistics, between 1973 and 1981 the Bank funnelled more than $2.6 billion into 61 projects.

1976: After severe dislocations in 1975 — a trade deficit of $1,196.56 million and a balance of payments deficit of $161 million — as well as heavy loan repayments of $1,462.3 million over two years (1973-1975), the Philippines was in a monetary mess. It had gone beyond the 100 per cent IMF quota and there was no way out but to accept the onerous conditions of the Extended Fund Facility (EFF). The Philippines qualified for the special credit line because of "structural maladjustment in production, trade, and prices," said the IMF Survey in 1976.

Chastened by IMF directives, the Philippines accepted corrective measures and incorporated these in a three-year economic plan described in a letter of intent. Main points agreed upon were: 1) to shift exports to processed agricultural goods and mineral products; 2) to continue with heavy capital investments in infrastructure projects; 3) to raise taxes to finance government deficits.

It is not surprising how both the World Bank's book, The Philippines: Priorities and Prospects for Development and NEDA's* Four Year Development Plan, FY 1974-1977, as well as the new NEDA plan for 1978-1982, echoed the same points. For its willingness to carry out directives assiduously and to subject the economy to close scrutiny every six months, the Marcos government was granted EFF loans of $117 million in 1976 and $141.37 million in 1977.

The virtual surrender of RP sovereignty to the IMF-World Bank conglomerate was an accomplished thing. A confidential 1976 "Country Program Paper" mentioned the Bank's hand in

* National Economic and Development Authority

this. Its strategy covered massive lending for "rural development" (a political ploy to ward off agrarian unrest); labour-
intensive, export-led, foreign-dominated "industrialization";
energy and infrastructural projects to lay the underpinnings for
the agricultural and industrial advance of transnational corporations. The well-co-ordinated move made sure that the Philippines would keep its place in the international division of
labour and remain basically an agricultural producing country,
supplier of raw and processed agricultural and non-traditional
products at very cheap prices.

The World Bank's macroeconomic hold

1980: The Philippines was at a crossroads as it entered the new
decade. On one hand, the World Bank's high-powered "Poverty Mission" that visited the country in 1979 had described in
no uncertain terms the plight of the Filipino people, bluntly
referring to "the possible direct and indirect consequences of
policy and project recommendations upon the poverty process". On the other hand, the Fund and the Bank were pushing
for the very strategy of liberalization that had wrought tremendous havoc.

External conditions added to the contradictions. The
Philippines was being encouraged to delve deeper into export-
oriented industrialization at a time when goods could not be
absorbed in the global capitalist market due to world recession.
It was also being asked to dismantle protective barriers just
when the advanced industrialized nations had restricted the
entry of imports to protect their own economies. What direction was it to take?

Since the Philippines had a $2.7 billion current account
deficit and a $15.2 billion external debt, it was driven in des-
peration once more to avail itself of $654 million worth of IMF
assistance and to accept the program loan of the World Bank.

Of great significance in 1980 was the Bank's winning leverage over macro-level policy, whereas before it generally operated on a project-to-project basis. World Bank control over one
or more sectors of the nation's economy was finally formalized.

A $200 million loan was given by the Bank for "structural
adjustment", part of a proposed $1 billion financial assistance.
Before this loan was approved, conditions were specified and

negotiations held in Manila in August 1979. A confidential World Bank *aide mémoire* of the meeting records:

The Government of the Philippines broadly agrees with the general analysis and policy recommendations contained in the World Bank's report.... The World Bank is prepared to consider Industrial Programme ... lending to support the implementation of these policies.

The Bank's directives, echoed by Minister of Finance Cesar Virata's letter of intent, were to: 1) lower protective tariffs; 2) liberalize commodity imports; 3) increase indirect taxes; and 4) maintain a flexible exchange rate. The direction went one way: heightened export-oriented industrialization.

To qualify for the loan, Philippine domestic legislation faithfully implemented tariff reform and import liberalization and other measures. There were also organizational changes, such as the fusing of the Ministry of Industry and the Ministry of Trade with the Board of Investment, a move geared towards diverting resources to export promotion and away from domestically oriented output. Revisions in Central Bank policies provided for the siphoning of local funds, scarce as they were, to finance industries with no linkages to the domestic economy. Export processing zones and industrial estates throughout the country were envisaged to maximize cheap Filipino labour for the use of transnational corporations. Selected industries that were manufacturing non-traditional exports like textiles, footwear and processed food were slated to be modernized and rationalized to make them internationally competitive.

The World Bank released $200 million, the first installment of which went to the development of free-trade zones and industries for export, and towards the practice of subcontracting the more labour-intensive stages of production.

Meanwhile, by January 1981 the Philippines had kept its word by reducing tariffs on 472 imported items, mostly processed goods and raw materials. Fourteen industries previously protected were denied protection. The goal was to reduce tariffs from 100 to 120 per cent to as low as 18 per cent.

The irony is that the very cause of the current account deficit in 1978 and 1979 was the import of inputs: raw materials and intermediate goods, rising from $100 million in 1975 to an estimated $440 million in 1979. The main beneficiary of tariff reduction would be this category of inputs. The World Bank explicitly stated that tariff charges were meant to be "specialized arrangements for the export processing industries".

The reduction and eventual removal of licensing of imports by the Central Bank would facilitate the entry of all kinds of imported goods, even of non-essentials like baby pacifiers and watermelon seeds. Obviously the end-result would be an increase in sales for American and Japanese corporations.

The reorganization of the whole financial system of the Philippines was another requisite of the World Bank loan. For this financial reform, $300 million known as the "Apex loan" was to be administered by a Central Bank unit, the Apex Development Finance Unit (ADFU). It would channel the loan to the Philippine Development Corporation, the Development Bank of the Philippines, and the Philippine Investment Systems Organization, which in turn would reloan to labour-intensive, export-oriented medium and large-scale industries. The financial innovations included: 1) the floating of interest on loans; 2) the decreasing of bank reserve requirements; 3) the increasing of rediscount rates for small- and medium-scale industries and traditional exports and the lowering of rediscount rates for non-traditional exports.

The banking industry was also reoriented towards greater concentration of economic power and a shift from the local capitalist to the foreign capitalist. This was done through the establishment of universal banking or expanded commercial banking. The objectives of this were: 1) to encourage greater competition among financial institutions by eliminating legal specializations that limit their scope of activities; and 2) to increase the availability and use of long-term funds.

A Bank-dictated mandate was transmitted as Circular 739 from the Central Bank promulgating the consolidation of banks so as to be able to pool together a minimum capital of P500 million. This was one step towards drawing the Philippines into international banking and making domestic financing resources available to a wide field of corporate investments.

Another recommendation of the World Bank's Country Program Paper for 1980 stated: "The foreign exchange accounts could be balanced by a moderate devaluation. This, rather than a default on debt service obligations, would be the probable consequence of a liquidity problem should it arise." Once again the peso was said to be "overvalued" and the solution was simply to devalue it.

The trampling of people's rights

The ravage of the Philippine economy by the IMF-World Bank policies has had pernicious effects on people's rights. More than being simply isolated cases of human rights violations, the result has been the collective bondage of Filipinos of all sectors.

In the Philippine experience, World Bank President Robert McNamara's goal to eradicate absolute poverty was not realized during his 13 years at the helm and there is doubt if the incumbent president, A.W. Clausen, will do any better. The application of the "diffusion theory" of Walt Rostow, Mc-Namara's buddy during the Kennedy years, has not succeeded at all in our part of the world. Whatever "trickling down" that may have occurred has had questionable "good effects" on the various sectors of Philippine society.

The rural poor

Almost four-fifths of all the poor in the country live in rural areas. Did their lot improve because of IMF-World Bank policies?

Take the World Bank strategy for "rural development". Rather than truly answering the needs of the rural poor, it was more a political response to agrarian unrest. The "development projects" in the countryside were undertaken mainly to prevent the repetition of the Vietnam experience of a mobilized peasantry.

In the past 20 years, while the IMF demanded an export-led industrialization, World Bank projects concentrated on encouraging subsistence farmers to become small-scale market producers. Linked to other sectors through the market, they were expected to desist from disrupting the national economy for fear of harming their own "businesses".

A catchy name for this strategy is "Green Revolution". The packaged solution has been backed by agricultural research stations like the International Rice Research Institute (IRRI), which was founded by the Ford and Rockefeller Foundations. It is a subtle scheme of building dams and roads, introducing rural credit and enforcing the purchase of farm inputs — all to the benefit of transnational corporations. It boils down to people's subsidy for the underpinnings of big business!

A "miracle" rice was promised on condition that farm inputs be purchased. Here was how the farmers were milked: from a P28 fertilizer expenditure per hectare in 1966, farmers paid 16 times more in 1981 — or P455 per hectare. Over the same time, the price of palay rice increased by less than four times from P0.41 to P1.55 per kilo. The national average increased only a little less than two times from 26 cavans in 1966 to 43 cavans in 1977. As a result, farm income deteriorated. In 1973 rice farming income could provide only one-sixth of what a farming family of six needed to live decently, but by 1982 it could only provide one-eighth of family needs. Farm income increased by only three times whereas the cost of living was already four times the 1973 level. The value of the official increase over eight years was only nine centavos.

The logical thing to do for people-oriented developmentalists would be to provide subsidy for the hard-pressed farmers. The irony of it is that fertilizer companies have been the recipients of the poor farmers' tax money, a total of P2.52 billion from 1973 to 1980.

The building of huge irrigation projects was also encouraged. It came to a point that money practically poured in. As a National Irrigation Authority person said: "We have no problem with funds. Our problem is where to build the irrigation systems the World Bank wants us to construct."

Affected by these projects are the tribal Filipinos. The destruction of their villages is a desecration of sacred ground. When their villages become part of a dam site, they face major upheavals: physical and cultural uprooting. The Bank admits in its report *Economic Developments and Tribal Peoples: Human Ecologic Considerations* that "Little or no systematic attention has been given to tribal peoples per se in Bank-assisted projects." In the Philippines we have seen how tribal groups dare resist annihilation in the name of development. The Chico River Irrigation project, where they have been valiantly struggling for their ancestral rights, is a case in point.

But of course there was also "land reform", which in the Philippine case meant the transfer of ownership from landlords to tillers of agricultural lands devoted principally to rice and corn, similarly aimed at "converting mere share-croppers to small agricultural entrepreneurs". The program has been labelled "primarily a public relations effort" as it involved only 14.5 per cent of all farmers and 9.1 per cent of all farm lands. It has turned the land valuation process into a market transaction, enabling landlords to realize for their land a cash value that is 30 per cent above the capitalized value of future rents. This has also sunk 80 per cent of "tenant-beneficiaries" into debt arrears. What happens to the farms of those in arrears is not clear; the logical result appears to be a transfer of ownership to government. Perhaps a most satisfying end for the perpetrators of a program with dubious objectives.

Export-oriented incentives and encouragement by the Philippine government were positively received in the agricultural sector. The 1970s saw the massive expansion of areas under export crop cultivation. While agribusinesses, foreign and Filipino, were raking in profits, agricultural workers and landless seasonal labourers continued to wallow in centuries-old poverty. Government legislation has pegged agricultural (including plantation) labour to the lowest wage rates in the country. One and a half million families are dependent on the coconut, which has been an export crop since the colonial period. Add to this figure the millions of families dependent on available work on a seasonal basis in the country's vast sugar estates, or banana, palm oil and other corporate farms producing export agricultural products.

Have Filipino farmers been reduced to sheer docility? Not really. On October 16, 1981, delegations from the Central Bulacan Area Marketing Co-operative, with a membership of 5,029 farmers, confronted the Fertilizer and Pesticide Authority with a protest against the increased cost of farm inputs.

The new World Bank recommendation is to create "reserves". In the Philippines this is being done in the style of Vietnam "hamletting". Not only tribal groups but Christian settlers as well get enclosed in some kind of concentration camp. This happens in areas rich in natural resources — minerals in particular. But since these areas have become the territory of the New People's Army or the Moro National Liberation Front, the villagers who are suspected of sustaining the guerril-

las with food supplies are subjected to strict military control.
Their movements are curtailed by curfew hours and they live in
fear of being liquidated, tortured or raped.

Meanwhile the problems of the rural poor remains unresolved. Low incomes, landlessness, unemployment and
underemployment plague them more than ever. The consequences for the masses are greater hunger, malnutrition, ill
health, homelessness and illiteracy.

The urban poor

For decades back, the metropolis — centre of commerce,
growth pole of the economy and, to impoverished rural folks, a
centre of opportunity — served as a magnet to those whose
labour was not needed on the family farm and for whom no
work in the village was at hand. And a major problem upon
reaching the city was finding a place to live. They built where
they could and became squatters, for the land was not theirs.

The Manila press has recently been covering the mass ejec-
tion of squatters. By December 1982, the "eyesores" were supposed to disappear, according to government directives.

The case of 1.6 million squatters in 415 blighted areas of
Metro Manila is pathetic. Squatters comprise 30 to 40 per cent
of the Metro Manila population. It is the most obvious proof of
Philippine underdevelopment. Because of the land problem in
the rural areas, these ex-rural poor have been pushed to the city
where they suffer the squalor of the slums. According to the
Ranis Report, "The existence of urban squatter colonies is, in
other words, a symptom of a labor surplus economy." The same
report recognizes the value of such colonies: "Squatters play a
certain useful role, frequently in the service sector, and . . . to
banish them from the cities would be technically difficult and
economically costly."

While foreign visitors are shocked by living conditions that
look horrendous to their eyes, some believe that "Living in
absolute poverty with the barest amenities is in itself the example of the Filipino's resiliency and ingenuity," as the magazine
Business Day put it.

How does the World Bank/IMF conglomerate come into the
picture?

In 1974, Philippine strongman Ferdinand Marcos created

the Housing and Urban Development Team, part of a two-year
project study of the Tondo Foreshore area — Southeast Asia's
largest slum. The study eventually led to a World Bank loan of
$32 million with counterpart funding of the same amount from
the Philippine government. It was the World Bank's first urban
upgrading effort in the Third World.

Considerations of return on investment, that sacrosanct
measure of profitability, led to the concept of "cost" recovery.
Beneficiaries should pay back what was spent, with interest. As
in the case of land reform, almost all the supposed beneficiaries
could not meet the financing requirement. As a government
official said: "Don't be fooled by glamorous names. These
much glorified projects are mere duplicates of what we've been
offering. The difference, however, is that they're run as a business proposition!"

One has to have sufficient income to be able to pay. Most of
the squatters are service workers: sidewalk vendors, itinerant
peddlers, pier and hotel workers, salesladies. A number work
in manufacturing firms.

The first big confrontation was over the people's claim to
land that they had been occupying for years. Backed up by the
law (Republic Act 1597, later amended to RA 2438), they
looked forward to buying a part of the Tondo Foreshore area at
P5 per square meter. The token payment, a fraction of the current market value, was not to the Bank's liking. The Bank therefore came up with a counter-proposal: that "Due to past governmental promises and conflicting legislation on the subject of
land tenure in the Tondo area, a Presidential Decree apparently
be required to implement any proposal." In a short while the
government took up the case and came out with Presidential
Decree 1314 repealing the premartial law acts and promulgating 25-year leases at $6.40 a month for a 48 square mile plot
and the sale of this at market value after a five-year lease.

This of course infuriated the Tondo people who protested
through their organization, ZOTO. Whereas the Bank believed
75 per cent of the residents could afford the rental rates, a
German government mission affirmed the fact that only 4 per
cent of squatter households could possibly pay the rents regularly.

What was hoped to be a showcase World Bank slum

upgrading project has turned out to be a fiasco not at all answering the needs of the poor, far less the poorest of the poor.

Industrialization and working people

More widespread are the effects of export-oriented industrialization, an IMF-World Bank scheme. Cases in point are the free trade zones and the bonded villages where the burden of development is especially laid on the workers.

One of the main features for attracting foreign investors is the low labour cost. The Canadian-based Ford Ensite came over because of "the Philippines' inexpensive labour which is less than $2 daily as against Norway's $8 an hour".

In protest against this kind of exploitation the Ford workers staged the first strike in the zone, in spite of the banning of strikes. They may be receiving relatively high wages but compared to the superprofits of Ford, what goes to them is but a pittance, making them the most exploited of all workers in the zone.

As a rule workers are not encouraged to unionize (they even suffer harassment if they do). Job insecurity is high; lay-offs are frequent and apprenticeship, which costs less than the minimum wage, can stretch for a year and even longer. Workers' morale is very low. They suffer from forced overtime and the quota system, which racks their nerves and works them to ill health. There is an abnormally high percentage of women to men (9:1). The women are hired to work on the tedious, meticulous, non-traditional exports — electronics and garments. Married female workers are discriminated against in employment, so abortions are common. Managers and supervisors take advantage of the very young girls who work (most between 16 and 25) and exploit them sexually. The choice is to give in or to lose one's livelihood. In one zone it is common to find unwanted babies strangled to death and thrown to the creek or garbage pile.

Another way of implementing the export-oriented industrialization prescribed by the IMF/World Bank has been through the bonded villages. There was a plan to establish a hundred such villages for various product lines and to put in operation the re-export system. The companies import the equipment used, as well as all raw materials. Cheap and high quality labour is added to these materials to produce the "value-added". Whatever the external buyers pay for the "value-added" represents the Philippines' foreign exchange earnings from the industry. Not only is the price paid for work done determined by foreign buyers, but also the profit for the local sub-contractors and the wages of the workers.

Concretely speaking, in the case of garments, about 56 per cent of the export values are actually imported raw materials and only 44 per cent (the value added thanks to the Filipino garment workers) originates from the Philippines. In other words, for every $1 reported as value of exports, only 44 cents really are export earnings. Of said export earnings, about 30 per cent are profits which may be repatriated to the mother companies so that only 70 per cent remains from which wages and other local overhead expenses are taken. For every $1 therefore, the "net benefit" to the country (in terms of incomes paid to Filipinos and which remain in the country) is only 31 cents. This "net benefit" is wiped out entirely by low wages and cruel treatment of garment workers and smuggling and transfer pricing through the "consignment system".

The World Bank Mission's Report, *Industrial Development Strategy and Policies in the Philippines* (1979), is a blatant proof of the Bank's hand in the re-export scheme, which benefits foreign investors at the expense of the Filipinos.

Indeed, the Filipino people have been asked to subsidize export-oriented industrialization directly by the cheap price of the sweat and blood of workers, farmers and those in the service sector, and indirectly by bearing the effects of inflation. For example, when copra exports went up by 20.5 per cent in volume for an increase of 10 per cent in dollar earnings during the first semester of 1978, there was a corresponding increase in prices of coconut-based products such as cooking oil, milk and soap — items needed by the ordinary Filipino. What happened was that as a result of increased exports, artificial shortages were created, which pushed prices up. Thus Filipino consumers were forced to subsidize the expansion of great industrial firms like Procter and Gamble and Franklin Baker.

It is no wonder the vast majority of Filipinos are finding it most difficult to survive. From 53 to 90 per cent of the population in 1975 did not even have the minimum income to satisfy the family's essential needs. As the World Bank itself admits, "The 1975 poverty incidence in the Philippines... was, in fact... above the average for middle income LDCs.... The Philippines had a significantly higher poverty incidence than the other large developing countries of the East Asian Region except for Indonesia."

According to Dr. Mahar Mangahas of the Development Academy of the Philippines, the real income per family in the bottom 30 per cent fell from P957 in 1971 to P762 in 1980. This means that the poorest 30 per cent of Filipinos have a real income of only P2.09 (U.S.$.25) per day.

Local entrepreneurs

Who really benefit from the strategy of export-led industrialization?

• The main trading partners of the Philippines are the United States and Japan, who together account for 52 per cent of RP foreign trade in 1978. Japan bought about 24 per cent of RP exports and sold 27 per cent of RP imports in 1978; that same year the U.S. bought 33 per cent of RP exports and sold 21 per cent of RP imports.

• American investments in the Philippines dominate the principal export industries: mining — copper, gold, nickel (Atlas Consolidated Corp., Benguet Consolidated, Inc., Marinduque Mining and Industrial Corp.); agriculture — coconut, bananas, pineapple, sugar (Legaspi Oil Co., Stanfilco, Castle and Cooke/ Dole, Victorias Milling Co., Bogo-Medellin); forest products — logs, lumber and plywood (San Jose Timber Co., Nasipit Lumber Co.).

• Japanese investments in the Philippines are tied with American interests in export interests, for example: mining — Atlas Consolidated Mining and Development Corp. and Mitsubishi Metal Corp.; Marinduque Mining and Industrial Corp. and Marubeni Corp.; agriculture — Legaspi Oil Co. and Mitsubishi and Co.; Stanfilco and Stanfilco Itok Ltd., Tokyo Seiki.

• The Filipino partners of these foreign investors belong to the elite, people such as Zobel, Cojuangco, Cabarrus, Soriano, Yuchengco, Ossorio, Araneta.

Investments are controlled and owned through equity or loans. The law requires that Filipinos should hold 60 per cent

of equity investments and that foreigners should not exceed
having 40 per cent of equity investments. In fact, according to
one tabulation the balance turned out to be 39 to 61, not in
favour of the Filipinos but in favour of foreign investors!

In a worse strait are local entrepreneurs in domestically-
oriented industries. They are being squeezed out of business.
Although small- and medium-scale industries numbered
around 20,000 units in 1980 and comprised 97 per cent of the
total number of manufacturing establishments in the country,
they accounted for only 29 per cent of manufacturing output
while 71 per cent of that output was produced by the 3 per cent
composed of 481 large-scale industries which have foreign
equities. The legitimate gripe of Filipino entrepreneurs is that
they are given no incentives at all.

There definitely is a bias for capital-intensive industrial
development. The 1980s show a trend towards the merging of
small companies. The giants swallow up the small ones in
practically all industries, including banking. The restructuring
of individual industries in the so-called "non-traditional
exports" (textile, cement, food processing, furniture, and footwear) was dictated again by the World Bank to render them
internationally competitive. This is another way of harnessing
profits for transnational corporations at the expense of the
national economy.

Consequently the core of national businessmen who still
have a share in the domestic market of consumer goods are
disgruntled. The more courageous among them have voiced
their complaints and exerted some political pressure, but to
little avail. Even the old-time cronies of President Marcos and
the First Lady found themselves edged out by the creation in
1981 of a cabinet made up of World Bank favourites, technocrats like Virata, Ongpin, Laya and Mapa.

After 20 years of manipulation by the International Monetary Fund and the World Bank (agencies controlled principally
by the United States government), the Philippine economy is at
its lowest ebb. The consequences of the export bias and the
retardation of the development of the domestic market, of the
control by transnational corporations of crucial industries, and
of tariff liberalization on the supply side and low wages on the
demand side have been disastrous. The past two decades have

seen the country go from bad to worse. No one denies the nightmarish financial crisis. Everyone feels in the gut level the increasingly difficult struggle for survival. We dread to imagine what sufferings await a country whose future has been mortgaged to the International Monetary Fund and the World Bank. Any way out?

Nicaragua: The Risks of Debt Renegotiation

Oscar Ugarteche

Oscar Ugarteche, a Peruvian economist, is a New York-based special consultant on debt problems for Latin American governments — most recently Bolivia and Nicaragua. He was formerly a consultant for the Economic Commission for Latin America (CEPAL) as well as being the founder of Actualidad Economica, *a Peruvian journal.*

The relationship between Nicaragua and the international banking community has always been somewhat out of the ordinary. During the 1970s the Ultramar Banking Corporation, acting in the name of the government of Nicaragua, managed to obtain credits from international banks at levels surpassed in Central America only by Costa Rica. These funds, needless to say, were not always spent in the most useful ways. Ultramar was, in fact, associated with the Somoza family and partially owned by them. The credit transactions included very high fee charges — over 5 per cent of the amount of the loan. Hence the company had a vested interest in obtaining all the credits possible. The combination of credits obtained by Ultramar and capital flight led Nicaragua in 1978 to a very severe crisis of foreign exchange and a bleak economic outlook.

Nicaragua's per capita foreign debt increased 22 per cent per annum between 1975 and 1978, reaching U.S.$515 million in that last year. On the other hand the level of international reserves between 1977 and 1978 dropped by $276 million dollars: roughly half of the total export income for 1978. This was a result of negative private capital movements, which totalled $338 million dollars in those two years. The country's export income did not cover the loss in reserves and capital flight.

Thus, with a foreign debt service of $588 million dollars payable to the international, private banking community alone, in September of 1978 the Somoza government called for a special mission from the IMF to evaluate the economic situation and recommend a stand-by loan. This would give the country's Central Bank fresh funds to cover the gap in foreign exchange.

Nicaragua's request to the IMF was for $20 million dollars. The purpose was to obtain the stand-by agreement and, using it as a "good housekeeping seal of approval", convene the international banks for a meeting in which a part of the foreign debt would be restructured. However, after its visit to Nicaragua, the IMF did not recommend a stand-by agreement. In December of 1978 Nicaragua's Minister of Finance sent a telex to the banks stating that it was impossible to pay back capital or interest over the existing balances, but that in the next few months the country would be ready to pay interest due and renegotiate capital. This proposal was based on Nicaragua's foreign exchange earning season, which is in the first five months of the year, when crops are sold abroad.

In February 1979 the Central Bank called for another mission from the Fund. This mission recommended that the government take some orthodox economic measures, such as: devaluing the currency by 43 per cent; contracting the government budget deficit; eliminating subsidies; and restricting internal credit. It left for Washington with the recommendation that Nicaragua get $65 million in a stand-by agreement. In March 1979 the government made current its debt to multilateral agencies (such as the World Bank and the Inter-American Development Bank) and to most governments.

In the meantime, the *Insurrección Final* had begun on September 9, 1978. As a result the country was running up an intense shortage of foreign exchange due to capital flight; and the government budget was affected adversely by major military spending. In the last few months of the war, in May of 1979, the Fund approved a $65-million dollar credit. Out of that, $20 million was disbursed immediately. At a meeting convened by the President of the Central Bank and the Minister of Finance, at Citibank, New York, the General Manager of the Central Bank proposed a steering committee of banks to restructure the existing debt. They sought to refinance $176.6 million in long-term credits and $76 million in short-term lines. While these conversations were being held in New York, Somoza resigned. Immediately after the *Frente Sandinista* marched into the capital, Managua, on July 19, the international financial community froze the accounts of Nicaragua.

The Sandinista government was faced with this financial crisis immediately upon coming to power. It did three things vis-à-vis the debt: First, it quantified it to have an idea of the magnitude of the problem; secondly, it discussed the political convenience of recognizing or repudiating the debt; and finally it sought a solution that would best serve the interests of the country. Five months after coming to power, it chose to recognize the debt to the banks. A month later it started to negotiate the conditions for its restructuring.

Debt recognition and renegotiation

In July of 1979 there was no consensus on what to do with the debt. Before the *triunfo*, in a document titled *Programa de la Junta de Gobierno de Reconstrucción* written in San José, the upcoming government suggested restructuring and renegotiating the foreign debt estimated then at $1.3 billion.

The government's policy statement read: "The renegotiation of the debt will include its change in the terms and conditions which are most favorable to the national interest and will be closely linked to the economic recovery process of the country and to the gradual restoration of its repayment capacity."

However, at the UN General Assembly in September of 1979, Daniel Ortega stated that Nicaragua would recognize only that part of the debt free of corruption. More precisely, he stated that all the foreign debt would be recognized except that part used for the purchase of weapons and contracted in a corrupt manner, and the funds that did not enter the country.

With this framework the government would define a refinancing policy, taking as a reference a detailed analysis of each contract from each loan; of all the funds that entered or did not enter the country; of the fees and the manner and terms in which loans were obtained. Equally, a study was done to determine how many loans were intermediated by Somoza's partner at Ultramar Banking, and which might not be subject to recognition. However, in the end political pressures both internal and external — and particularly a certain optimism — led the government to recognize all the debt and leave aside the elements that Ortega had introduced at the UN.

The Nicaraguans expected that if they recognized the debt, the international banking system would open its credit-lines again for foreign trade. They also believed that if they did not recognize the debt, those lines would be closed and the country forced to pay cash for all its imports.

In December 1979 at the Mexican Ministry of Foreign Affairs, where all international creditors were convened, the government of Nicaragua, represented then by the Minister of the International Reconstruction Fund (in charge of the foreign debt), gave a speech recognizing the debt. The bankers felt relieved. Nicaragua appeared not to be another Cuba, which had disavowed its debt on the grounds that the money had benefited a few and because of the undue pressure the American government had placed on it. In the case of Nicaragua the bankers still could not be sure, however, that in the next few months things might not change and that the move to recognition wasn't a bluff. One year later, in December 1980, they were reassured when Nicaragua signed the First Tranche of its debt renegotiation, which covered the medium and long-term debt of the Republic to the international banks. It was indeed not another Cuba.

For renegotiation purposes the foreign debt of the country was broken up into four separate sections: Tranche I, as above; Tranche II-A, short-term debt of the nationalized banks with the international banking community; Tranche II-B, debt of former Somoza-owned or related enterprises with the banks; Tranche III, private debt held with the international banks. Each Tranche was negotiated independently.

The Tranche I negotiations began in Mexico in January

1980, concluding in Panama in August 1980. None of the meetings were held in New York or London — the usual practice. This change in location was a precedent set by Nicaragua.

Table 1
FOREIGN DEBT INDICATORS

	1970	1975	1976	1977	1978	1979
Per Capita Foreign Debt in U.S.$	90	295	314	402	515	640
Exports (millions of U.S.$)	179	375	542	637	646	617
GDP per capita U.S.$	875	955	974	991	891	649
Private Capital Movements (millions of U.S.$)	-	45	27	-63	-275	-503
Variations in International Reserves (millions of U.S.$)	-	-31	39	-58	-218	-584

Source: Developed from Table 1 of the ECLA Report:
Nicaragua: Repercusiones Económicas de los Acontecimientos Politicos Recientes, E/CEPAL/ g. 1091, Agosto 1979.

The obsession of the bankers with Nicaragua was that a precedent was not to be set. They entered the negotiations knowing that they had to negotiate, but that the situation "demanded and justified" conditions that would be less harsh than usual, in the words of economist Richard Weinert. The banks wanted to impose market conditions and market interest rates. This, however, clashed with the reality presented by the flow of foreign exchange of the economy and the country's need for five years to build up its foreign reserves again and increase imports, all in order to allow the economy to recover.

The initial proposal, made by the banks in March 1980, was in the same terms that Turkey had just negotiated: two years' grace period, five years' payback; at the rate of 1.75 per cent over LIBOR. The initial Nicaraguan proposal was 23 years' payback.

Starting as they did from two opposite positions, soon both sides took a common approach which allowed for a quick signing of the agreement. Nicaragua recognized past-due interest since 1978, when Somoza's regime stopped payments. The calculation for all past-due interest were done at a fixed 10.875 per cent rate rather than at the market rate. At the time, LIBOR was at 20 per cent. For the first five years, Nicaragua was to pay 7 per cent interest, capitalizing the difference with the market rate to be repaid from 1986 onwards. This was a precedent that gave the country a relief from debt repayment for five years.

A third precedent was that the country did not negotiate payments due in one or two years, which is the tradition in country refinancing. Rather it opted for restructuring the entire volume of debt. This was cheaper for the economy and more just for a government that was not forced to recognize its foreign debt in the first place. This, indeed, became one of the most painful precedents for the banks.

Finally, there was no front-end flat fee paid at the conclusion of the agreement which again is the usual practice. Normally this fee is between 0.5 and 1.5 per cent of the renegotiated amount. This precedent was followed by Senegal in 1982 when it concluded its renegotiations.

What was most enlightening in the Nicaraguan negotiations is that it opened a discussion of the difference between a country and a company in relationship to banks. For banks there is one major difference: Countries cannot go bankrupt.

From the banking point of view, the difference is the realization that the banks are in a monopolistic bargaining position vis-à-vis the country immersed in a balance of payments crisis. When a country does not agree to the bank's terms, the banks can embargo exports or, more realistically, enforce their right to offset using the accounts of the country. This means that the money coming into the accounts of the country can be withdrawn to cover up the country's debt position with the bank. This has occurred recently in the conflicts around Iran and Argentina. In the Iranian case the accounts were offset in U.S. banks. In the Argentinian, the accounts were offset in London.

In all cases the interventions are with accounts held not only by the central banks but by the government and in some cases private nationals.

The pressure the banks can exert over a country in this manner is large. To a certain degree but often less dramatically than the cases cited, banks do exert their right to offset and the Nicaraguan case was no exception.

In the case of companies, banks know that if such pressure is exerted the firms might fold, which does not solve the impasse. The point is to recover the amount lent or, if not, receive interest on it. The banks don't want to write off non-performing loans. The case of the large firms is clear. The government backs up the position of the firm with a subsidized loan to pay back the banks. Or it gives the company a guaranty. In the United States, this kind of support has happened in the automobile and aircraft industry. In cases where the employment and productive structure of the country is at stake, the state fulfills a role of moderating banking pressure towards the firms. However, in the case of a less developed country, there is no bailout, no major sovereign state or institution that will serve in this fashion.

A recent example of one sovereign state bailing out another was U.S. support for Brazil; similarly, Mexico. If the U.S. did not bail them out, its own banking system as well as the international financial system would collapse. The pressure was exerted in the opposite direction. So, there is a monopolistic negotiating position vis-à-vis a country as opposed to a major firm. Because of this monopolistic position the banks can charge higher fees to the weaker countries, impose more severe conditions and, finally, obtain relatively more profits from a smaller base.

We note that the sovereign concept becomes non-existent when the accounts of central banks and commercial banksof LDCs are held in the major banks of the industrialized countries, where the accounts can be taken over with the legal support of the government of that state. This does make both sides aware at the initiation of negotiations that they are in an unequal position. In the case of Nicaragua, it obtained parity to negotiate as a result of its revolution and the international support it had at the time: Moreso by the fact Nicaraguans knew that if an agreement was not reached with the banks, or if the banks exerted undue pressure, the population could be told and it would support the government's position.

Nicaragua recognized the debt of Tranche II-A and negotiated it between January and September 1981. The agreement was signed in December of that year. An option Nicaragua did not take was to declare its commercial banks bankrupt — even though that was what they were. The reason was more to keep the international community at ease than an economic one. The debt of the Tranche was $182 million.

For the same political reasons, the debts of Somoza-owned or related enterprises were recognized and renegotiated in Tranche II-B. These businesses as well were left bankrupt, practically without exception. However, Nicaragua proceeded to assume the debt of up to $53 million. Total assets of all these firms did not amount to more than around $20 million.

Table 2
PUBLIC DEBT
Nicaragua
(in thousands of U.S.$)

	Creditors	12/31/79
I	Official Sources	316,217.6
II	Multilateral Agencies	434,674.0
III	International Financial Community	
	A. Suppliers	15,234.0
	B. Commercial banks*	
	I	584,812.3
	II-A	182,692.2
	II-B	53,552.9
	TOTAL	1,587,682.9

Source: *Banco Central de Nicaragua*
* Renegotiated. It includes past-due interest capitalized.

Through the agreement of Tranche III, the Central Bank of Nicaragua promised to provide the private sector with foreign exchange for the payment of foreign debt.

In March of 1982 Nicaragua concluded its renegotiation process for an amount totalling $821 million (see Table 2) out of a total public debt to July 1979 of $1.6 billion.

Country risk analysis: economic indications

The elements taken into account by the banking system to evaluate the degree of risk in a country are two: economic stability and political stability.

Economic stability relates to the leading growth indicators, the balance of payments and the level of international reserves. The political risk concept is more subjective. It is defined as the permanence of the government and the political system including its ongoing viability.

Table 3
GDP
RATE OF GROWTH

	1979	1980	1981
Costa Rica	4.9	1.2	-0.9
El Salvador	-1.5	-9.6	-9.5
Guatemala	4.7	3.5	1.0
Honduras	6.7	2.5	1.3
Nicaragua	-25.1	11.5	7.8

Source: *Consejo Monetario Centroamericano*, Memorandum CMCA/192/81, San José, Costa Rica, 11 December 1981.

The rate of Nicaragua's GDP growth (Table 3) shows that the country was very hard hit by the war but still held a sustained rate of growth in the subsequent years. The Central American region, as a whole, was affected by a sharp fall in commodities prices. However, Nicaragua's economy was less badly hit. The region as a whole also observed a massive process of capital flight, which affects its movement of capital account. Nicaragua, on the other hand, had a positive movement of capital in the form of long-term loans from governments and donations which served to balance out the previous capital flight. Despite 60 per cent of the economy being in private hands and lack of investment by the private sector, the rates of growth for the first two years after the revolution were on an average over 9 per cent. Growth was achieved in these years through foreign credit at subsidized rates used for government investment.

According to SIECA, the loss of international reserves during 1981 was $298 million and the only country that saw an improvement in its level of reserves was Nicaragua. During 1982 Nicaragua lost $60 million in reserves, out of a total of $143 million for the region. This problem of reserves is a derivative of the international trade problem. In this sense it must be pointed out that trade improved in volume yet also fell in absolute value.

Table 4
TOTAL EXPORTS
$ (millions of Central American)

	1979	1980	1981
Costa Rica	1,122.1	1,223.9	1,289.1
El Salvador	1,224.2	968.5	792.0
Guatemala	1,551.9	1,834.2	1,608.7
Honduras	859.2	967.8	975.1
Nicaragua	690.1	528.7	582.0

Source: Ibid.

The prices of raw materials exported by the region fell by about a 40 per cent average in the period between July 1980 and December 1982. Hence Nicaraguan exports that increased 11 per cent in 1981 fell by 5 per cent in 1982. Its leading exports are coffee, cotton, sugar and beef. Total exports went from $450 million in 1980 and $500 million in 1981 down to $476 million in 1982.

In volume, however, there has been improvement. The cotton crop increased from 427,000 quintales* in 1980 to 1.6 million quintales in 1981. Sugar production increased from 1.3 million quintales in 1980 to 2.1 million in 1981 and 2.7 million in 1982. Coffee increased from 1 million quintales in 1980 to 1.1 million in 1981 and 1.2 million in 1982. The panorama, though bleak on the side of foreign exchange, is quite promising on that of domestic productivity.

* Quintale: 100 kilograms

On the other hand, inflation has been kept under control, being held at the 27 per cent level. The economic policy does not allow for a deficit of more than 10 per cent of GNP; a level above could trigger a higher rate of inflation.

Table 5
INFLATION
CONSUMER PRICE INDEX

	1979	1980	1981
Costa Rica	9.2	18.1	30.0
El Salvador	8.6	17.4	20.0
Guatemala	11.4	10.7	12.5
Honduras	12.1	18.1	10.0
Nicaragua*	70.0	34.0	17.0

Source: *Ibid.*
* *Nicaragua: A Challenge to Reconstruction*, BIRF, Washington, D.C., October 1981.

Table 6
NICARAGUA
LEADING ECONOMIC INDICATORS

	1979	1980	1981	1982 (est.)
GDP Growth%	-25.1	10.7	7.8	0
General Price Level				
1974=100	180.6	244.4	317.7	-
Total Population				
(in thousands)	2,479	2,568	2,648	2,812
Economically Active				
Population				
(in thousands)	716	789	813	863
External Public Debt				
(in thousands of $)	1,202.7*	1,579*	2.163.9**	2.238.2

Source: *Banco Central de Nicaragua*, 29 July 1982
* Does not include past-due interest
** Includes the refinancing effect and capitalization of interest.

Political risk

The element of political risk is defined, as we said, by the perceived stability of a given government and its political process and by its ongoing capability. However, a bank's perception of risk is also related to the foreign policy of the country where the bank originates. It is repeatedly said that capital is not national any longer; it is transnational. However, after the experience of work meetings with about 120 banks around the world, it could be said that banks belonging to countries that have a friendly attitude towards Nicaragua are likely to be more open. However, this is not an exclusive condition.

Banks that originate in countries with a bad relationship with Nicaragua tend not to have any relationship or want any relationship with the country. That is to say, an important part of the political risk consideration would be the relationship between the countries rather than the events in the country itself. The political risk would be defined by the occurrence of a conflict between the bank-originating country and the recipient country. In the case of Nicaragua, there is a covert war against that country by the United States.

In the period between March 1981 and December 1982 the Nicaraguan government and its representatives made repeated contacts with the international banking community. European banks to a certain extent opened up their trade credit-lines to the country, restoring partially its capacity to import. This has occurred because of the foreign policies involved and perhaps because of the old trade relationship existing between coffee and cotton markets and growers in Europe and Central America.

It is not clear what the economic viability of the country will be if the trade finance lines are not fully restored with the majority of banks; or if Nicaragua does not fully restore its financial relationships to support foreign trade. A failure to do so could have a polarizing role in Nicaraguan foreign policy and financial relationships.

There is an understanding between banks and countries. If a country stops paying its short, medium and long-term debt, all credit is suspended and the country must pay cash for its imports. However, the moment that the debt is updated or restructured, credit is restored almost automatically. Nicaragua today is treated by most banks as if it had not renegotiated its debt. Worse yet, it is treated as if it was not currently meeting its obligations. Thus U.S. banks are acting as a destabilizing force — as a tool of foreign policy.

Tanzania: Origins of a Financial Crisis

John Loxley

John Loxley teaches economics at the University of Manitoba
and is the author of External Finance and Structural
Adjustment in Third World Countries, written for the
North-South Institute. He has served as economic advisor to
the commercial banking system of Tanzania; as director of
the Tanzanian Institute of Finance Management; and as
economics professor at the University of Dar es Salaam. He
is an editor of and contributor to Towards Socialist Planning
(Dar es Salaam, 1972) and from September 1981 to May
1982 worked in Tanzania as a member of the Tanzanian
Advisory Group.

For the last three years, Tanzania has been in dispute with the
IMF, a dispute that raises a number of very fundamental questions. First of all is the question of the validity of the analysis
used by the IMF when dealing with underdeveloped countries
and the prescriptions put forward based on that analysis. Secondly are questions about the IMF's understanding of the historical and structural problems that underdeveloped countries
face. Thirdly are questions about the ideology underlying the
IMF's analysis and prescriptions. And finally come a number of

important questions about the links between the Fund and World Bank policies. This paper seeks to deal with each of these questions.

The symptoms of the crisis in Tanzania are fairly well-known and not by any means confined to Tanzania at this particular point in time. For one thing, there is an extremely acute foreign exchange shortage. Secondly, there is a huge budget deficit resulting in the printing of money on a fairly large scale. Thirdly, there is a shortage of both imported and local goods and therefore a very high rate of inflation. In recent years, in sectors where price controls exist, fairly extensive black markets have developed. For those people who knew Tanzania years ago, there has been an obvious increase in the level of corruption, although it is debatable just how deep and how high up it goes. Certainly in day-to-day dealings corruption is common. It never used to be a few years ago.

Finally, there is evidence of declining productivity and a reduction in the operating surpluses of public sector corporations. Since most of the major means of production are in the hands of the public sector corporations, this is a fairly serious symptom of crisis. One aspect of the crisis that makes it difficult to discuss Tanzania intelligently is that the statistical system seems to have collapsed, so that hardly any figure at all is reliable these days in Tanzania. This is simply a symptom of the general malaise in the economy.

These symptoms are not really in dispute and the Tanzanian government acknowledges all of them. What *is* in dispute is the origin of the crisis and what should be done about it. It would appear that there are three schools of thought on this. The first is the IMF approach, which is shared by a number of other important donors. The World Bank shares this view, by and large, as do a number of bilateral donors, particularly the U.S. Agency for International Development (AID), but others as well. The second is the approach we might call the Tanzanian school. The third one, to be dealt with last, is the view of the left about what's happening in Tanzania.

The IMF package for Tanzania

The IMF approach sees the origins of the crisis in Tanzania as largely domestic. That approach sees the crisis as the product of economic mismanagement and, more indirectly, of the policies of socialism being pursued in Tanzania. This is articulated most clearly not in IMF publications but in the World Bank's Berg report, "Accelerated Development in Southern Africa", which demonstrates that the approaches of the IMF and the World Bank are very, very similar. It is not that these institutions are blind to other factors having an impact on the Tanzanian economy, but by and large they see the problems as domestic in origin.

The prescription that follows is, of course, based on their view of the nature of the problem. Thus, they emphasize the movement to free-market solutions, a move away from the public sector controls and "socialist" policies that they see as responsible for many aspects of the crisis. One could take any of the symptoms of the crisis and demonstrate how they argue their case. Thus, for instance, they would argue that the budget deficit is a product of overspending by the bureaucracy; of the introduction of universal programs that Tanzania can't afford in health, education and water supply; of the need to subsidize maize-flour consumption by urban workers. All of these would be important considerations in the IMF's interpretation of the causes of the budget deficit. The IMF and World Bank would apply similar arguments to the problems of black markets and shortages; they would see these as the result of price controls, poor planning or poor management. So the solution they advocate is to rely very heavily on the free market and, in many respects, to attack the interventions of the government in the economy.

Now, this conflict is very clear from President Julius Nyerere's New Year's day speech to diplomats in 1980, reprinted in *Development Dialogue*, where he lays out very clearly what the problems were with the IMF as early as 1980. Each of Tanzania's objections to specific IMF proposals had an ideological ring, and the President concluded by telling the IMF that if it couldn't be useful, then at the very least it should "stop meddling".

In spite of these ideological differences over which sections of society should bear the burden of adjustment, Tanzania reached an agreement with the IMF in August 1980 and made a stand-by arrangement for about $235 million. It is interesting to see that this particular arrangement did not contain any of the issues that the President objected to; it did not, for instance, contain any requirements to devalue, did not contain a requirement to drop price control or to abolish import control, and did not specify that the burden of adjustment should be placed on the poor. These were items objected to in the New Year's Day speech. In spite of that, the stand-by arrangement broke down because, after drawing only one quarter's loan, about $25 million, Tanzania could not meet the budget target or the required restraint in its money-supply target.

Since then, relationships between the IMF and Tanzania have deteriorated quite considerably and this is now common knowledge. There were demonstrations in Tanzania against the IMF and in discussions between Tanzania and the IMF things have become quite acrimonious on each side. The IMF has, on occasion, been quite undiplomatic and its reports are singularly unsympathetic. On the Tanzanian side, we have witnessed a public outrage over IMF conditionality. None of that has helped discussions but, of course, underneath there are some very important differences of analysis and idelogy.

In fact, the recent conditions laid down by the IMF in negotiating a different and larger agreement, though still a relatively small agreement by international standards (less than half a billion dollars compared with about five billion each for Mexico and India), are particularly harsh and clearly very ideological in their orientation. That ideology is at odds with Tanzania's ideology. It is crudely inequitable and quite deflationary.

For instance, this time the IMF is asking for a devaluation of over 100 per cent for the Tanzanian shilling relative to the U.S. dollar; or else they would like to see the Tanzanian exchange-rate float freely. The IMF is asking for the abolition of the subsidy on maize-flour production and suggesting that the price of maize-flour, which is part of the staple diet of workers, be raised from 3.50 shillings a kilo to 8.0 a kilo. Some people in Tanzania feel that this is a prescription for street riots.

The IMF is asking that wages not be adjusted in the first year of the program so that the inflationary effect of the devaluation would be shouldered squarely by workers. It is asking that import controls, exchange controls and price controls be loosened. It is asking that interest rates be adjusted for inflation; this means that, relative to 1981, interest rates would rise from 10 per cent on overdrafts to 40 per cent (and Canadians were worried about their 18 per cent mortgages!).

The IMF has conditions for cutting the budget deficit and money-supply growth that go well beyond anything that Tanzania feels it could successfully achieve, certainly as regards money supply growth. Finally, the IMF is calling for an end to public sector deficits so that subsidies would no longer be paid through the budget to public sector corporations.

That is the IMF package for Tanzania, a package on which the Fund has so far stood firm for almost a year. But this view of the problem and its solution is not confined to the IMF. The World Bank, when approached by Tanzania for a structural adjustment loan, laid down a condition that there should first be agreement with the IMF before that loan be considered. Other donors are beginning to jump on the bandwagon and echo the IMF view, although the donors are still not unified on this.

The case against the IMF

The Tanzanian position is somewhat different. Tanzanians argue that the origins of the crisis in Tanzania are largely external — and they are not the only ones who think so. A book by Green, Rwegasira and Van Arkadie makes roughly the same kind of argument.* Those authors do not deny that there are domestic management problems, nor does the Tanzanian government. But in arguing that the origin of the problems is essentially external, they point to a very marked deterioration in terms of trade. In 1980 there was a major increase in the price of oil, primary-product prices collapsed and industrial prices continued to grow significantly. The result was that Tanzania lost a very large amount of ground simply in prices received for international commodities. It also had a series of bad harvests, drought and floods three years in a row, and therefore had to import food, putting pressure on scarce foreign resources.

In 1979, to the applause of the world, Tanzania assisted in

* R.H. Green, D.G. Rwegasira and B. Van Arkadie, *Economic Shocks and National Policy Making: Tanzania in the 1970s*, Institute of Social Studies, The Hague, 1980.

the removal of Idi Amin; but the applause was not accompanied by any country offering financial assistance. So Tanzania footed the bill for a major war — and there have been very few wars fought this century without serious disruptive effects on budgets and inflation.

Finally, the East African community collapsed and Tanzania had to make significant investment outlays in railroads, airways and so on to replace the community assets. These are Tanzania's arguments, that most of their problems are caused by external shocks. They also point to the fact that Zambia and Uganda owe them roughly the amount of money they're seeking from the IMF in one year's assistance.

Their argument is that the balance of payments problems that have led to subsequent domestic problems in the budget, in inflation, etc., can be explained by these kind of random events. At the same time, in recent months there has been an acknowledgement that things are not as good as they might be internally in certain sectors. The government does have a program now to improve economic management. It's fairly explicit and fairly detailed, and in effect is an acknowledgement that not all its problems were externally induced.

Given their approach, the Tanzanians have been very reluctant to devalue. They did devalue earlier this year simply because they were tied to the dollar while the dollar was appreciating. They made what is called a technical adjustment to offset that. They didn't feel it was appropriate for the Tanzanian shilling to appreciate relative to other currencies simply because the dollar was appreciating. But, beyond that, they've refused to devalue. They argue that a devaluation is inherently regressive. While this need not be so, certainly, in the IMF case, devaluation would be regressive, because the burden would fall on the poorer sections of society.

Secondly, the Tanzanians argue that devaluation is irrelevant to imports because while it raises import prices this does not have significance because imports are controlled. Every dollar of imports is controlled by licensing authorities and consumer imports are negligible. Everybody agrees that Tanzania does not import large quantities of luxury consumer goods. Most of its imports are essential intermediate goods such as gas, food and oil.

The Tanzanians also argue that a devaluation is not relevant in the short run on the export side because there are physical problems restricting the output of the three major crops: coffee, cotton and sisal. It would take up to five years to expand coffee and sisal output. Cotton is said to be limited by the physical constraints of land available to cultivation. So in the short run, they argue, devaluation would simply put more money in circulation for every ton of coffee and sisal produced, without really increasing the output of these crops.

Thus, the Tanzanians argue that devaluation would be quite inflationary — and especially so if the devaluation was as large as the IMF is asking, given the context of inflation rates that are already between 20 and 35 per cent a year, depending on the figures used.

Turning to interest rates: Tanzanians reject the IMF argument that they should raise interest rates to 35 or 40 per cent. The IMF report advocating this was really quite a poor piece of work and Tanzanians feel that this recommendation is irrelevant in a context where 90 per cent of all credit goes to the public sector. The IMF model is based on an assumption of private savers responding at the margin to alternative returns — private savers looking at the rate of interest in neighbouring countries and shifting their funds around to take advantage of slight differences in real rates of interest. This model simply does not bear any relationship to reality. In Tanzania, private savers are negligible and people moving money in and out of the country are doing so for reasons other than marginal returns on saving. So it is a wholly irrelevant model and the Tanzanians have rejected it.

The Tanzanians are standing firm on minimum wages; they're standing firm on subsidies on maize flour. On deflation, they see the need to trim the budget deficit, but apart from defence, which has inevitably been quite large since the Uganda war, there's not a great deal of room to trim the budget without cutting into health, education or water programs. These are progressive programs that Tanzania has been most successful in developing and it's here that serious ideological disputes come in again.

Quite clearly, if Tanzanians were to meet the guidelines of

the IMF, they would have to cut back on these programs and they are not prepared to do this. That was made clear in the President's 1980 New Year's day speech. Tanzania is also not prepared to levy charges for these services, at least not up to now, although there are people in Tanzania advocating this. Tanzania also quarrels with the IMF over the *phasing* of assistance, arguing that as much foreign exchange as possible should be provided *before* policy changes are made or, at least, *as* policy changes are made. They argue that economic adjustment would be easier if they could have the money in advance.

If the IMF did in fact put out the money up front, it would enable the government to solve its balance of payments problems quite quickly. It would enable industrial production — which is equal to 30 per cent of capacity at the present time — to increase significantly. In the process this would raise sales tax, the most important source of revenue for the government. So the budget deficit would be closed simultaneously, at least to some extent, by the provision of foreign exchange up front. Also, of course, with the inflow of this money the local currency equivalent could, to some extent, be used to reduce the budget deficit.

Increased industrial production would also enable Tanzanians to increase agricultural production, because farmers would have something to buy when they sell their crops. At the moment, there is very little for them to buy of local products and imports, and this is a serious problem. Tanzania also argues that such a boost in production would enable them to reduce black market prices by flooding the market with goods now scarce, so this would reduce inflation to some extent.

Such an expansion in industrial production would, however, need to be financed by bank credit as inventories of raw materials and finished products increased. Thus the Tanzanians argue that credit restraint as demanded by the IMF would choke off recovery.

The Tanzanians also insist that certain types of controls are necessary to ensure equity and efficiency. Hence they are not prepared to dismantle those controls to the degree desired by the IMF. They are, however, prepared to relax price controls on scarce luxury items.

An analysis of the IMF model

These are the disputes. Negotiations continue as the crisis persists, with the IMF position hardening as time goes by, giving the impression that it is *either* not interested in a settlement with Tanzania *or* that it is attempting to force an agreement that would undermine what remains of the government's popular support. As the crisis deepens, of course, Tanzania may have little option but to capitulate. Before considering the view of the left on the crisis, it might, therefore, be useful to pause and consider the nature of the model that the Fund is seeking to impose on Tanzania.

First of all, it is very much a demand-oriented model and essentially (though not unambiguously) monetarist in character. Thus, demand restraint through credit and fiscal restraint are its key features. But, although it focuses explicitly on demand, it has, nevertheless, important structural implications. It serves to reinforce the entrenchment of underdeveloped countries in the existing international world order by strengthening traditional export trade links and possibly by encouraging the export of manufactures for those few countries with appropriate production structures. The wisdom of stimulating farmers to produce more for export in the context both of serious declines in their terms of trade internationally and of world depression is highly questionable.

The burden of adjustment in IMF stabilization programs is usually borne by urban wage earners, whose real income is cut by price hikes, subsidy abolition, cuts in money wages, reductions in government services or increases in unemployment due to demand restraint. This is often accompanied by increasing rates of profit in the urban and traded goods sectors. Because of these effects on income distribution can be large and sudden, IMF programs have on occasion caused serious social disruption leading to state repression as a requirement for "successful stabilization".

The IMF model is market-oriented and favours private enterprise. This is in a context in which neither the market nor the private sector has been particularly successful in alleviating poverty or other aspects of underdevelopment — quite the opposite. As such, it is particularly distasteful medicine to swallow for those countries that have attempted to overcome underdevelopment by more active state intervention.

The IMF's approach is highly consistent with that of the World Bank, which also favours private enterprise and use of market forces. The World Bank's structural adjustment loans carry, if anything, even more stringent terms than those of the IMF. They reach down to the sectoral level in requiring policy adjustments, whereas the IMF tends to confine its "advice" to broad macro-variables.

Tanzania and the left

These, then, are the models that may be forced on Tanzania because of its lack of options in securing the foreign exchange it requires. The third view of the crisis, that of the "left", argues that Tanzania was moving slowly in the direction of the IMF/ IBRD model anyway and that the crisis is not the outcome of pursuing socialism but just the opposite. It is precisely Tanzania's failure to implement its declared socialist policies that is responsible for creating the domestic causes of crisis and leaving Tanzania exposed to the external shocks that have buffeted the economy in the past three years.

The left would argue that Tanzania's ruling Party for the Revolution failed to transform the relations of production in agriculture and, in the process, to deal with the food problem and create a surplus for reinvestment. Instead, a forced villagization program in certain areas of the country had all the negative attributes of Stalinist collectivization *without* achieving collective production or an increase in the surplus. Returns to farmers in traditional export crop production have been reduced significantly, largely by the growth of unproductive, inefficient and bloated crop authorities. As a result, production has fallen.

In other sectors, productivity has been low because of the failure to allow workers' control over management after tentative efforts in this direction in 1971 were reversed, sometimes quite ruthlessly. The management model is essentially the private-sector type model. Workers do have checks and balances, in the system, but the result is that nobody takes responsibility; nobody has any initiative.

Of course, the system could move in two directions from

where it is — it could move towards a pure private-sector model by getting rid of workers' involvement and security of employment and by introducing more discipline and more material incentives. It could also move in the other direction and give workers the power they were asking for in the early 1970s. This is a cause of some dispute in Tanzania. There are groups advocating each position and it is a debate one should look at quite carefully to see how it might be possible to solve problems of inefficiency in the public sector.

The left would argue that Tanzania has not done what it said it would in other respects too. The economy does not produce for need. Most of its production is for demand, meaning export demand. The economy is not integrated in any planned fashion with agriculture-supporting industry and vice-versa. The industry developed in Tanzania has a very high import dependence, which is responsible in part for the crisis the country is facing over foreign exchange.

The left would also argue that Tanzania became over-dependent on foreign aid, which finances the bulk of the nation's capital budget. Foreign aid provides about 40 per cent of the imports coming into Tanzania. There can be no question that many of the problems of domestic mismanagement and shortages of foreign exchange could be traced back to external advice from aid donors and to aid projects. Of course nobody admits that; aid donors are not prepared to take the responsibility for the problems in Tanzania. But there is clearly an over-dependence on aid, which Tanzanians now seem to recognize, although this is hardly the time to do anything about it — when the most immediate problem is to keep foreign exchange flowing in order to keep vital imports coming in. Certainly in the longer run, however, foreign aid is to be dealt with.

Such would be a "left" interpretation of the crisis. The left abandoned Tanzania long ago and moved to seemingly more promising pastures. Tanzania had its ten years of building socialism: It didn't accomplish it, so it was divorced. It is clear that many Western socialists have failed to appreciate the *relative* progressiveness of the government in Tanzania even as it stands. There is definitely a problem of the large gap between rhetoric and reality in Tanzania. There are clear signs of some form of class formation developing. The problems outlined are

real. On the other hand, there are many progressive attributes
to the government, in its international policy in particular, but
also in its domestic program. These attributes are at stake, I
think, in Tanzania.

The left has probably underestimated the difficulties of
social and socialist transformation in underdeveloped
countries; particularly the ones with a very, very small political
base to begin with. The left will probably find exactly the same
problem in what now appear to be greener pastures. So perhaps
the expectations were somewhat unrealistic. The IMF dispute
brings into focus the fact that there are still these progressive
attributes; in attacking these attributes, IMF conditionality is
reactionary and quite suspect.

The push for solutions

The sad part of the story is that Tanzania has very few alternatives. It may well be that, structurally, Tanzania should not be
where it is, but the fact is that it *is* where it is, and in that
context, it is very difficult to find alternatives. That there
appear to be many similarities with Jamaica under Michael
Manley is apparent from the work of Norman Girvan, Richard
Bernal and Wesley Hughes. There are, however, also some
major differences. Public ownership and controls are much
more deeply entrenched in Tanzania. These are not about to be
dismantled. Secondly, there is no right-wing opposition party
in Tanzania chomping at the bit, funded from abroad, waiting
to take over. It is a very different political situation.

One would have to be very cynical to argue that Tanzania is
resisting the IMF simply because not doing so would mean
dismantling parts of the bureaucracy and therefore reducing
the power of a certain class interest in Tanzania. The issues
involved in the dispute with the IMF do concern ordinary people in Tanzania. There is, for instance, no fuel or kerosene, the
basic cooking and lighting fuel in Tanzania. There are primary
schools all over Tanzania — it has a very good record of establishing primary schools and training teachers — but at this
point there are no school supplies, no books, no crayons or
pencils. There are clinics and hospitals without basic drugs.
There's a complete shortage of insecticides. Serious public
health problems are developing.

These are very, very human problems; very real problems that affect ordinary Tanzanians and that could be ameliorated in the short term by an inflow of foreign exchange. After that, of course, Tanzania would have to deal with its own internal domestic problems and in a more fundamental manner deal with the social system and development strategies that have brought on this crisis.

Whether the government's current program for setting its own house in order would work remains to be seen. It may well be that the movement to the right in Tanzania cannot be corrected in the foreseeable future and may be given a boost by the crisis. But there are alternative leftist strategies and the IMF program, with its implied harsh burden on urban workers and assault on what remains of progressive social initiatives, can hardly be regarded as an acceptable direction in which to move. It seems that on the balance of the evidence, the international community, including the left, has an obligation to give critical support to Tanzania in its dispute with the IMF.

Jamaica: Democratic Socialism meets the IMF

Richard L. Bernal

Richard Bernal teaches economics at the University of the West Indies in Jamaica. He was a consultant to the National Planning Agency during the Manley administration and is co-author of "The IMF and the Third World: The Case of Jamaica, 1974-80", published in Development Dialogue (1980:2)

Jamaica's experience with IMF programs has been described by *The Economist* as the "IMF's most publicized and traumatic experience in the 1970s". The experience was traumatic for both the country and the institution because they were never able to bridge the gap between two significantly different approaches to economic development. This failure is often not recognized, because in many eyes, and particularly the IMF's, the immediate issue was correcting a balance of payments deficit. But it is crucially important to realize that each strategy of balance of payments adjustment involves a strategy of economic development.

The development strategy of the IMF's programs of balance of payments adjustment was and is that of dependent capitalism. This strategy was in contradiction with the Democratic Socialism of Michael Manley and the Peoples' National Party (PNP), which formed the Jamaican government between 1972 and 1980. The IMF did everything in its power to derail Democratic Socialism behind a facade of objective scientific economic analysis and political neutrality. This point has been made* but what has not been explained is: What is the development model of the IMF, how did it seek to bring this model into place and why?

The IMF has attempted to camouflage the profound disagreements between itself and the Manley government. Indeed, an article G. Russell Kincaid published in the IMF/World Bank magazine *Finance and Development* in 1981 makes the spurious claim that Jamaica was an example of "how the Fund made available an unprecedented volume of resources and adapted its conditionality practices for a member in difficult economic circumstances". The IMF has gone as far as stating, in an article by the same author in *IMF Survey,* that "The selection and combination of policies undertaken to achieve the objectives of the programs — and indeed, even the targets of the programs — were varied in response to priorities set by the Jamaican authorities themselves." The IMF poses itself as a neutral technical advisor. "The Fund remained conscious of the country's circumstances and social priorities," wrote Russell Kincaid in *Finance and Development:*

The particular structure of policies developed was based on the authorities' understanding of the relative social costs and benefits, while the Fund staff provided technical assistance as to the likely economic impact on the balance between resource demands and available resources.

These claims are contradicted by information from Jamaican sources. The negotiations for both the stand-by agreement of 1977 and the Extended Fund Facility of 1978 were bitter and protracted. There were fundamental differences over appropriate policy measures and sizable differences in target figures. Statements by political leaders indicate that there was

---

* See, for instance, Norman Girvan and Richard Bernal, "The IMF and the Foreclosure of Development Options: The Case of Jamaica", *Monthly Review,* Vol. 33, No. 9 (February 1982).

never any genuine unanimity on the direction and content of macroeconomic policy nor on the goals of such policy. In his 1980 budget speech, Hugh Small, the last Minister of Finance in the Manley government, bemoaned the fact that IMF programs "cut across those things that were fundamental to our philosophy and beliefs" and that "their implementation interrupted the programmes of the PNP". When the PNP government abandoned negotiations with the IMF in March 1980 it was because it believed that the terms required were completely untenable. According to a party statement at the time, it knew that "The PNP cannot be true to its social and economic goals and objectives within the framework of an IMF programme."

The government bitterly resented the IMF's efforts to force Jamaica to accept its prescribed measures. In a national broadcast in January 1977 Manley stated indignantly:

We are now facing a situation in which some of the people who could lend us money will apparently do so only on the condition that they should be able to tell us how to conduct our affairs. . . . The International Monetary Fund, which is the central lending agency for the international system, has a history of laying down conditions for countries seeking loans. . . . This government on behalf of our people will not accept anybody anywhere in the world telling us what to do in our own country.

Differences over economic targets were clearly revealed in the Minister of Finance's nationally broadcast comment in May 1978: "Some of the conditions on which they [the IMF] have been insisting appear to us to be unduly harsh, but negotiations are continuing."

At issue was the extent of the devaluation of the Jamaican dollar. Jamaica eventually succumbed to the IMF's target of a 40 per cent devaluation. The IMF exploited the dire need for foreign exchange to coerce a government into accepting its terms. As the *Washington Post* reported, on July 24, 1978, "The Jamaican Cabinet expressed deep concern at the shock which the resultant devaluation would have on the prices of basic essentials," but, ultimately "[David] Finch [chief IMF negotiator] was determined about what Jamaica could and couldn't do." On January 4, 1978, in explaining the 10 per cent devaluation of the Jamaican dollar, Manley said: "The IMF feels the devaluation should be somewhat larger than we think necessary and justified at this time. . . . We would have preferred a small adjustment, but in the end, the fundamental consideration is that we must have access to foreign exchange in the future."

These differences over devaluation were camouflaged by the "letter of intent" — a letter from Jamaica's Minister of Finance to the Managing Director of the Fund requesting an agreement and outlining what policies the government would pursue during the duration of the proposed agreement. This letter, as the standard legal fiction presenting the IMF-designed economic program as that of the government, exonerates the Fund from having coerced the government into accepting its policies. Furthermore, the letter obliges the government to profess its belief in the feasibility and appropriateness of the measures proposed.

The "letter of intent" from finance minister Eric Bell to then IMF managing director Johannes Witteveen on May 11, 1978, declared: "The Government of Jamaica believes that the policies set out in the annexed memorandum are adequate to achieve the objectives of its programme."

In IMF procedure a letter of intent is accompanied by what is called "prior action" — some measure undertaken to demonstrate the government's seriousness. The action taken is preferably in the area where there has been the greatest difference of opinion with Fund officials. The extent of devaluation, as one of the most bitterly disputed issues, hence became a precondition for opening negotiations for a second IMF agreement. Jamaica had devalued its currency by 13.6 per cent in January 1978. The Extended Fund Facility, signed in May 1978, involved a further devaluation.

In addition, the "letter of intent" involves a solemn promise by the government to submit to IMF direction of its economic policy. In the 1978 "letter of intent" the government stated: "During the period of the intended arrangement they ["the Jamaican authorities"] will also consult the Fund concerning the adoption of any measures that may be appropriate, either at their initiative or whenever the Managing Director of the Fund requests consultation because any of the criteria referred to ... are not being observed, or because he considers that consultation on the programme is desirable." The binding document is the actual IMF agreement (Stand-by or Extended Fund Facility), which contains binding performance criteria (or targets). That agreement is an IMF document and therefore its interpretation is the sole prerogative of the IMF, while the letter of intent is the member country's document.

What the IMF portrays as a difference of opinion with a member country about the specific policy mix and the exact performance criteria and targets was really, in the case of Jamaica, a clash of diametrically opposed development strategies. What the IMF presents as a close and co-operative endeavour to find solutions to difficult problems was a bitter process of negotiation which the IMF deliberately stretched out to increase its leverage. What the IMF calls intransigence by a government that found it difficult politically to do the right thing economically — that is, to introduce deflation — was a struggle by Jamaica to utilize IMF facilities without completely abandoning its development strategy.

The making of the Jamaican economy

The Jamaican economy is small. The country has a land area of 4,411 square miles, a population of 2.2 million and a Gross Domestic Product (GDP) of J$4.73 billion (U.S.$2.65 billion). This small size has been an additional constraint on development because of the limited amount and range of resources available and the small size of the domestic market. This situation has prevented the realization of economies of scale, limited the emergence of a capital goods sector and facilitated the existence of monopolies.

The structure of the Jamaican economy has four main features:

1) A lack of intersectoral linkages, that is, sectors which use each other's outputs as inputs. This is reflected in the high import content of production and the large share of output for export. The economy does not have an internal dynamic because expansion in one sector does not stimulate expansion in other sectors. Export sectors — plantation agriculture, for example — and sectors producing for the domestic market — manufacturing, for example — are very dependent on imported inputs. This is especially the case in capital-intensive sectors such as the bauxite alumina industry, but even in labour-

intensive, service sectors such as tourism, the import content is over 40 per cent. The ratio of imported raw materials to gross value of output in the manufacturing sector in 1978 was 43 per cent. The overall import content is over 60 per cent, because all capital goods and technology are imported.

2) The economy is very open. International trade is large in relation to total economic activity and consequently there is a serious disjuncture between aggregate consumption and aggregate production. A substantial portion of consumption is satisfied from imports. In 1978 the ratio of imports of goods and services to GDP was 33.9 per cent, exports/GDP was 29.2 per cent and total trade/GDP was 63.1 per cent. The agricultural sector illustrates the gap between what is produced and what is consumed: In 1975, 28.3 per cent of agricultural production was for external markets while the country imported J$118.1 million worth of food, most of which could have been produced locally.

3) The economy is dominated by the capitalist mode of production, with its attendant monopolization of means of production and income by a capitalist class, the core of which consists of 21 families, and which leads to gross maldistribution of such basic needs as farmland and household income.

4) Up to the mid-1970s the economy was dominated by foreign capital, predominantly U.S. Foreign capital controlled the most important sectors: bauxite/alumina, manufacturing, export agriculture and banking. In 1975 U.S. direct private investment in Jamaica was U.S.$654 million of which U.S.$390 million was in the bauxite/alumina industry. In 1977, Canadian investment amounted to C$112 million.

Import capacity determines the functioning of the economy because of the high import content of consumption, of production for the domestic market and even in certain lines of export production. The dependence on imported inputs is compounded by the lack of a capital goods sector. This means that investment depends on the capacity to import. A further complication is the almost total dependence on imported energy.

The import capacity is determined by the quantum of foreign exchange available to the economy. The amount of foreign exchange available is determined by exports of goods and services, and capital inflows.

The main exports are bauxite/alumina, sugar, bananas and tourism. Bauxite and alumina accounted for over 70 per cent of merchandise exports from 1977 to 1979. The export of sugar and bananas stagnated during the 1970s and declined considerably as a percentage of total merchandise exports. Earnings from tourism increased in size and importance during the same period. Exports of manufactured goods are of limited significance, confined almost entirely to the Caribbean Community (CARICOM) region.

Capital flows have a double significance: They increase investment and provide foreign exchange. These capital flows take three forms: direct private investment; aid (or loans on concessionary terms); and loans (on commercial terms). Private capital inflows — almost entirely in the form of direct foreign investment in the bauxite/alumina industry — were particularly important during the 1960s. Foreign investment accounted for an average of 32 per cent of total investment from 1953 to 1972, with a peak of 45 per cent in 1972. During the 1960s private capital inflows were enough to cover the current account deficit. Between 1960 and 1971 the cumulative current account deficit was J$511.8 million and private capital inflows amounted to J$604.7 million. The current account deficit increased throughout the 1960s and early 1970s, moving from J$16.6 million in 1960 to J$275.2 million in 1976.

During the 1960s the Jamaican economy experienced high rates of growth. The real rate of growth per annum of GDP was 3.6 per cent between 1960 and 1968. However, the country did not achieve economic development, which is a process of quantitative and qualitative change. Within a nationally controlled economy economic development is an internally dynamic process of self-sustained capital accumulation and should provide an increasing level of material welfare for the majority of the people. In Jamaica the failure to experience economic development is reflected in the external dependence, disarticulation, dominance of foreign capital and increasing extent and degree of poverty. Unemployment increased from 13.5 per cent in 1960 to 23.6 per cent in 1972. Indeed, between October 1969 and April 1972, the number of people employed declined by 26,100. Income distribution worsened: It is estimated that between 1958 and 1968 the share of the poorest

40 per cent of the population in personal earned money income declined from 7.2 per cent to 5.4 per cent. Absolute poverty grew during the same period: The average income of the poorest 30 per cent of the population fell from $32 to $25 per capita, in constant 1958 dollars. In mid-1968, roughly 65 per cent of the employment labour force was earning less than $25 per week.

The government of Jamaica between 1962, when the country became formally independent of Britain, and 1972 was formed by the Jamaica Labour Party. This party subscribed to a political program that rendered whole-hearted support for the continued existence of dependent capitalism. The JLP government pursued a policy of "foreign investment by invitation", attracting foreign investment by offering generous tax incentives, such as relief from income tax for periods up to 15 years. The development strategy was outlined in 1969 by Edward Seaga, then Minister of Finance: "The first essential is that developing countries should ensure that a favourable climate exists for foreign private investment" and "The second essential is for the establishment of the necessary institutional framework to facilitate foreign, private investment."

This policy was rationalized by the specious argument that because of Jamaica's small size its resource base was inadequate, and that rapid population growth had locked the country into a "vicious circle of poverty" that meant inadequate levels of domestic savings and investment. The strategy of an economy propelled by foreign investment failed to make growth self-sustaining and beneficial to the majority of the population while economic decision-making was increasingly dominated by foreign capital.

The PNP and democratic socialism

In February 1972, the Peoples' National Party led by Michael Manley became the government, committed to a policy of growth with redistribution within dependent capitalism. The policy of the Manley administration from 1972 to 1974 consisted largely of several social programs aimed at alleviating the worst aspects of poverty and to a much lesser extent of measures to redistribute income through transfer payments and increased access of the poor to the means of production. In September 1974 the PNP declared its commitment to democratic socialism.

The ultimate objective of any form of socialism is to create a society in which people can realize the fullest development of their potential, that is, a social environment in which they are free from alienation, exploitation, material want, political oppression and social injustices. According to its own statements, the PNP's democratic socialism consisted of the following tenets:

1) Democratic socialism as not a phase between capitalism and communism, but an objective in itself.

2) A democratic political system such as that of a multi-party electoral system. Democracy and socialism are complementary because political and economic freedom are complementary.

3) The abolition of exploitation of man by man, an exploitation which is inherent in capitalism.

4) National self-determination and sovereignty over resources, to enable the construction of a self-reliant economy capable of providing increasing material welfare for the majority of people.

The problems that democratic socialism hoped to solve were caused by the operation of dependent capitalism. The socialist goal could only be achieved by the transformation of capitalism and the elimination of dependence. Capitalism is a mode of production in which most of the means of production are privately owned by a small minority: the capitalist class. The majority of people — the working class — do not own any means of production and live by selling their labour power for wages. During the production process, capitalists appropriate surplus value as the basis of profits: This is exploitation. Resources are allocated and production determined by the play of market forces and the profit motive.

Inherent in capitalism is economic inequity, social injustice, alienation and exploitation. For example, in 1968 some 293 owners of farms over 500 acres held 43.2 per cent of total farmland, while 151,705 owners of farms of less than 5 acres

held 15.4 per cent of total farmland. The richest 5 per cent of
the households received 30 per cent of the total income, while
at the other extreme 60 per cent of households received 19 per
cent of total income.*

In an address to parliament in 1977 Manley warned, "The
capitalist economic system does not possess the kind of
dynamic which can resolve the basic contradictions which
exist in the Jamaican economy." His party viewed dependence
as the major barrier to economic development. The PNP General
Secretary Dr. D.K. Duncan stated: "The major obstacle in the
path of our development is the domination of our economy by
the imperialist system by which foreign interests have
exploited our people and natural resources for over 300 years."

The party's diagnosis was that underdevelopment was
caused by and inherent in capitalism and dependence.
Dependence was seen as a situation in which the economy's
performance was conditioned and determined by external factors. If democratic socialist goals were to be achieved, an economic strategy of structural transformation was necessary. The
economic strategy of democratic socialism consisted of:

1) *A mixed economy made up of a state sector, a co-operative
sector and a private sector.* The state and co-operative sectors
were to transform the pattern of ownership and control of the
means of production. The PNP's *Principles and Objectives*
states that in "the economic sphere, socialism requires social
ownership and/or control of the means of production, distribution and exchange which must begin with a dominant public
sector which owns and/or controls the commanding heights of
the economy". The party would promote co-operatives "since
they serve to widen the basis of ownership and change the
relations of production as well as lessen the inequalities in the
distribution surplus". Private enterprise would operate in sectors not defined to be in the commanding heights, providing it
was "socially responsible"; earned a "fair" return on investment; instituted worker participation; and conformed to
"national goals and objectives".

* The statistics are dated but more recent estimates reveal no significant change. See *Jamaica Socio-Economic Report*, (Washington, D.C.,
Inter-American Development Bank, July 1979), Vol. 1, p. 49.

2) *Economic sovereignty and self-reliant development, by reducing the openness of the economy, its integration with particular developed capitalist countries, foreign ownership and the import of content of production.* This would lead to a re-articulation of production and consumption and an internalizing of the dynamic of capital accumulation and reproduction. Two issues were crucial to this process: the diversification of

Table 1
SOCIAL PROGRAMS OF THE MANLEY GOVERNMENT

OBJECTIVE	PROGRAM	YEAR ANNOUNCED
Alleviate worst aspects of poverty	Special Employment Program	1972
	Skill Training Program	1972
	Literacy Program	1972
	Youth Training	1972
	Community Health Aides	1972
	Free Education	1973
	Rent Controls	1973
Transfers of Income	Food Subsidies	1973
	Uniforms for Primary School Children	1973
	Increased Pensions	1974
Redistribution of Means of Production	Land Lease	1972
	Loan to Farmers	1974
	Construction of Small Industries Complex	1974

international economic relations; and the elimination or control of foreign ownership in certain sectors, such as bauxite/alumina, finance and public utilities. The state would permit new foreign investment on condition that it was consistent with the national goals and policies of the government; that it operate on the basis of "good corporate citizenship"; and that it be willing to enter into partnership with local private interests, the state or both "as may be required by the Government of Jamaica". Foreign investment would also be monitored to ensure compliance.

The purpose of these measures was to reduce the drain or surplus out of the country by the repatriation of profits and to minimize the denationalization of decisions about resource allocation. International economic relations would be diversified to reduce dependence on developed capitalist countries, and to strengthen economic links with socialist and Third World countries. State intervention in international trade would be exercised through a State Trading Corporation.

3) *Planning must be instituted to achieve increased control of the economy and to restructure the economy, to reduce "the acute external dependency" and create structural interdependence and self-reliance.* The need for planning arises not only from underdevelopment but from the monopolies and oligopolies that dominate the markets in Jamaica.

The implementation of a democratic socialist economic strategy required the expansion of the role of the state. The party's *Principles and Objectives* states: "In the transition to a Democratic Socialist Economy, the State sector leads the way in planning, directing and transforming the economic structure." The state was to own and control the "commanding heights" of the economy: mineral resources (bauxite, gypsum), strategic industries (alumina, cement, sugar), public utilities, financial institutions and foreign trade. By 1979, there were 185 public enterprises with gross assets by 1980 of approximately J$4,400 million. By 1980 the state owned all the public utilities, the largest commercial bank, 51 per cent of bauxite mining companies (Kaiser, Alcoa, Alcan), 75 per cent of sugar output, 48 per cent of hotel industry capacity. Along with this it had established the State Trading Corporation.

Jamaica and the IMF

After 1974 Jamaica experienced balance of payments difficulties, which reached crisis proportions two years later when the deficit was J$231.3 million. Net foreign reserves fell from

J$136.7 million in June 1975 to minus-J$181.4 million in December 1976.

The causes of this balance of payments deficit were external and internal. First, world inflation had a serious impact on imports, which increased by 125.7 per cent between 1972 and 1976. Part of this inflation came from OPEC price increases, which had tripled the oil import bill in one year from J$64.5 million in 1973 to J$177.6 million in 1974. In addition, export volume declined by 27 per cent between 1974 and 1976. Receipts from tourism declined sharply between 1975 and 1977, with holiday arrivals falling by 30 per cent, room occupancy declining from 43.5 per cent to 28.9 per cent and tourist expenditure decreasing by 9 per cent, from J$116.8 million to J$95 million.

Also contributing to the balance of payments deficit was an increase in investment income payments during 1975 and 1976, an increase due to capital flight and higher interest payments on government direct and guaranteed external debt. External debt repayment increased from J$49 million in 1974 to J$100 million in 1976. There was also a substantial increase in the net inflow of private capital in 1976 at the same time that transnational commercial banks ceased lending to the government.

In December 1976 the government opened discussions with the IMF and agreed on a two-year stand-by arrangement in June 1977. In September Jamaica made its first drawing and in December failed the net domestic assets test by exceeding the ceiling of J$355 by J$9 million or 2.6 per cent. The IMF terminated the agreement and negotiations began for a new arrangement. In May 1978 the government agreed to an External Funding Facility to provide U.S.$240 million over three years. This was increased to $429 million in 1979, but in December of that year Jamaica failed to meet the stipulated target, this time when it exceeded the ceiling on the net international reserves. The IMF suspended the EFF agreement, having disbursed only $172 million. The failure was due principally to external factors: namely, increased oil prices, increased world inflation, increased interest rates and flood rains.* For

* For more details see N. Girvan, R. Bernal and W. Hughes, "The IMF

one and a half years, from May 1978 to December 1979, Jamaica fulfilled all the requirements of the IMF's Extended Fund Facility Program, but experienced no growth or improvement in its balance of payments. Real GDP declined by 1.7 per cent in 1978 and 2.2 per cent in 1979. The balance of payments deficit increased by U.S.$40 million in 1978 and by a further $78 million in 1979. After six months of discussions with the Fund, the government decided in March 1980 not to seek a new IMF agreement but to pursue a "Non-IMF Path".

The policies of the IMF were in contradiction to those of the PNP government. The IMF policies were a comprehensive prescription for preserving dependent capitalism in Jamaica, which the PNP's Democratic Socialism sought to reform — and which it had the potential to transform. The IMF and those classes that supported dependent capitalism argued that IMF policies were based on principles of sound economic management that could be applied to any economic system. After all, the argument goes, the IMF is concerned with balance of payments adjustment and does not advocate any particular strategy of development or any particular economic system. This argument, however, is incorrect and untrue: The IMF has, implicit in its balance of payments adjustment program, a specific development strategy, that of dependent capitalism.

The IMF development model

The IMF model for its diagnoses and policy prescriptions is based on the monetary approach to the balance of payments and income determination. It sees the balance of payments as a monetary phenomenon and a deficit or surplus as a stock disequilibrium between the demand for and supply of money. Demand for money is a stable function of a few variables; therefore the main determinant of macroeconomic performance is the money supply, which is determined principally by domestic credit creation. Real factors are secondary and their importance limited, and the economy has a tendency towards equilibrium in the long run.

Hence, as American economist Harry G. Johnson states:

and the Third World: The Case of Jamaica, 1974-80", *Development Dialogue*, 1980:2, pp. 128-129.

Any balance of payments policy must be conceived of as aiming at speeding up a process of adjustment that would be occurring anyway (unless deliberately frustrated by policy); and that it must work by reducing or reversing the initial disequilibrium between quantity of money demanded and supplied.

The IMF approach is formulated in the Polak model* which emphasizes monetary factors, internal factors, and the short-term nature of the adjustment process.

The IMF has denied that it is a development institution. This is because in its view, the cause of underdevelopment is a shortage of capital, and the IMF itself is not concerned with mobilizing or providing capital. Indeed, a suggestion made by India at Bretton Woods, which would have amended Article I(ii) to require the Fund "to assist in fuller utilization of the resources of economically underdeveloped countries", was rejected. The objective of the IMF as stated in its Articles of Agreement is:

To facilitate the expansion and balanced growth of international trade, and to contribute thereby to the promotion and maintenance of high levels of employment and real income to the development of the pro-ductive resources of all members as primary objectives of economic policy.

The Fund's role was to ensure international and national monetary stability because this was regarded as the environment most conducive to economic growth. This was clearly understood by the founders. In March 1943, Harry Dexter White explained: "Stabilization is not an end in itself, but only a means to full employment and a rising standard of living." The *Annual Report* of 1965 confirmed, "Monetary stability must be regarded as a prerequisite for sustained economic expansion, rather than as an objective in itself." Per Jacobsson, managing director from 1956 to 1963, in explaining the role of the IMF in development emphasized, "Monetary stability is an essential condition and indeed the only reliable basis, for sus-tained growth." Other IMF backers have stressed that this is particularly the case in less developed countries.

* See J.J. Polak, "Monetary Analysis of Income Formation and Pay-ments Problems", *IMF Staff Papers*, Vol. 6, (November 1957) pp. 1-50. This model was subsequently modified: See "The Monetary Approach to the Balance of Payments", (Washington, D.C.: IMF, 1977).

The IMF's concept of economic development is based on the view that economic *growth* is synonymous with economic *development*. To the IMF, economic growth has two dimensions, external and internal.

The external dimension is concerned with the beneficial effects of expanded international trade. It is implicitly assumed that if trade is based on comparative advantage all countries will be better off. International trade is likely to grow most

Table 2
POLICY DIFFERENCES BETWEEN THE MANLEY
GOVERNMENT AND THE IMF

Issue	Manley Government	IMF
I. Type of Economy	Mixed	Dependent Capitalist
Dominant Sector	State	Capitalist
Ownership of the Means of Production	State/Cooperatives/ Capitalist	Capitalist
Allocation of Resources	Planning/Market	Market
Openness	Reduce	Complete
II. Accumulation and Distribution	State Directed Capitalist/ Co-operatives	Laissez Faire Capitalist
Investment	State/Co-operatives/ Capitalist State/ to Invest in Production Distribution and Infrastructure	Capitalist Investment in Production and Distribution. State Confined to Infrastructure Investment
Savings	Public and Private	Emphasis on Capitalist Savings out of Profits
Foreign Capital Inflows	Aid, Loans & Regulated Foreign Investment	Direct Foreign Investment
Income Distribution	Increase the Share to Labour	Increase the Share Accruing to Capital
III. Economic Management	Increased State Intervention and Planning	Laissez Faire with Emphasis on Monetary Policy

Issue	Manley Government	IMF
Monetary Policy	One of Several Policy Instruments	The Most Important Policy Instrument
Fiscal	Expansionary	Contraction
Exchange Rate	Dual Exchange Rate	Devaluation
Exchange Controls	Yes, to Effect Foreign Exchange Budgeting	Elimination of Controls
Trade	Import Restrictions and Licensing	Removal of Import Restrictions and Licensing
Prices	Control and Subsidies	Removal of Controls and Elimination of Subsidies
Wages/Incomes	Increase Pegged to Cost of Living Increases	Decrease in Real Terms

rapidly if there are no barriers to trade and if there is an international payments system of multilaterally convertible currency, with payments being made on a current basis. In addition, exchange rate changes must be kept to a minimum and competitive devaluations prevented. In this view, maximum economic growth in the world economy and in individual member countries can only be achieved by free or perfectly competitive markets within countries and at the world market level.

It is implicitly assumed that the real conditions do and can be made to approximate this ideal state. The General Agreement on Tariffs and Trade (GATT) has responsibility for elimination of tariff barriers and quantitative restrictions on trade, and the IMF, according to its own charter, has the task of "The elimination of foreign exchange restriction which hampers the growth of world trade." Free markets are a necessary but not sufficient condition for the growth of international trade and capital flows. The sufficient condition is the arrangement of stable international payments. Here, balance of payments deficits and inflation are the main cause of exchange rate problems. Therefore the IMF attempts to maintain internal monetary stability and finance a speedy balance of payments adjustment. This is enshrined in Article IV, section I:

Recognizing that the essential purpose of the international monetary system is to provide a framework that facilitates the exchange of goods, services and capital among countries and that sustains economic growth, and that a principal objective is the continuing development of the orderly underlying conditions that are necessary for financial and economic stability, each member undertakes to collaborate with the Fund and other members to ensure orderly exchange arrangements and to promote a stable system of exchange rates. In particular each member shall:

i) endeavour to direct its economic and financial policies towards the objective of fostering orderly economic growth with reasonable price stability, with due regard to its circumstances;
ii) seek to promote stability by fostering orderly underlying economic and financial conditions and a monetary system that does not tend to produce erratic disruptions;
iii) avoid manipulating exchange rates or the international monetary system in order to prevent effective balance of payments adjustment or to gain an unfair competitive advantage over other members; and
iv) follow exchange policies compatible with the undertakings under this Section.

The IMF seeks to ensure that if there is a deficit in the balance of payments, that deficit does not lead to a situation in which the country cannot make payments on "current transactions" on an immediate basis. Current transactions are:

payments which are not for the purpose of transferring capital and include, without limitation:
i) all payments due in connection with foreign trade, other current business, including services and normal short-term banking and credit facilities;
ii) payments due as interest on loans and as net income from other investments;
iii) payments of moderate amount for amortization of loans or for depreciation of direct investments; and
iv) moderate remittances for family living expenses.

Immediate settlements will be facilitated "by making the general resources of the Fund temporarily available to them under adequate safeguards, thus providing them with opportunity to correct maladjustments in their balance of payments without resorting to measures destructive of national or international prosperity". If a country's balance of payments deficit deteriorates to the point where payments are delayed or not made, the international movement of goods and capital will be disrupted or turnover time lengthened. The IMF therefore emphasizes the speed of adjustment "to shorten the duration and lessen the degree of disequilibrium". The importance of the speed of adjustment is revealed by the short duration of adjustment provided by IMF stand-by agreements. Indeed, the original stand-by agreements were limited to periods not exceeding six months.

The internal dimension of growth involves increasing capital formation. The IMF feels this is best achieved by free markets, which are supposed to be the most efficient mechanism of resource allocation. The Fund also diagnoses the cause of underdevelopment to be insufficient domestic capital formation. Therefore it sees inflows of foreign capital as indispensible. Since developing countries cannot borrow sufficient amounts, these flows must take the form of private direct foreign investment. The major dangers to capital formation and foreign investment are exchange rate changes and inflation, both of which result from monetary instability.

Competitive markets free of state intervention and monetary stability are the foundations of the IMF's strategy of development. Monetary stability encourages investment because it provides an environment conducive to domestic savings and investment. It is also supposed to stimulate foreign capital inflows by reducing the risk of repatriation difficulties, for example the problem of being credit-worthy and the risk of exchange rate fluctuations. Monetary stability is meant to enable the country to minimize inflation, which in turn permits appropriate domestic prices, and to maintain a realistic exchange rate and unrestricted external payments. The IMF defines monetary stability as a rate of growth in money stock which is compatible with the demand to hold money and to execute transactions.

To the IMF, monetary instability — the existence of persistent inflation — causes price distortions which result in the misallocation of resources. It leads to a reduction in domestic savings and investment and to the diversion of investment into relatively unproductive ends. If inflation exceeds that of the rest of the world, it leads to a shift in consumption from domestic goods to imports, which may lead to an adverse trade balance. It also distorts international capital movements by discouraging capital inflows and fostering capital flight. The IMF has always argued that inflation in developing countries is caused by excessive credit operation, usually to finance a budget deficit. Its *Annual Report* of 1966 states: "Excessive credit expansion to finance private investment or to meet wage demands, has at times been an important factor in generating inflation. However, unduly large fiscal deficits financed by bank credit have been by far the more common cause."

Whether these deficits arise from deliberate Keynesian expansionist fiscal policies or operating losses of public enterprises or by social programs to alleviate poverty, the IMF views them as unsound. The Fund regards budget deficits as causing excess aggregate demand, which in turn cause inflation and a balance of payments deficit. The IMF therefore blames the government for creating economic problems that retard economic growth.

Again, according to this view, economic growth will be maximized where the allocation of resources is optimal. The most efficient mechanism of resource allocation is price — generated by free markets. Any form of intervention, such as price controls or subsidies, leads to a misallocation of resources and hence lower rates of growth and even balance of payments difficulties. Therefore, any situation of misallocation of resources is the result of government interference with the operation of the market.

The IMF's economic strategy is based on support for private enterprise, private ownership of the means of production and capitalist social relations of production. It is therefore based on the support of capitalism. Complementing this is the IMF's distaste for the qualitative and quantitative expansion of the state in production, distribution and regulation of the economy. It confines the role of the state to providing infrastructure, law and order and to protecting private property, thus rendering impotent the very instrument that could be utilized to transform capitalism. It portrays any state-dominated economic system such as socialism as aberrant and inefficient.

What the IMF advocates is laissez-faire capitalism. This was explained by one-time managing director Per Jacobsson who said:

If we conclude that some government regulation is useful, and even indispensible, we must insist with equal force that government action must not be arbitrary; it must conform to the basic principles of the market system. As the philosopher Francis Bacon told us about the year 1600: "Nature can be commanded only by obeying her." We have therefore to know and understand the basic laws and principles of the price system in a free economy; and only if we act in conformity with those principles can we expect useful results from government action.

The IMF philosophy of development, with its open economy and markets free of any government intervention, guarantees the dependent character of capitalism. The openness permits the penetration of foreign capital by multinational corporations. IMF policies also frustrate the development of an articulation of production and consumption. What is more, dependent capitalism, while it can experience periods of economic growth, cannot provide development.

Diagnosis and prescription

The IMF is able to have its development strategy implemented by unwilling governments because it exploits their desperate foreign exchange situation and coerces them by its apparently scientific diagnosis of the causes of the balance of payments deficits. The IMF prolongs the negotiations until the foreign exchange situation becomes so desperate that the government surrenders to the demands of the Fund.

The IMF prescriptions and diagnosis are virtually identical for all developing countries: Studies both by the IMF and critical of IMF programs demonstrate this. The IMF's diagnosis is that balance of payments deficits are caused by: 1) excess import demand generated by excessive aggregate demand, and fuelled by a budget deficit financed by excessive credit creation; 2) inability to increase foreign exchange earnings because of uncompetitive exports due to an over-valued exchange rate.

According to the IMF, the country's exchange rate becomes inappropriate due to inflation generated by excessive demand and reinforced in some cases by excessive wage increases not matched by productivity increases. Capital flow is disrupted by inflation, an overvalued exchange rate, restrictions on payments and trade and price controls. There is inefficient resource allocation and insufficient capital formation because of incorrect pricing produced by state intervention in the operation of markets. The ultimate underlying cause is state intervention, which results in excessive credit creation and interference with the market mechanism.

The IMF's diagnosis of the causes of Jamaica's balance of payments problem, as stated in IMF documents, was excessive wage increases, overvalued exchange rate, excessive fiscal deficit, excessive monetary expansion, restrictions on external trade and payments, state intervention, price controls and a lack of private sector confidence.

This standard IMF diagnosis provides the justification for measures that constitute the IMF strategy of dependent capitalism. The standard package, applied in Jamaica and elsewhere, involves devaluation, wage restraint, removal of price controls, elimination of exchange controls and import restrictions. Along with these measures come reductions of government expenditure, the elimination of the budget deficit, the contraction of credit creation and limits on borrowing by the state and public enterprises.

That the diagnosis serves to justify the policies prescribed is revealed by the fact that the Fund pursues these same policies even where its diagnosis proves to be wrong. In Jamaica the IMF's emphasis on excessive import demand is contradicted by the fact that import volume declined by 24.3 per cent between 1972 and 1974. Exports did not decline because they were uncompetitive but because of declines in U.S. demand for bauxite and because of problems with technological obsolescence and decreased quotas (assigned by industrialized countries) in the case of sugar and organizational difficulties in both sugar and bananas. The unscientific character of the IMF derives from ignoring structural factors and by its complete bias toward internal and monetary factors.

The results of IMF programs were to:
1) Reduce state intervention in the economy, restoring the market to dominance in the resource allocation and preserving economic opportunities for private enterprise;
2) Force the government to compromise in pursuing its own development strategy, bringing its credibility into question and generating splits within the political directorate;
3) Deflate the economy and terminate social programs, thereby weakening the support of certain classes for the government, dismembering the class alliance which had supported the rul-

ing party and strengthening social forces committed to dependent capitalism.

In October 1980, Manley and the PNP were defeated in a general election by the Seaga-led Jamaica Labour Party (JLP), which had announced its total commitment to IMF policies and dependent capitalism before the election.

Role of the IMF in the world economy

The IMF both monitors and regulates the international payments system in a manner conducive to maximizing international trade and thereby promoting growth in the world capitalist economy. The character of the IMF's balance of payments adjustment programs is that of prescribing a dependent capitalist economic strategy based on free markets, private enterprises and an open economy. This strategy — while it may provide growth — cannot provide development. In cases where the IMF's economic strategy is different from that of the government's, the Fund exploits the foreign exchange crisis to coerce the government to change its policies and implement those of the Fund. It justifies these policies through an apparently scientific diagnosis. For the country in question, the result of implementing IMF policies is to abandon its own development strategies. The compromise and the accompanying deflation dismembers the class alliance supporting the ruling party and can result in a change of government by democratic or violent processes. Jamaica's experience illustrates how the IMF preserves dependent capitalism in the Third World.

Jamaica: Manley's Defeat — Whose Responsibility?

Kari Polanyi Levitt

Kari Levitt teaches development economics and is a fellow of
the Centre for Developing Areas Study, McGill University.
She is the author of Silent Surrender: The Multinational
Corporation in Canada (1970) and has worked as a
consultant for governments in the English-speaking
Caribbean and for ECLA (Economic Community for Latin
America).

I would like to raise one or two questions about the role of the
IMF in the defeat of Jamaica's experiment with democratic
socialism. With respect to that experience we must evaluate a
little more carefully and critically the degree to which the Fund
was or was not responsible for the failure of the Manley project.

This is important not only for Jamaica and the politics of
Jamaica. It raises a more general question: If the Fund is really
as powerful in imposing open capitalist economies on
countries seeking more social justice, and in forcing political
changes, as Richard Bernal's analysis would make it appear,
then I think it would follow that progressive governments

should not deal with the IMF at all. Indeed, perhaps the cause of progress and human rights would be better served by the abolition of the IMF? Now, I suggest such a conclusion is not realistic, nor do I think anybody is seriously proposing the abolition of the Fund. However, I believe that the degree to which the Fund is reformable and has to be reformed is an important question and so is the matter of the degree of power which rests on the side of Third World governments in dealings with the IMF.

Take, for example, the recent very large IMF loan to India, some $5 billion to $6 billion. Is it therefore given and determined that India will have to bend and bow down to the extreme model of the IMF? Tanzania is currently negotiating with the Fund. Does that mean that the government of that country is 'selling out' to international capitalism? I don't think so. The Peoples' Revolutionary Government of Grenada has requested a three-year Extended Fund Facility from the Fund. Does that mean that Grenada must go the way of Michael Manley's Jamaica? I think not.

The questions I want to raise in the Jamaican context therefore are the following: Did the IMF really deal the kind of death-blow to the Manley experiment which one might infer from Richard Bernal's paper, or were there other and ultimately more basic reasons for the failure of the Manley government? Secondly, what are the implications of this for future relationships between Third World governments and the IMF?

The key actors in Jamaica

In order to set the role of the Fund in Jamaica into perspective, I think it is useful to make a simple listing of the principal actors whose combined opposition was in no small measure responsible for the failure of the Manley government. More exactly, and with the wisdom of hindsight, I believe that it was Manley's naïvety and the absence of a realistic and consistent strategy in the face of the combined forces of domestic and foreign opponents of democratic socialism that projected Jamaica into a long slide of economic decline culminating in eventual defeat at the polls in 1980. The International Monetary Fund was not the only major participating factor in this story.

Here then is a listing of the principal actors which the Manley government had to contend with. I have classified them as economic and political on the one hand, and foreign and domestic on the other.

External economic actors: Here we have, firstly, the transnational corporations. In the case of Jamaica these are principally the major North American bauxite-aluminum companies. Secondly, we have the fraternity of international commercial banks. And thirdly, of course, the International Monetary Fund. These were not the only external actors in the Jamaican scene, but they were the principal ones.

*External political actors:*The principal external political actor was without question the government of the United States. The postures of the President and the state department toward the Manley government underwent a number of changes between 1972 and 1980. The Nixon-Ford-Kissinger administration was unambiguously hostile. The early Carter administration was conciliatory. In the last year of the Carter administration, the 'hawks' devoured the 'doves', and U.S. governmental support was withdrawn from the Manley government.

Domestic economic adversaries: The local capitalists or — if you prefer other language — the local private sector became increasingly unco-operative and hostile. Capital fled the country and eventually significant sectors of the organized local private sector united in efforts to destabilize the government and replace it with a Jamaica Labour Party (JLP) administration.

Domestic political forces: Here we have, firstly, the Jamaica Labour Party. Secondly, the privately-owned *Daily Gleaner,* which was transformed from a prestigious daily newspaper into an instrument of relentless and unceasing anti-government propaganda. The role of the *Gleaner* has been compared with that of *El Mercurio* in the campaign to destroy the credibility of the Allende government in Chile in the early 1970s. Thirdly, we have the state bureaucracy: the public service, police and army. As economic decline proceeded and the popularity of the government declined, individuals within the state apparatus became disillusioned. Critical sectors in the police force and army became actively disaffected.

Ultimately, and perhaps most importantly, there was the nature of the Peoples' National Party itself. The PNP is a broadly-based nationalist populist party with a class base and ideological spectrum ranging from the political centre to the far left. The symbiotic relationship between the various strata and key personages within the party and its charismatic leader resulted in frequent shifts in policy, as contradictory advice was offered and accepted by Mr. Manley. All elements of the party needed the popular leader, and he in turn was unwilling to disappoint or reject any part of his wide-spectrum political base. Thus conflicts within the party were perpetually discussed but seldom resolved. Ultimately this contributed to a sense of insecurity and uncertainty, an absence of firm direction, as contradictory policies were simultaneously adopted and explained by ever less-convincing exhibitions of magnificent rhetoric.

What I want to do with the aid of this little classification of principal actors is to put the IMF story into context, because all the actors identified here played important roles in the eventual failure of the Manley government. Furthermore, as I've already said, ultimately the principal responsibility for the failure to implement the declared policies of 1974 and 1975 of democratic socialism on the domestic front, and anti-imperialist non-alignment as a foreign policy, must be laid at the door of the Peoples' National Party and its leader Mr. Manley. The party and leader were responsible for a lack of realism and a failure to seriously mobilize the popular and economic resources of Jamaica to face the combined opposition of domestic and external capital, which perceived its privileges to be threatened — and ultimately pulled out all the stops to destroy the Manley government.

First phase: redistributive reform measures

The eight years of the Manley government fall into three subperiods. The first period, from 1972 to 1974, saw massive programs of long overdue social reforms that had the support of the overwhelming majority of the population: special employment programs, literacy programs, school feeding, equal pay, minimum wages, land lease, food subsidies, free secondary and university education, increases in pension and poor relief and a number of other similar social measures.

The degree of internal redistribution of income is reflected in the fact that the share of wages and salaries in total disposable income increased from a level of 58 per cent in 1968-71, to 64 per cent by 1976. The share of profits, interest and capital consumption in national income declined from 36 per cent to 29 per cent over the same period. In the years 1972-74 the mass of real wages (adjusted for price changes) increased by 3.7 per cent, while real input was stagnant or declining. Employment increased by 35,000 and the number of unemployed declined by 11,000 — the first decline in unemployment registered in over a decade.

Personal consumption rose steadily from 1972 to 1976 while gross fixed capital formation started to decline dangerously from 1974 onward. This very substantial increase in real income of the masses of the people over the period 1972 to 1976 was the result of a heavy program of redistribution without growth. Indeed, the economy started its downward path in 1974, and by 1976 real output per head had declined by 10 per cent as compared with 1972.

Second phase: democratic socialism and non-alignment

The second phase of the Manley administration commenced in 1974 and terminated in 1977 with the signing of the first IMF agreement. The year 1974 saw a shift of the PNP from its traditional role as a centrist populist party to a domestic policy of democratic socialism and a foreign policy of non-alignment. It was also the year when Jamaica responded to the oil price-rise by a well executed move to impose a six-fold increase in tax on its giant bauxite-alumina industry.

Here we must recall that Jamaica was, at that time, the world's leading exporter of bauxite and alumina and that all four of the major North American companies — Alcoa, Alcan, Reynolds and Kaiser — had important facilities in Jamaica. The unilaterally imposed bauxite production levy and the partial, although largely, cosmetic nationalizations as well as Jamaica's role in the establishment of the International Bauxite Association aroused the fury of the companies and the U.S. government. It must be recorded, however, that this move was supported by the Jamaican capitalist class as a fair and reasonable response to the OPEC initiative, and that prominent members of Jamaica's business community were active participants in the negotiations with the aluminum companies, serving on the government side of the bargaining table.

The bauxite levy was an adroit move and produce an instant increase in government revenue from $35 million in 1973 to $200 million in 1974. The contribution of the bauxite industry to government revenue increased from 12 per cent to 35 per cent, and the returned value of bauxite-alumina in total Jamaican export earnings rose from 35 per cent in 1973 to 75 per cent in 1979. The point, however, that I want to make is that if you pick a fight with powerful international capitalist interests, you have to be prepared for retaliatory measures. Retaliations came in the form of litigation in the United States, and a press campaign claiming breach of contract on the part of the Jamaican government. More directly, the companies cut production levels from a peak of 15 million tons in 1974 to 11 million tons in 1975.

This cutback might have been excused on the grounds of the prevailing recession but 1976 witnessed prolonged strikes, a major unexplained explosion and a consequent further reduction of production levels to 10 million tons. Production has never regained its 1974 levels. The production cuts by the transnational aluminum companies prevented the government of Jamaica from reaping the full advantage of increasing levy yields from rising ingot prices. The companies moreover stopped replacement investments and proceeded to pull out as much money as possible.

All of that was to be expected and is not said in criticism of the bauxite levy. Where, in my opinion, the government acted irresponsibly and with an eye only to short-term political advantage, was in its spending of the Capital Investment Fund set up with the proceeds of the bauxite levy. This money went into various items of current expenditures of immediate attraction to its political constituency. There was no effort to limit the foreign exchange expenditure of the middle class nor to practise budgetary restraint. In 1975, real wages rose by 5 per cent while real output fell by 2.6 per cent. Government expenditures continued to increase and net foreign reserves continued to decline. In a difficult international climate, with rising oil prices, and facing the hostility of the key foreign-controlled export-earning industry, the government was prepared to deliver further economic benefits to its mass political base, without hurting its middle class supporters, in preparation for the crucial election year of 1976. From then on, government expenditures were increasingly financed by central bank borrowing, that is, by what we colloquially call printing of money.

The U.S government was highly displeased with the Jamaican move against the American aluminum companies and was particularly concerned that the International Bauxite Association might duplicate some of the successes of OPEC. It soon became apparent, however, that the IBA was a paper tiger, a cartel without teeth because of its inability to control production levels. Of even greater concern to the Nixon-Ford-Kissinger administration was Jamaica's new foreign affairs posture of non-alignment: in particular, Manley's evangelical advocacy of a New International Economic Order and most particularly his newly formed friendship with Fidel Castro.

The year 1975 was when the government of Angola requested and received military assistance from the government of Cuba to defend itself against South African invasion. Unlike Forbes Burnham of Guyana, Manley was not able to offer material help to the Cuba-Angola airlift, but certainly expressed the popular sentiment of Jamaicans in his uncompromising support of all efforts to check South African aggression. Henry Kissinger came hot-footing down to Jamaica with a retinue of assistants for a brief holiday. His major concern was Jamaica's new relationship with Cuba. It has been said that Mr. Kissinger offered Mr. Manley $100 million dollars of U.S. assistance. If that was the carrot, then what was the stick? We were reminded that Kingston burned in 1976! There is no question that there was massive destabilization and physical sabotage in Jamaica in the election year of 1976. The full details will probably have to await the opening of U.S. archival records many years from now, but it is interesting to recall that the Prime Minister of Canada personally announced $100 million of Canadian development aid to Mr. Manley on the eve of the 1976 election, a move interpreted as a gesture of moral support by Mr. Trudeau to Mr. Manley.

The destabilization campaign of 1976 was seriously damaging to Jamaica. We have already mentioned the strikes and explosions in the bauxite-alumina industry. The tourist industry was destroyed for several years to come by widely disseminated adverse and exaggerated publicity concerning violence in Jamaica. The violence speeded the flow of out-migration. The propaganda campaign about 'Cubans', which started in 1976, continued unabated for the remainder of the Manley administration with anticipated adverse effects on the investment climate.

Prior to the turn in policy signalled by the announcement of 'democratic socialism', the local private sector was generally supportive of the government. When, however, Mr. Manley announced that there was no room for millionaires in Jamaica and reminded his listeners that there were "five flights a day to Miami", the exodus started. There was a flight of capital, and of capitalists, large and small — mostly small because there were not many large capitalists in Jamaica and in any event powerful and well-connected business people were able to ship their funds out of the country without necessarily giving up their luxurious Jamaican residences.

Many professionals and skilled workers joined the panic parade of emigrants. The drain of migration started in 1975 and accelerated throughout the remainder of the Manley era. Between 1972 and 1979, 14,000 trained personnel emigrated to the United States and Canada. Miami became a suburb of Kingston. The Toronto suburbs of Mississauga and Scarborough became minor satellite settlements of emigrant Jamaicans. Ultimately the non-co-operation of the private sector in a mixed economy — in which that sector controlled a by far larger share of productive activity than did the government — was critical.

By mid-1976 the commercial banks had suspended credit to Jamaica. By the end of 1976, the Bank of Jamaica reported that $300 million had left the country in capital flight, and that net foreign exchange reserves were negative for the first time in the history of the country. After the smashing electoral victory of the PNP in 1976, which gave him a powerful political mandate, Mr. Manley was forced into secret backdoor negotiations with the IMF because his foreign exchange kitty was empty, the banks had blocked credits and the windfall gains of the bauxite levy were blown away, and domestic political expenditures were financed in large measure by credit creation. To all of this we must add the havoc caused by the CIA-assisted destabilization campaigns of 1976, which had largely wrecked the tourist industry and had escalated urban violence, plus the vindictive cutbacks of production by the North American bauxite aluminum companies, and more generally the threat to the supply of essential food, raw materials and fuel due to acute foreign exchange shortage.

In 1976 the PNP won a massive electoral mandate for a second term. It was a mandate for democratic socialism and self-reliance. Mr. Manley's campaign was very specific: Jamaica is not for sale! No devaluation! Jamaica will not bow down to the IMF! A team of dedicated PNP university economists were commissioned to draw up a production plan and more generally a strategy for economic survival, without IMF assistance. Appeals to the population brought forth many thousands of useful individual suggestions of how the country could be better organized to achieve greater efficiency, equity and popular mobilization.

But it was later discovered that throughout the first six months of 1977 Mr. Manley was secretly negotiating with the Fund. Mr. Manley appears to have been persuaded by his more conservative advisors that it would be impossible to continue without the IMF's "seal of good housekeeping". This at the very same time that it was believed, even within the party, that Manley had chosen to reject the IMF. While people in good faith were preparing for a non-IMF alternative, the decision had been made, in effect, to go the old way, to deal with the Fund, to borrow more money, to accept conditionalities.

The deal was sweetened in various ways. Messages were passed down from the Carter White House that Mr. Carter and his wife and the ambassador to the UN, Andrew Young, wanted to be nice to Mr. Manley. It was the liberal administration in Washington at that particular point in time which perhaps persuaded Mr. Manley that this was the safer path to take, rather than the more risky venture of self-reliance. In May 1977 the government of Jamaica signed its first agreement with the Fund. Jamaica was permitted a dual exchange rate, and the conditions were not harsh. It was the first step on the road to the destruction of the political support which had so recently been reaffirmed in the election of 1976.

Whether we date the turning point in the fortunes of the Manley government to the period 1975-76, when the government could have — and in my opinion should have — imposed strict measures of exchange control and budgetary austerity instead of encouraging a public and private sector spending spree with a consequent mounting internal and external public debt; whether we date it to the post-election months, when the government failed to convert its newly won political mandate into a radical popular mobilization of the country and when it demoralized crucial sections of party activities, is debatable. What, however, is inescapable is the fact that the vacillation of Mr. Manley during these crucial two years lost him the support both of the private sector, which was mortally afraid of 'socialism', and cut the ground out from under the possibility of popular mobilization and a non-IMF strategy. From May 1977 onward, the Manley government locked itself into IMF policies designed to encourage a private sector, which would not however play ball, while attempting to maintain its popular political base without the economic capacity to continue redistributive policies. The redistribution of 1972 to 1976 now went into reverse gear. Devaluations, wage restraint, fiscal austerity, and all the rest of the IMF package effected a shift from labour to capital, but failed to bring about the 'turn-around'. From 1977 to 1980, it was a case of reverse redistribution in an economy of negative growth.

Richard Bernal describes the standard IMF package applied to Jamaica. It was a package biased towards the establishment of free enterprise capitalism. It is important to understand that IMF programs are not designed to increase the welfare of the population. They are designed to bring the external payments account into balance, and ultimately to free it up so that profits and interest can be freely remitted. The objective is a freed-up system of external payments — that is the optimal situation for foreign capital. That is the ultimate guarantee that the banks and other creditors will be able to collect their loans, and interest on their loans, and that the real resources to service these foreign loans and other debts will be squeezed out of the hide of the population by a reduction in their real standard of living.

The IMF doesn't really care whether there is economic growth, or no growth, or whether unemployment decreases or increases. The principal concern is to ensure that good 'hard' currency does not get locked in, so that it can continue to circulate and earn remittable profits and interest. Devaluation is advocated in all cases where the 'free' or black market rate of currency is cheaper in dollars than the official rate. Devaluation in an open economy has the effect of an immediate cut in real wages, because prices go up instantly while wages and salaries are subject to control. Public sector wages are kept in check insofar as governments are prohibited to borrow more than a prescribed ceiling amount, either in foreign or in domestic capital markets. The deeper the external indebtedness of a country, the tighter the reins of the IMF straitjacket are drawn. The IMF is the ultimate guardian of the interests of capitalists and bankers doing international business.

Having said that, I must state that I believe that the Fund officials thought their prescription could and would produce a turnaround in the economy. I don't think they set out to embarrass Mr. Manley by speeding the decline of the Jamaican economy. I don't think they wanted to see the economy decline year by year. For one thing, it looks bad for the competence of the Fund. Yet this is exactly what happened. The deliberate effort to damage the Manley government by discrediting it in business and banking circles was the special contribution of Edward Seaga and of his Jamaican and American friends.

The final phase: the long march to defeat

The third period of the Manley era began with the first IMF agreement in May 1977. The screws were tightened after the failure of an IMF test in December 1977, on a technical triviality. After that, an Extended Fund Facility (EFF) agreement was negotiated. It commenced in May 1978 and included a substantial devaluation and all the rest of the standard IMF policy package, with the result of a 40 per cent increase in the cost of living and a 20 to 30 per cent reduction in the real value of total wages and salaries. The second year of the EFF started in May 1979, and the agreement broke down in December 1979.

We now have to look at the shifting policy of the U.S. administration in 1979 and 1980. You will recall that 1979 was the year of the Iranian revolution, plus the victories of the Sandinistas in Nicaragua and the New Jewel Movement in Grenada. The hardliners came into ascendancy in Washington. Andy Young, a good friend of Jamaica, was fired in August 1979 and Secretary of State Cyrus Vance was forced to resign some months later.

Manley attended the Non-Aligned Summit in Havana in September 1979 and got somewhat carried away with his own rhetoric. In any event, the fall of 1979 appears to have been the proximate time at which all forces combined to close in for the kill. From September and October 1979 onward, the Seaga JLP, the *Daily Gleaner,* the private sector, the commercial banks, and disloyal Jamaican security forces combined in an orchestrated campaign to checkmate Mr. Manley. The Carter administration withdrew its previously lenient and mildly supportive position of Manley in the councils of the Fund. IMF officials who were inclined to bend the rules to give Jamaica one more last chance at economic recovery were criticized for being too soft on Jamaica. The death-blow was delivered by the commercial banks.

In the autumn of 1979 the fraternity of international banks refused point-blank to roll over a massive amount of external debt due for repayment, even though Jamaica had abided by its IMF agreements as closely as could reasonably have been expected given the second oil shock of 1979. The banks made little secret of the fact that they were preparing to deal with the next government of Jamaica — and in fact discussed rescheduling with the leader of the opposition party, Mr. Seaga.

Early in 1980 Mr. Manley was forced to call an election, three years after having commenced his second term as Prime Minister. The conditions required by the Fund for reactivating negotiations were rejected by the ruling councils of the Peoples' National Party. Self-reliance and the 'non-IMF path' were once more on the agenda. These policies — which would have stood a fair chance of success in 1974 and 1975 before Jamaica entered the debt trap, and again in 1977 when Manley was riding high on a fresh political mandate — were clearly doomed to failure by 1980.

Meanwhile Mr. Seaga had launched his election campaign some months before Manley declared the premature election of 1980. Seaga's campaign was conducted principally in the United States. Key speeches were made in Miami, New York and Washington — and they were designed to damage the already very shaky credit of the government of Jamaica. The main weapon of the opposition party was the mobilization of financial and economic leverage with intent to damage the Jamaican economy. I am not here talking about the Fund, but about the deliberate campaign of the Jamaican private sector and the Jamaica Labour Party, in alliance with banks, and perhaps also with the government of the United States, to stage a strike of capital — domestic and foreign.

The management of the _Gleaner_ escalated its campaign of psychological warfare and assumed the role of a shadow government. Throughout 1980 violence reigned in the streets of Kingston, and 800 people — mostly poor people in the poor areas of the city — died at the hands of gunmen. The government was unable to contain the violence. It could not declare a state of emergency because Mr. Seaga had threatened that, in the event of such a move, he and his friends in the private sector would "lock down the country tighter than a sardine can". In the last months before the election, the government was moreover reluctant to provide more arms to the security forces, because the loyalty of the police force was dubious — and possibly that of the army also. There was a mini coup d'état in the army, believed to be a dry run for a more serious one to follow.

The outcome of the election was a foregone conclusion. In retrospect it was perhaps the best possible outcome, because I personally believe that if the PNP had won the election — which was, however, highly unlikely given the state of affairs in the country — there would have been a Jamaican version of the coup which had toppled the Allende government in 1973.

The social democratic model: Is it feasible?

The Jamaican experiment raises important questions, not only for the future of Jamaica, or of other Caricom (Caribbean Community) countries, but more generally for Third World countries seeking justice and reform within a hostile international environment. Is the democratic socialist model, with a mixed economy and an open political system, a realistic one, particularly for countries in the American hemisphere which the United States perceives as its geopolitical sphere of influence? What lessons are to be learned from the Jamaican experience? Was the IMF primarily responsible for the economic decline of Jamaica and the eventual defeat of the PNP government? Is it inevitable that the local private sector will sabotage democratic socialism? Was Manley realistic in expecting a New International Economic Order to solve the problems of his government on external commodity and financial markets? Can the IMF be reformed, and if so, would this make a crucial difference to events as they transpired in Jamaica? Must a democratic socialist government be as ineffective as the Manley administration in mobilizing domestic resources and avoiding excessive external debt? And most crucially, what are the limits to sovereignty when it comes to domestic political structures?

In the case of Jamaica, the combined forces of the Gleaner, the international media operating under the implicit protection of the government of the United States, and a disaffected private sector with access to virtually unlimited funds and powerful external connections, were able to take advantage of a highly open political system to speed the electoral defeat of the PNP. As for Mr. Manley, he seemed to believe that the debating points he was able to score in the national and international arenas could convince his adversaries of the superior logic of his case. He was captive to his commitment to operate the Westminster model in the gentlemanly manner of a cricket match, with minimal use of state powers to defend the government against a barrage of deliberate destabilization. He permitted his opponents a measure of freedom which was downright irresponsible.

The Gleaner was allowed to mount a scurrilous propaganda campaign, designed to undermine government credibility and the economic viability of the country. The campaign worked to destroy the investment climate, to wreck the tourist trade and generally to escalate the atmosphere of fear and violence. At one point in the conflict with the Gleaner, the PNP organized a protest demonstration in front of the offices of the newspaper,

led by a number of cabinet ministers including the Prime
Minister himself. At the time I had to ask myself just who is in
charge of this country? Such a measure of 'press freedom'
would not be tolerated even in more stable democratic
countries.

One of the most disgusting aspects of the opposition's
media campaign was the charge by the *Gleaner* and the international press that the Manley government was abusing civil
liberties. I have never lived in a country which was so completely free with respect to what anybody anywhere could say
or print — and that includes Canada. Just cast back your mind
to the 'apprehended insurrection' in Quebec in 1970, and the
Draconian measures taken, including the charge that the editor
of *Le Devoir* was part of a supposed 'provisional government'.
The Jamaican experience had many similarities with Allende's
Chile. Although nominally Marxist, the Allende government
was a popularly elected constitutional government. It was vio-
lently overthrown by combined internal and external forces
after three years in office. Likewise, the Sandinista government
in Nicaragua has been the victim of American-supported external military aggression and a tightening economic boycott. It
has been forced to curtail press freedom and postpone elections.

The easy, and perhaps tempting, conclusion is that democratic socialism is an impossibility, a liberal illusion, and that
the Cuban model is the only one with a chance of survival. This
view is held by a number of North American and European
intellectuals who do not have to face the complexities of reality
and can pass simplistic comment from the comfort of their
academic or editorial posts. The reality is that there is no one
model of socialism such that progressive governments based
on a wide spectrum of populist forces will continue to accede
to power in Latin America and the Caribbean — whether
through elections as in Chile and Jamaica, or by armed struggle
against an entrenched oligarchy as in Nicaragua. Mixed economies are likely to be the rule; and the widest measure of democratic expression and respect for civil liberties is essential to
achieve popular mobilization and confirm the legitimacy of the
government.

The basic problem, of course, is vulnerability to external

interference and external intervention. It is precisely in defence
against external destabilization and ultimately against external
military aggression that popular governments are forced to curtail freedoms and to take measures to defend their national
security. Far from protecting civil liberties and human rights,
the activities of the Reagan administration and its friends in the
Caribbean and Central America have made a mockery of
democracy and of elections. The first conclusion to be drawn is
that the most important single precondition for stability and
democratic, economic and social progress in the Caribbean and
Central America is the respect by the United States of the right
of peoples to choose their own form of government, without
external interference.

Could the Fund have saved Manley?

I have been asked whether I think the Fund could have saved
Jamaica, if the United States had been less hostile to Manley.
Frankly, I do not think so, taking into account the constellation
of forces, the policies of the Manley government and the lost
opportunities and mistakes. And I do not think that the Fund
will save Mr. Seaga's neck either, because from what I have
seen and know of current developments in Jamaica, Mr. Seaga
and his policies are going to be a great failure.

Ultimately, capital and capitalists are after money. They are
not interested in ideology. You can have all the Rockefeller
committees, and Mr. Reagan can endorse Mr. Seaga till the
cows come home, but if the capitalists do not think they can
make money in Jamaica and take it back home, they will not
put their money there. And I do not think that foreign
capitalists are putting any amount of money into Jamaica at this
time. There are some 500 investment projects, but if you go and
look at how many investments there are, you will discover that
there are not very many — except perhaps in real estate and
high-income residential housing.

I don't think a different IMF would have saved Manley and I
don't think the generosity being extended to Mr. Seaga by the
Fund will solve his problems, because they are embedded in
the malfunctioning of that model of dependent capitalism
which Richard Bernal describes, and which we know so well
from the 1960s. And if it didn't work in the 1960s, it is certainly

not going to work in the 1980s. In the 1960s, the Jamaican model was based on incentives designed to build up an import-substituting industry and was fuelled by massive bauxite-aluminum investments. The action in the international bauxite-aluminum industry has shifted to Australia and Brazil.

As for the import-substituting industries, although they were not very efficient and required a lot of imports as inputs, nevertheless, they provided some measure of employment. The policies currently favoured by the Seaga government and his patron in the Reagan White House have flooded the Jamaican market with foreign imports, and many Jamaican business people are having a more difficult time of it than even in the worst days of the Manley era. Jamaican domestic agriculture has seriously regressed since 1980. No, the IMF could not have saved Manley, nor will it save Seaga.

Some of the lessons

It is clear that there are a number of lessons to be learned from the mistakes of the Manley government. The first and most obvious one is that there is a limit to redistribution if the economy cannot maintain and increase production. Increased real wages and costly increased social services financed by credit creation and heavy outlays of foreign exchange are steps on the road to the debt trap.

The political mandate and immense popularity of the first Manley government of 1972 could have been converted into a national project to secure the independence of the country through a partial closing of foreign transactions and a lessening of vulnerability to external creditors. The political temptation to deliver immediate economic benefits to the masses of the people, without restraining the expenditure of the middle classes, should have been restrained. The windfall gains of the bauxite levy of 1974 should have been invested in strengthening the productive base, particularly in such key sectors as domestic food production.

Secondly, effective exchange controls and state purchasing agencies should have been have been put in place long before the foreign exchange kitty was empty in mid-1976. Inessential consumption expenditures and foreign travel should have been curtailed long before necessity forced such measures, and all

loopholes to capital flight should have been plugged. If necessary, commercial banks should have been nationalized to prevent them from assisting in the flight of capital, as they did. As
recently as 1976, Jamaican visitors to the Montreal Olympics
were permitted a travel allowance of $500. Given the critical
foreign exchange position, this was ridiculous.

It is a fact of open dependent economies that foreign
exchange is essential for just about all private and public sector
transactions. For this reason, foreign exchange budgeting is an
essential preventive measure to avoid an eventual, uncontrollable foreign exchange shortage.

Thirdly, the government should have run a far tighter fiscal
ship, with greater accountability and a stricter check on the
implementation of projects. Jamaica was replete with excellent
but often unimplemented projects. Where projects are financed
with foreign loan funds, there has to be an evaluation procedure which strictly ensures the capacity to service these loans.
Because money is fungible, there is a temptation to accept any
and every project offered by donors, simply in order to cream
off some foreign exchange which is urgently needed for other,
usually very current, purposes. At the end of that road, the debt
trap awaits. The ultimate choice is between a self-imposed fiscal discipline in accordance with the priorities of democratic
socialism, or a discipline imposed by the banks and the Fund
based on the very different priorities of external creditors.

Fourthly, there was a measure of naïvety in dealings with
the local private sector. In the autumn of 1979, for example, Mr.
Manley attended the Non-Aligned Summit in Havana and
indulged in some magnificent rhetoric concerning the
inequities of imperialism in general, and the policies of the
United States in particular. A week or two later, he attended the
annual private-sector get-together in Miami to explain
Jamaica's guidelines for private investment and to invite and
welcome foreign investments. Mr. Manley's actions on these
two occasions were honest and principled and strictly in
accordance with the declared policies of the government. But
they were not very realistic.

The fact is that the private sector is very sensitive about the
security of its money. You can tell them about guidelines, very
genuinely meant, but the fact is that American and Jamaican

investors are particularly turned off by 'socialism' of any variety, and have been conditioned by two decades of relentless propaganda to distrust anything 'Cuban'. The Jamaican economy was in a most precarious situation at the time. Essential food imports were not secure. The banks were refusing to roll over debt. The IMF programs were predicated on an upturn in private sector investment, which had not materialized. The public sector was too broke to offset the virtual strike of capital by the private sector. Further borrowing was difficult because even friendly sources were reluctant to lend to a government so clearly at the point of disintegration. So was that really the best time for Mr. Manley to grandstand to the world from a stage in Havana?

Fifthly, and finally, I return to my earlier comments about the Peoples' National Party and its incapacity to opt for a clear and consistent policy. Eventually, technocrats and other skilled workers became disgusted and many migrated. Party supporters and even party activists were demoralized. The private sector was confused, because capital — even small capital — wants to know exactly what the rules of the game are.

As for the masses of the people, Michael Manley and his Peoples' National Party were able to draw on an enormous fund of trust and goodwill, in spite of the suffering of the people from unemployment, shortages and horrendous urban political violence. People were willing to trust, to follow, to sacrifice in the belief that 'better must come'. But it is clear from this brief account of Jamaica's experience that by 1979 and 1980 there was no light at the end of the tunnel, no sense to continued sacrifices, and the majority of the people decided to give Mr. Manley and the PNP a rest on the opposition benches.

A final word or two about the Fund. Briefly, within the last 15 years the IMF's leverage in the international monetary system has diminished substantially. The Bretton Woods system of 1944, or even of 1965, has disintegrated because the United States is no longer able to play the role of top metropole effectively. Its currency is no longer secure and stable. Since the beginning of the 1970s there has been an orgy of credit creation, principally by the international commercial banks, in off-short currencies, the so-called Euro-dollars which are not only Euro and not only dollars. The banks were unbelievably greedy in pushing their loans on anybody who could be persuaded to take them, at high real rates of interest. As recently as 1965 the reserve position of all countries in the Fund, as a percentage of total world reserves was 19 per cent. By 1980, this percentage had dropped to 5 per cent (excluding gold).

The IMF is no longer the powerful monitor and stabilizer of the international monetary system envisaged at its founding. It is a wreck, whose programs are now exclusively confined to developing countries. The Fund was unable to prevent the United States from demolishing the stability of the fixed exchange rate system, and from financing its own enormous external deficits with its own currency. Nor was it able to check the international banks from overextending themselves by excessive lending. Today the Fund is acting largely in the service of the commercial banks, and its objective is to assist the banks to collect their loans from countries which are increasingly unable to repay their debts — and thus to prevent the burden of adjustment from falling on the banks.

There is no doubt that the international financial system is a shambles, and that reconstruction and reform are on the agenda. The burden of my argument, however, is that Third World countries undertaking basic social reform should not expect the forces of international capital to be supportive of such efforts, and that little can be expected from appeals to the North to assist the South at this time. This is particularly true in the Caribbean and Central America, where the government of the United States is using its financial leverage to bring pressure to bear on governments based on its own short-sighted perception of its geopolitical interests.

PART FOUR

Dependency or
Development?
The Case of Canada

Monetarism and Change — Canadian Style

Mel Watkins

Mel Watkins is professor of economics at University College
of the University of Toronto as well as an editor of and
regular contributor to This Magazine. He first became widely
known as chief author of The Watkins Report, a study of
foreign ownership in Canadian industry carried out in
1967-68. In 1974-76 and again in 1980-81 he was a consultant
to the Dene Nation.

I sometimes wonder why anyone any longer expects economists to have any worthwhile answers. Whenever I speak
these days on the economy, I expect someone to get up and say:
If you people have the answers, then how come we're in this mess
in the first place?

On this matter of economists and policy — as on many other
matters — there is a relevant pronouncement by John Kenneth
Galbraith in his memoirs. Galbraith writes of "the greatest
source of banality in economics and business writing, which is
the obligation to be constructive". He insists: "One should be
permitted to identify absurdity or error without being required
to correct it." There being at the present time no shortage of
absurdity and error, Galbraith's dictum at least gives me a
rationale for warming up slowly to a discussion of positive
policy.

The title of this section, "Dependency or Development", also makes me pause. For a moment I thought: But no one would choose dependency. Then I remembered something, which is that choice is exactly what Canadian bankers have demonstrably taken — perhaps we should say the Canadian business class in general has taken. They've found dependency very profitable, they've operated as junior partners first in the British Empire and then in the American Empire. Our problem (to anticipate a leading theme of my remarks) is what to do now that being in the American Empire is no longer so prosperous and benign a fate.

It is also useful to remind ourselves of why the Canadian situation is part of this conference, that is, why the question of the impact of the International Monetary Fund and World Bank is not simply confined to the Third World, where the impact is unquestionably most evident. Is what happens at the IMF meeting in downtown Toronto of any direct relevance to ordinary Canadians? The answer is that the ideology of the IMF — which is monetarist or neoconservative, or so-called supply-side economics — is very much part of the Canadian landscape. Canada is not a poor Third World country that has had an IMF package imposed on it. Rather, we've imposed one on ourselves. In an issue of *This Magazine* (September 1982), Professor Tom Naylor of McGill University says that an IMF package for Canada would involve:

... measures to hold down wages through public sector freezes and attacks on the right to strike; pushing prices of key commodities like oil up to world 'market' levels; chopping down government budget deficits; dismantling state enterprises like the Canada Development Corporation; upward pressure on interest rates; and measures to eliminate controls on foreign investments of the type represented by the Foreign Investment Review Agency and the National Energy Program.

"And if the IMF really had its way," says Naylor, "it would impose either a Joe Clarke Conservative or a John Turner Liberal government as a successor to the current one." But as Naylor concludes: "Lucky for us, we don't live in that kind of world."

In planning this conference we feared the very fact that the IMF meeting was taking place here in Canada would further legitimize that neoconservative ideology, and would do so just at a time when it was coming under increasing public attack here. We had reason to be concerned. The Managing Director of the IMF, Mr. Jacques de Larosière, had spoken here in March to the (significantly) Investment Dealers' Association. On that occasion, with Bank of Canada Governor Gerald K. Bouey present, de Larosière lauded Canadian policies of restraint as practised by Messrs. Allan MacEachen (Canadian Minister of Finance) and Bouey. Now that he is back in Toronto for these IMF/World Bank meetings, Mr. de Larosière is in effect doing more of that. The only criticism offered by him of Canadian policy — and, in the nature of these events, any criticism is implied — is that it has not been tough enough in bringing down the rate of inflation.

The IMF — monetarism at work

These same sentiments permeate the just-released 1982 *Annual Report* of the IMF. The report blames the economic crisis on "various rigidities and structural imbalances". The list thereof explicitly includes minimum wages and unemployment insurance benefits — which the IMF thinks are too generous! The report is written in the kind of flat yet flabby prose that flows right by you, but if you can keep your mind concentrated you will find some most revealing sentences. Take the paragraph on page 38 that begins, "To reverse the secular rise in unemployment it may also be necessary to make sure that incentives for seeking employment are adequate." Someone might imagine that the next sentence would talk about the need for higher wages, because real wages in Canada and elsewhere have been falling now for some time. But no, it reads rather: "Unemployment benefit levels have tended to increase and to apply to a larger share of the labour force in recent years."

This is monetarism with a vengeance, in its new guise as supply-side economics. Is it not enormously revealing of the true nature of supply-side economics that incentives for capital mean bribing it more (with lower taxes) while incentives for labour mean paying it less? That is, if you're unemployed, by cutting benefits; if you're employed, by imposing wage ceilings well below the rate of inflation (like the notorious "six and five" formula imposed on the federal public sector in Canada) or by demanding wage concessions (which the auto companies are attempting with the United Auto Workers).

You sense at some point, as you read the IMF report, that when the IMF writes about *structural rigidities* it casts the net very widely. You come to suspect that it would put the whole trade union movement in that category, as a kind of market imperfection. In fact, the first example the report does give of a rigidity is "wage bargaining". I suppose it's part of the bankers' mentality to like what U.S. President Reagan did to the air controllers. At the same time, the IMF gives the back of its hand to anyone with the effrontery to protest this.

On the first page of the report we are told: "The increasing social and political strains associated with high unemployment are creating pressures for a relaxation of the restrictive, anti-inflationary financial policies that have been pursued during the past few years by many Fund members, including several of the major industrial countries." In the next sentence we are told that this is "a very worrisome development"; the "this" refers not to the social strains themselves that are associated with high unemployment but rather to the pressures for change.

You will not be surprised to learn that the IMF report launches a veritable tirade against government deficits. That is, after all, the hallmark of the conservative mind; indeed, even some non-conservatives are worried about this, particularly with the Reagan administration (of all governments) creating unprecedented deficits. You and I know, however, that in the short run these deficits are the result of the recession, not the cause of it, and in the longer term, in the U.S., they result from tax cuts for the corporations and the rich on the one hand, and from massive increases in arms spending on the other.

But in the IMF report, a reference to the rapid growth of government expenditure is followed by the words "particularly on social programs". I could not find a word, not a single solitary word, about arms spending. Conservatives are always talking about how financing the government deficit crowds out productive private investment, but it is arms spending which truly crowds out productive investment and destroys the economy — unless of course it is first destroyed by the increasingly probable nuclear holocaust.

There was a risk, then, that this kind of dangerous nonsense would be further legitimized by the IMF meeting being held here in Canada. Actually, I don't think that has happened. In the last few days we've been told too often by the big bankers that things are not as bad as they seem. It's like those ads of the Bank of Nova Scotia that say the sky is not falling in. Or the interview in the *Globe and Mail* (September 8, 1982) with Mr. Richard Hill, Chairman of the First National Bank of Boston. Mr. Hill said that the banks have a lot of concern about Third World and corporate debt, but he did not feel there is any sense of panic. However, he went on to say: "It is rather like being the manager of a nuclear power station. You are aware of what could happen."

Peddling unemployment

That certainly raises the question, germane to any discussion of policy, as to how severe is the present crisis. I take it that its severity is no longer in doubt. I've thought that for some time. True, a few weeks ago interest rates began to fall, and the Canadian dollar began to rise on the foreign exchanges, and there were record gains on both Wall Street and Bay Street. Suddenly there was even talk about the great boom of the 1980s. (I'd been on holidays and taking it easy and I began to wonder if I'd overslept and missed the lower turning point of the business cycle.) But then I noticed how the mining corporation Inco told a workforce already on temporary layoff that, as of January 1983, 1,185 of them would be permanently laid off. Inco said this was necessary because of slack demand for nickel, but if the economy had bottomed out and was truly on the road to recovery, then how come Inco could look six months down the road and see that much slack?

Nor was this simply a minor contradiction. All the major economic forecasters, including those at the IMF and the World Bank, are predicting no significant lessening of unemployment even if there is a reasonable recovery, with the latter itself still being problematic. For Canada, this is true one and a half, two, two and a half years ahead. It is true at a time when the official unemployment rate is 12 per cent, with the real rate half as high again; when the number of unemployed is up a staggering 66 per cent from one year earlier; when the bureaucrats have popularized a new term — "exhaustees" — to describe those people who have been unemployed for so long that they have exhausted their unemployment insurance benefits and face the prospect of going onto the welfare rolls, which are also being rapidly exhausted. These facts make utter nonsense of the IMF allegation that unemployment results from too generous unemployment insurance benefits.

It is this crisis of unemployment that we should concentrate on in our discussion of policy. Let's begin with policies we don't like. I have already said enough about monetarism for it to be obvious that it must be rejected. The case against monetarism, though it is still accumulating, is already overwhelming. It is a cure that is worse than the disease. It says that inflation is *the* problem, and it wrestles inflation to the ground, or tries to, over the bodies of the unemployed. The effects on inflation are uncertain, as we have come to know in Canada. That is, inflation remains very high in spite of heavy-handed monetarist policies. At least in the U.S., inflation has moderated. But it is not news that some level of slack in the economy, some high level of unemployment, leads to lessening pressure on prices. And if recovery begins, as it surely must sometime, will not inflation go up again? Such eminent American economists as Galbraith and Nobel Prize winner James Tobin of Yale University fear so.

The effects of monetarist policies on unemployment, on the other hand, are certain and deeply adverse, as we also have occasion to know in Canada. The most damning point that we can make against the monetarists is that they created this present recession. They drove interest rates up to the point where they strangled the economy. Arguably the economy skated to the edge of a major collapse and was pulled back (for how long?) when interest rates moderated recently.

This whole monetarist madness in Canada must cease. To the extent it results from close ties with the U.S., then loosen those ties. If that move risks capital flight from Canada, bring in exchange controls. We are willing to control labour in this country — as we have recently been forcefully reminded by the federal government; I prefer we should control capital.

Controls: the new-look monetarism

This leads us to the question of controls as a policy alternative, both comprehensive wage and price controls in general and the present "six and five" in the federal public sector in particular. The six and five controls are clearly simply wage controls, albeit still partial. Comprehensive controls, including prices, are not necessarily better (meaning less bad); they easily degenerate into wage controls, while eroding the basic rights both of collective bargaining and the right to strike. Controls, of either kind, are said to be necessary to fight inflation, but wage controls do not strike at its prime cause, given that workers are only trying to catch up with escalating prices and not being all that successful as their falling real incomes show. Therefore, the effect of controls on prices is indirect and uncertain. At the same time, the controls on wages have the certain effect of limiting purchasing power and hence increasing unemployment.

This is beginning to sound suspiciously like monetarism in a new guise. In fact, trade unionists do say that controls are not an alternative to monetarist policies but rather are part of the monetarist package, and they are right. This is clearly an important point because the public opposes monetarism and supports controls when it should, in fact, oppose both. Also, some economists — the so-called post-Keynesians — argue that workers and their unions should accept controls, at least as the lesser of evils. But the real world does not seem to offer a choice; instead, it gives us both at once.

But even if there is a choice, why should workers be constrained to choosing between evils? The trade unions don't run the economy. They didn't create this mess. Government and business take credit when things are going well. Let them take responsibility when things are going badly, and not blame the victim and try to push all the costs onto workers.

We should, then, say NO to controls. We should say YES to unions fighting them, such as the British Columbia Government Employees' Union. We must also say NO to wage concessions, and YES to unions like the United Auto Workers which are leading that fight. Wage concessions must be seen as an extreme version of controls. They attempt to solve the recession by cutting wages. It was exactly to counter such error that Keynes invented Keynesianism 50 years ago; if Keynesianism is now insufficient, that is no excuse for retreating to Herbert Hooverism.

In saying all this — above all, in saying that we must deal centrally with the crisis of unemployment — I don't mean to be cavalier about inflation. Indeed, inflation itself can be seen as a form of wage control, since rising prices lower real income. But what must be rejected are anti-inflation policies that increase unemployment and worsen the distribution of income. It presumably does not lie beyond the human imagination to conceive of policies which lower inflation and increase employment and improve the distribution of income. We might be so bold as to call such a program economic planning; the labour movement, while saying NO and properly so to monetarism cum controls, has frequently been on record as being only too willing to countenance that. Concretely, the government should propose now an industrial strategy to create jobs.

Restructuring the economy

What is needed, of course, is an economic strategy that is linked to the specificity, or peculiarities, of the Canadian situation. This means, concretely, the realities of Canada's present dependency and of the need for genuine development. It is that dependency, and consequent underdevelopment, that is the real structural rigidity or imbalance in the Canadian economy.

But it is in the nature of dependency that any attempts to change it will encounter the wrath of the international business community, and of the IMF. Such national policies are labelled "protectionism", and it is alleged that they are the *cause* of the present crisis, rather than a response to it. The so-called "beggar-thy-neighbour" policies of the 1930s are conjured up. But it is the monetarist policies that, by cutting back on markets, are true beggar-thy-neighbour policies. It is worth remembering that the same Keynes who was an architect of Bretton Woods (and thus of the IMF and World Bank) nevertheless worried that the world was too interdependent economically. At least in his more philosophic moods, Keynes saw virtue in greater national economic autonomy and less vulnerability.

The character of the Canadian economy is such that, though rich by global standards, it is not mature and not highly industrialized; we are not an efficient producer of manufactured goods. Rather, we are what historians have called a staples economy, or a resource hinterland serving more advanced metropolitan areas. We were, of course, born that way. In the past century, we have added an industrial sector but to a significant degree it is of a branch-plant nature, truncated and inefficient. To an important extent, both our resource sector and our industrial sector are appendages of the American economy.

Now however — and this is central to understanding the present global economic crisis — the U.S. economy is waning. When the British Empire declined we jumped ship and joined the American Empire. Where are we now to go? The answer would seem to be: the pursuit of a more autonomous path. Lest this be thought merely a radical idea, a couple of days ago (on September 7) at a panel discussion sponsored by the Canadian government in conjunction with the IMF/World Bank meetings, Gerard Adams, a professor of economics and finance at the University of Pennsylvania (since he was a guest of the Canadian government we can assume he is no radical) was quoted in the press as saying: "The world can no longer count on the United States to provide the demand stimulus needed. . . . The old (U.S.) locomotive theory is no more. What we need is a train of self-propelled vehicles, each country making its own effort to stimulate growth."

In fact, what has been the Canadian growth strategy in recent years? The answer has been megaprojects, the contemporary version of the staples model. Did we have an industrial strategy — at a time when a frightening process of deindustrialization was underway? The answer was: yes, spinoffs from the megaprojects.

Under the best of circumstances this did not seem like much of a growth strategy. In any event, it now lies in shreds. The megaprojects are on hold, indefinitely. Even the rich oil-based economy of Alberta is in trouble. We no longer have the pretense of an industrial strategy. The government of Canada issued an official book of information material for the IMF/World Bank meetings and included a section on economic prospects for the 1980s. It talks about our rich resources, which we will apparently sell off as always. It talks about linkages into transportation and machinery, about the further processing of resources, and about high-tech industries.

But centuries of resource export have not produced a capital-goods industry in this country; we do not even have a mining-machinery industry. On that matter, and on the whole question of benefits from the further processing of resources, ask the people of Sudbury as their city, founded on mining, moves towards becoming the biggest ghost-town in the long history of ghost-towns. If you look at that list of industrial prospects put forth by the government, what just happens to be missing are the so-called mature industries, like autos and textiles, where most of the jobs are today. The omission is ominous.

I do want to give credit to the government where credit is due, and the federal government did give us the National Energy Program (NEP) and specifically the Canadianization part of that program which I think merits our support. It came late in the day; then energy minister Marc Lalonde said at one point that the government should have Canadianized ten years earlier, forgetting that that's what some of us said then! Still, better late than never. But that initiative too is now on hold. The government's information material claims that the goal of Canadianization is ahead of schedule and that there is no need to press the case "in the years ahead" — which means presumably that Imperial Oil, as the dominant firm in the industry, and Gulf, Shell and Texaco will remain indefinitely in place.

Mr. Trudeau and another cabinet minister, Herb Gray, also promised us in the last election campaign, by way of an industrial strategy, a tougher Foreign Investment Review Agency (FIRA). The NEP was brought in and all hell broke loose. Though the government failed to bring in the changes in FIRA, that agency nevertheless became the whipping-boy of the right-wing in both the United States and Canada, in both the private sector and in the provincial governments. Herb Gray periodically surfaces in the letters column of the Globe and Mail replying, to his credit, to the latest libel against FIRA, but I've forgotten what he looks like.

The conclusion that I want to draw from all this is that in the tough world of industrial competition, we have to restructure the economy to make it more productive. To do that we have to confront its branch-plant character. We have to do something about foreign ownership, both its quantity and its quality. We have to deal with this fact of dependency, and opt clearly for development. This is not an easy strategy. Rather, it is a very hard one, for it risks the further wrath of the U.S., further charges of protectionism by the IMF, and so on. But unless we do this, I see little prospect for improvement in the economy for the foreseeable future. That in turn means little relief for the well over one million people and still counting who are officially unemployed in Canada.

When all is said and done, it is because of the lost production, because of the human costs and human misery that results, that we must reject the economic philosophy represented by the IMF.

Global Managers — Canadian Workers

Peter Warrian

Peter Warrian is executive assistant to the president of the Ontario Public Service Employees Union (OPSEU) and formerly the research director of the United Steelworkers of America (Canada). He has done research and consultation for Falconbridge nickel miners in the Dominican Republic and has written widely on labour economics and labour law.

Canada, the United States and indeed the world economy are in the midst of the deepest recession since the Great Depression of the 1930s. In Canada the current unemployment rate is officially 12 per cent; in real terms probably 18 to 20 per cent taking into account the underemployed and those who have given up looking for work.

Beneath these aggregate figures there is an even harsher reality in specific sectors, regions and communities. This harsh reality reflects structural weaknesses in the Canadian economy: our overdependence on resource extraction for export and the weakness of Canadian manufacturing. In northern New Brunswick, the unemployment rate is 46 per cent. The rate in Sudbury is close to this level. In the country as a whole, the

forest industry has 40 per cent of its workforce on layoff. The
mining industry was at this same level in summer 1982 and at
times higher. Virtually every mine in the country has been on
layoff or shutdown. We have lost approximately 400,000 jobs
mostly in manufacturing, since August of 1981. The largest
number of losses have been in Ontario.

Taken together, this means we are in a depression. It is
immediately obvious in the downtown of a major metropolitan
city like Toronto, but the depression has hit in industrial Canada, in the mining and forest communities, in the fishing villages and the industrial towns.

The social effects of the recession and unemployment are at
first those of discomfort and inconvenience: retail stores gone
out of business or short on stock (not carrying inventory),
declining consumer choice, boarded-up real estate and travel
agency businesses. At a harsher level, it is expressed in lost
hopes and opportunities as women and young people in particular go without work or are the first laid-off. The modestly
successful but important campaign to get women into non-
traditional production jobs in the steel industry has been
undercut by layoffs. More brutally, the underlying frustration
and anger are reflected in rising statistics on family violence,
wife-beating and child-battering in Canada.

The biggest single cause of all this, though obviously not
the only cause, is the economic slump. The economy is down,
and for everyone except statisticians, it is in all likelihood
going to stay down for at least another 18 months. The government's continued adherence to high interest rates, budget cutbacks, and the recent "six and five per cent" incomes policy
will guarantee that we stay down. The months ahead will see
even more unemployment, major bankruptcies and a crisis in
local government budgets as people come off unemployment
insurance and go onto welfare.

The restructuring of the economy

The current economic slump is not only quantitatively different from the nine or so other recessions we've had since World
War II. But it is also qualitatively different. The economy is
being reorganized. When it comes back up it is coming back up
in a different place from where it went down. Our economy is

being changed, reorganized in three dimensions: 1) the distribution of wealth and power; 2) technological change; and 3)
the international division of labour.

Wealth and power is being redistributed in Canada. That is
the hidden logic underlying the government's otherwise unin-
telligible economic policies. Labour incomes for wage and salary earners are being suppressed. The average industrial wage
has trailed the consumer price index since 1976, and the average industrial worker is $1 per hour behind where he or she
was in 1976. Canada had the lowest growth in labour compensation per unit of output in the OECD countries from 1971 to
1981. And now we have the "six and five" incomes policy to
put us further behind. At the same time, our social wage in the
form of social services, education, medicare, welfare and pen-
sions is being cut back.

On the other side of the ledger, sales and profits of the
corporations are certainly down. There is no doubt we shall see
major bankruptcies. However, capital is being reorganized as
well. In 1980-81 there was a major escalation of corporate mer-
gers and takeovers, only part of which had to do with the
National Energy Program. In the last two years, of the $32 bil-
lion in corporate lending by the Canadian chartered banks, $14
billion was related to the NEP, $18 billion was related to other
forms of corporate cannibalism. In addition, the short-term
debt-load of non-financial institutions escalated enormously,
going from $6 billion to $19 billion in 1981 alone. Some will
drown from it, others will take over a wider space at the trough.

On the other hand, things are also being reordered. One of
the unmentioned effects of Keynesianism and attempts at full
employment and welfare state policies since 1945 has been to
stave off a kind of capitalist house cleaning we haven't seen for
40 years. I expect that this is exactly what we are about to see.
The survivors in the next few years will then set out to re-
establish their profitability and consolidate their power.

The second area where the economy has been reorganized
is in the escalating rate of technological change. We associate
this with certain consumer products, particularly with electronic devices and games and industrially with micro-chip
technologies and robotics. In the workplace, workers are being
told "change or you won't survive", and for many out of work

there won't be jobs to go back to, even after the recession is over. Quite candidly, the extent of technological change ahead of us in this decade is something that we are unprepared for socially, and has placed labour on the defensive.

Trade unions are striving to deal constructively with technological change while wading through an ocean of unemployment, with no real protection under labour relations legislation. While academics and free-lancers such as Alvin Toffler speak of a *Third Wave* of opportunity for labour-saving services, energy efficiency, information processing and transfer, and liberation of a greater human potential in the global village, labour is unconvinced. Our members' experience with technology has been that it cuts off fingers, hands and limbs, kills lungs and hearts, deadens the mind and throws people out into the street. If the new technologies remain in the exclusive hands of management and the transnational or multinational corporation, we will more likely have a large workcamp than a global village.

The third aspect of economic reorganization is in the international division of labour, in the global system of production and trade. The post-World War II boom period, with its undeniable growth and prosperity, was predominantly based on the growth of domestic markets and trade between the advanced industrial countries of the OECD. Since the 1960s and increasingly in the 1970s, however, we have seen the rise of major industrial capacity in the so-called NICs, the Newly Industrialized Countries such as Brazil, Mexico, Taiwan, South Korea and Malaysia.

The industries where this capacity has been installed are steel, autos, shipbuilding and consumer goods. The heavy-industry, capital-intensive capacities in steel, auto and shipbuilding have come to threaten the "mature" industries of those sectors in North America and Western Europe. In consumer goods, especially electronics, textiles and light manufacturing, the capacity has often been set up in so-called EPZs (Export Processing Zones), which are free from duties, taxes and the environmental and labour standards regulations of the host countries. The Zones, which in 1980 employed a million people, the largest proportion being Third World women, are low-wage and "union-free". It has been reported that in

Malaysia the young women workers have a productive life of approximately four years because of the pace and intensity of the precision assembly work. When their usefulness ends, they are returned to their villages.

This development model of a "new economic order" (not the same NIEO we talked about in the mid-1970s) is associated in the economic literature with the concepts of "the new credit economy" and "export substitution". The strategy of industrial relocation and export substitution, which the IMF and the World Bank have encouraged and facilitated, poses a direct threat to the living standards and trade union rights of North American and Western European workers. Short of a social revolution and redistribution of income in the Third World, there is no way that this new industrial capacity can be digested by those countries.

Politics of the recession

The labour movement in Canada has been consistent, and almost alone in seeing the roots of the recession as political.

The policy of monetarism, with slight national variations (in Canadese, "gradualism") has been around since the mid-1970s. However, in 1981 there was a radical departure led by the Reagan and Thatcher administrations, whereby the governments of the OECD countries explicitly committed themselves to extend monetarism to the global level and run the economy into a recession. The mechanisms have been high interest rates, tight money, social cutbacks, incomes policies (wage controls) and contract concessions from labour.

There was to be a holy war against inflation, fought on the backs of the unemployed. The governments delivered a harsh message to their domestic populations: We must cut back, become leaner and more competitive in the national interest so that we can be internationally competitive, export and grow. Subsequently we have had a comparative race to see who can cut back wage and public spending the most.

The most obvious flaw in this strategy, beyond its social inequalities, is that it is self-defeating. If every economy dramatically constricts demand, where are these much-vaunted exports to be sold? The predictable result is that world trade came to a halt in 1981 and was falling by 1982. The policies of monetarism have not worked and the governments of the OECD are coming under increasing pressure to act on unemployment.

The IMF, in its *Annual Report,* expresses "widespread dissatisfaction and concern" with global economic conditions. However, the IMF is looking through the wrong end of the telescope. The IMF is urging governments not to yield to pressures to stimulate economies and reduce unemployment. The IMF calls for "courage" and continuation of monetarism accompanied by "appropriate adjustment policies". By this they mean social cutbacks, curbing of food subsidies and are addressing the "inflexibility" in the structure of wage rates. As an example of flexibility they put forward the Japanese model.

Let me say in passing that the "Japanese model" entails the following unacceptable features:

1) Bonuses rather than straight wages comprise the largest share of workers' incomes. The bonuses are dependent on corporate profitability, over which the workers have no determinative decision-making power;

2) The much-heralded form of lifetime job security applies only to a minority of workers, mostly males in large enterprises. The rest of the workforce is in small enterprises or contract labour, and mostly comprised of women who are regularly pushed in, then thrown out, of full-time work;

3) Japanese unions are enlisted to play the policeman role in suppressing dissent in the company and issuing industrial discipline.

Finally, on top of weak trade, the IMF says that protectionist measures by the industrialized countries "would be particularly injurious to the trade prospects of the developing countries" and their ability to earn foreign currency to pay off their debts. No doubt the preoccupation here is with the defensive reaction of unions in the mature steel, auto and textile industries of North America and Western Europe, unions pushing for job security and import restrictions. The beneficiaries of the IMF and World Bank "export substitution" development strategy are their clients in the NICs and EPZs.

The result of all of this is political polarization. The interests and policies of the IMF/World Bank are in conflict with unionized industrial workers in the OECD countries. Furthermore, the policies of monetarism, high interest rates and unemployment are causing increasing political conflict for the OECD governments on the home front. Indeed, in this regard Keynesianism was much more than simply an economic policy of full employment and counter-cyclical fiscal and monetary techniques. It was also a class political compromise. It was a deal: The ownership and control of the dominant menas of production and distribution remained and were legitimated in private hands, on the condition that employment and growth were sustained. If Keynesianism is over, then the deal is off. Politically we face a crisis in democratic capitalism. A new deal entails a fundamental shift in the "mixed economy".

Crisis in the world capitalist system?

We talk — I have talked — about an economic, social and political crisis. Is there a crisis in the world capitalist system?

I don't believe so, in the sense that the system is about to suffer collapse. It is, however, going through a major restructuring, with traumatic unemployment and social results.

If there is a crisis within the system, it is a crisis of accumulation that dates back to the late 1960s, prior to but accelerated by the OPEC crisis of 1972-73. From the mid-1960s, there was a slowdown in growth, and hence profitability, in the mature industries — steel and auto and so on — in North America and Europe. These had been the key industries in the industrial expansion both before and after World War II. "Western prosperity" was very much dependent on them. The problem we face is, if you have an economy dominated by privately-owned corporations, then their ability to grow, make a profit, accumulate and invest is fundamental to the maintenance of income and employment. What we have seen in the last decade and a half is multinational corporations, in league with the IMF/World Bank, developing their answer to the crisis of accumulation by a major shift to the NICs and EPZs.

If the crisis is real — and I believe it is — what do we do domestically and internationally? If there is a major international shift in the organization of capital, the formations of class are also changing, particularly the relationship of Third World workers and First World industrial workers. It is not too much to say that this changing relationship will dominate the political agendas of trade unions, popular movements and their political parties throughout this decade. Will the redistribution of income away from wage and salary earners and towards capital in Canada and the OECD countries work? If so, on whose terms and how will the social burden be distributed? Will North American and European workers construct a defensive wall against imports? Or, will trade union and human rights be achieved, along with social redistribution in the Third World? Will new mechanisms of financial allocation and trade emerge, on different terms than those of the IMF, World Bank and EPZs?

These are some of the questions flowing from the tentative analysis presented above. Trade unions will have to deal with them as a matter of practical necessity. Academics can contribute by deepening and broadening the analysis and arena of discussion for our options.

Canada / Third World Policy: Linking Strategies

Michael K. Oliver

Michael Oliver, a political scientist, has taught and held top administrative positions at a number of Canadian universities. He was first general president of the federal New Democratic Party (1961-63), director of research for the Bilingualism and Biculturalism Commission (1964-67) and president of the Association of Universities and Colleges of Canada (1975-76).

Only too often our thinking is divided into neat, separate compartments: domestic policy in one, international policy in another; a Canadian industrial strategy — or problems of Third World development. We switch models and assumptions with an uneasy awareness that we are enmeshed in inconsistencies but rarely do we confront ourselves with the challenge of reconciling our policies. So in the morning we make trade decisions that cut deeply into the export revenues of developing countries and in the afternoon virtuously vote new funding levels for CIDA. If we have twinges of anxiety about the net effect of these actions, we take refuge in somewhat specious statements like, "Oh well, Third World manufacturers are in the hands of the multinationals anyhow."

If we want lessons in inconsistency, we have only to turn to the two august bodies, the IMF and World Bank, that share the city of Toronto with us this week. Although neither of them was created with the needs of what was, in 1944, the colonial world in mind, they have become two of the primary global instruments that apply policies to the developing countries. In the case of the World Bank, we have been able to perceive a remarkable evolution in the way it looks at international development. Its initial concern was to help create small industrial revolutions throughout the Third World and to applaud any growth in GNPs as an indication that progress was being made. In its view, given the right infrastructure and some judicious investment decisions, Third World economies would reach the take-off point and rapidly move along a path of self-engendered growth.

But as the world entered the 1970s, it became evident that economic growth in a Third World country could simply mean sharper contrasts between an ever-richer, Western-oriented elite and a steadily impoverished mass of citizens: that the technological marvels of the Green Revolution, for instance, could produce concentrations of wealth and power instead of increases in general well-being; and that an increasing reliance on imports of both consumer goods for the developed enclaves and fuel, parts and semi-processed components for industry created fatal vulnerabilities when terms of trade worsened and a huge upset like the post-1973 increases in oil prices occurred.

The World Bank policies, in their development aspects, began to change. It promoted the satisfaction of basic needs for all the people in developing countries to the top of the list of development objectives. Its concern became the *distribution* of the fruits of growth and it abandoned faith in the theory that wealth and well-being would trickle down from the initial recipients to all levels of society. It favoured projects that directly met the needs of the poorest. Its spokespersons espoused and preached policies based on eliminating the privations of rural populations and sectors thus far insulated from the effects of development.

In the Third World, governments genuinely concerned with the welfare of all the people, and which sought to better the lot of the poorest, began to relax and expand in the warm glow of

World Bank approval. Until, of course, they got into a balance-of-payments problem — then things changed.

It did not matter *how* the problem was induced; it could arise from totally uncontrollable forces like a fall in staple-export prices on the world market; or a sharp increase in the cost of essential imports like oil. The point was: They were in financial trouble and the body to turn to was the IMF, the World Bank's sister institution. Given the World Bank's new outlook on the problems of developing countries and on appropriate development strategies, it might have been expected that the IMF would be especially sympathetic to the Jamaicas or Tanzanias of the developing world. *Or*, you *might* have had these expectations if you were naïve enough to think that consistency would rule in these twin organizations, the World Bank and IMF.

We know what happens when a developing country turns to the IMF when it is in difficulty. Its policies are scrutinized and the changes it will have to make, if rescue funds are to be provided, get laid out. What policies have to go? Those policies attempting to assure that the fruits of development reach *all* the people; those policies that try to increase the standard of life in rural areas and in impoverished sectors; those policies that try to establish some degree of self-reliance so as to lessen the country's vulnerability to severe and unpredictable shocks from outside. Overnight the World Bank's "white" becomes the IMF's "black".

If I seem to belabour this point it is because it is so revealing of the policy inconsistencies that characterize so much of the economic thinking in Western countries. The sad truth is that when the crunch comes, the protection of the interests of the wealthy and powerful is what counts.

What has happened in Canada? When times were good, you might have been led to believe that we were a society where certain humane values were beginning to prevail. Economic benefits were being spread by a process of free collective bargaining, by more equal access to education, by medicare and other social insurance schemes, and by equalization policies that enabled all regions to share in the returns from Canadian resources. Policies that promoted equality seemed to have a secure place. But then an economic downturn occurred — and

what were the policies that our governments-in-fright turned
to? Precisely those that *negated* the humane and egalitarian
elements that had begun to look secure in our system.

Our governments, both federal and provincial, have set control of inflation as a higher goal than alleviation of unemployment; they have begun to impose wage controls; they have
allowed medicare to be eroded by extra billings; they have
raised fees for universities and colleges without putting up
student assistance; they have turned the country into a cockpit
of regional contenders for shares of resource revenues; they,
and I am thinking especially of the federal government, have
backed down on closing tax loopholes and have reduced the
progression of taxes; and they are being urged to abandon
instruments like the Foreign Investment Review Agency
(FIRA), that we have begun to put in place to lessen our vulnerability.

"When the going gets tough, the tough get going," and it
suddenly becomes clear who is *really* tough. It is not the
unions; it is not the unemployed; it is not old-age pensioners. It
is those whose power seemed so benign a few years ago — the
banks, the large employers, the spokespersons for business
interests.

Canada and dependency theory

We are forced, then, to dig out those questions about what is
fundamentally wrong with our country, questions we had
allowed to be buried under a wash of optimism. We are com-
pelled to face the problems of how to ensure the gains we make
in social justice. We have to look at the underlying structure of
our economy and seek out the sources of weakness that make
our gains so insecure, our approaches to equality so readily
reversible.

It seems to me that there are two ways of going about this,
and neither is completely satisfactory in itself. The first way I
want to suggest is to ask ourselves what we can learn about
ourselves and the policies we should follow, using the model
that seems best to explain the plight of LDCs, *dependency*
analysis.

The analogies between Canada's political economy and
those of many LDCs are striking:

- We rely on exports of raw materials, of unprocessed or very lightly processed primary products: grain, minerals, forest products;
- Much of our resource industry is owned by multinational corporations;
- Branch plants of foreign firms have established an import-substitution industrialization behind a tariff barrier;
- We consequently suffer from cost structures determined by the multinational corporations' internal pricing policies for the importation of parts of semi-processed elements;
- We are recipients of a prepackaged technology engineered for others' needs;
- We are deprived of the benefits of investment in research, including both the range of high quality employment posts that research provides *and* the greater control research gives over where our society and economy will go in the future;
- Our financial pattern lures us into bringing more multinational corporate capital to compensate for the outflow of interest and profits that the foreign capital already engenders here.

The judgement made by Kari Levitt in *Silent Surrender* back in 1970 still holds: "Canada's position resembles more closely that of a less developed nation than that of other developed countries." We have, indeed, many of the characteristics of a dependent economy, of an economy of the periphery.

The explanatory power of dependency theory is impressive. Applied to South and Central America, and indeed to Africa and Asia as well, it provides remarkable insights into the way things are — the location of power and control, the contradictions, the conflicts of interests, the warped economic structure, the shocking inequalities that grow rather than narrow. And it provides equally remarkable understanding of how things got to be that way.

Let me stress how important it is for Canadians to work through this kind of analysis for ourselves, about ourselves. But when the analysis is done, let's admit that the analogy has real limits:

- We don't have the marked dualism of a modern sector combined with a traditional, exploited sector;

- We have our own multinational corporations, many of them, like Bata and Inco, extremely active in the Third World;
- And we could go on.

We can't press the analogy too far, and if we do, we give ourselves the aura of victims which, in comparison to the LDCs, we *are not*.

Let me also suggest that dependency theory is more impressive in historical explanation and in description than in prescription.

Although the analytical framework is global, the policy implications of dependency theory seem to focus on the state, on policy for one country. Because it judges all influences of capitalist states abroad as baleful, it calls for a maximizing of self-reliance that can easily be misinterpreted as a call for isolated autarchy. It has little to say on alternative international economic patterns and institutions.

I think, therefore, that we can derive many important policy conclusions by looking at Canada from this kind of international viewpoint. We can learn:

- It is important to strengthen our national self-reliance;
- It is vital to be willing to use public agencies to give us greater control of our economy;
- We must set limits and conditions on foreign investment.

But when we've gone this far, perhaps it is wise to pause. Let me give you a very simple example of why I want to push self-reliance only so far. In Canada we produce wheat, much more than we can possibly eat ourselves. What's more, it makes *sense* that we should produce a great deal of wheat. Those northern prairies are *made* for the crop. But if we are going to produce good hard wheat cheaply and efficiently *some* countries have got to be food importers. And those countries *won't* be self-sufficient in food. Instead, they will produce something else, more cheaply and efficiently than we can, and trade it to us for wheat.

Let me get to the point. What I am saying is that self-reliance is a second best solution. It's a vital solution in a world of wildly fluctuating commodity prices, of exploitation of poor weak states by powerful states. It's a crucial part of the contemporary strategy of any developing country, and a part of any sensible Canadian economic strategy too. But it's second best.

The best solution is an international system of secure, stable trade, and an international institutional framework that will prevent such a system from sacrificing the weak to the strong.

How far we are from that! Yet improvements in the equity, stability and ease of flow of international exchange are not just utopian goals, they are pressing necessities, especially for the developing countries.

Even if those developing countries devote themselves as strenuously as possible towards achieving a goal of self-reliance, in the here and now they *must* buy and sell abroad. Even if we deplore that they are dependent economies, that their trade is handled by MNCs which deny them many of the fruits of exchange; even if we recognize that their peripheral role makes them dance to tunes set in the dominant world centres; still, they have to trade.

We in Canada have both an interest and a responsibility to see that trade is maintained and increased and that a new international economic framework for this exchange is established as rapidly as possible. Our *interest* in trade is as consumers (who will be able to buy for less) and as potential sellers and investors. Our responsibility is to make sure that we don't abuse our power or side with others who *do* abuse their power.

Reconstruction: an international strategy

There is no time today to go into all the intricacies of the North-South dialogue, of the demands of the Third World for new rules, new institutions, new power-sharing as well as new wealth-sharing. North/South negotiations are badly stalled now. The meetings of the IMF and the World Bank, which, in a way, are part of those negotiations, are just the most recent evidence of the failures to reconcile interests. Perhaps talks won't move ahead until ways are found of bettering the Third World's bargaining position — South/South dialogues are in the immediate future likely to be more productive.

But because new, more equitable patterns of international trade and exchange are slow in emerging, it doesn't relieve national economic planners of the responsibility for attempting to foresee and, in the meantime, take account of international trade realities.

Here in Canada it is crucially important that those of us who in this time of economic crisis are seeking ways to fundamentally reconstruct our economy keep the needs and claims of the rest of the world in mind. Let's not take the steps one must take to make Canada more self-reliant, more equal, with a bigger public sector, without putting Canada into the context of an improved world order. Let's adjust our plans to a future where developing countries begin, more and more, not just to get control of their *own* resources and become more self-reliant, but begin to get a reasonable share of the *world's* resources through trade and exchange.

What I'm proposing as an agenda for the democratic left in Canada is to devise for our country an industrial strategy, indeed a complete strategy of reconstruction, which takes full account of the international setting. Which seeks to eliminate the inconsistencies we get ourselves into by putting domestic policy and international development policy in separate compartments. That means:

- looking in a clear-eyed way at our dependency and moving to greater self-reliance especially in investment;
- but *also*, promoting a Canada that is resilient enough to open its markets to the products of the developing world; that does not seek to conserve a pattern of domestic production that is high-cost and inefficient just because we fear change.

These are incredibly difficult tasks. We must build into Canadian society not just the more equal distribution of wealth and income and the welfare and security which all of our people are entitled to, but also the capacity to adjust equitably to change.

If we are honest in our desire to see the LDCs emerge from their poverty and share more equitably in the world's resources, we must be prepared to change. And because the same set of values that accepts the Third World's move to equality will insist that the equity also applies at home, we must build into our society an equalization of the risks and costs of change. We must be sure that those who are asked to adapt are compensated; that the pace of change be reasonable and humane; that people share in the decisions that affect them rather than having solutions shoved down their throats.

Our challenge is to fit the demands of international justice and the necessity to accept change into social democracy in the 1980s. Let me ask you to reflect on this agenda.

PART FIVE

The Search
for Alternatives

The Imperative of Reform

Kighoma Malima

Kighoma Malima is a Tanzanian economist and Member of Parliament with the office of Minister of State responsible for development planning and economic affairs. A former head of the economics department of the University of Dar es Salaam, he remains a member of the teaching faculty. He also sits on the national executive council of the ruling CHAMA CHA MAPINDUNZI (Party for the Revolution).

It is clear that the need for reform of the Bretton Woods institutions has become more pressing than ever before. The world economic situation is in such a turmoil that old conventional wisdoms and prescriptions have been found wanting. It is, however, in the developing world where the economic crisis threatens to unleash human sufferings of unprecedented proportions.

The lack of foreign exchange has created a chain reaction affecting practically all economic and social activities, putting in jeopardy the whole socio-political stability of these countries. In Sub-Saharan Africa, for instance, agriculture is the backbone of the region's economies. Not only does agriculture provide food for a rapidly growing population but it also provides critically needed foreign exchange as well as raw materials for the nascent industrial sector. Yet for agriculture to make its expected contributions, it desperately needs imported fertilizers and insecticides, as well as implements of various kinds. Without the foreign exchange to pay for such imported inputs, agriculture is the first to suffer, bringing untold misery to millions of innocent people.

Similarly, the provision of the so-called "basic needs" such as general education, health services and rural water supply, is also dependent not only on imported equipment and materials but also on the ability of a particular government to collect the requisite taxes. Tax revenues are inextricably tied to utilization of the available domestic productive capacity, which in turn has been adversely affected due to the lack of imported spare parts, equipment and raw materials. In other words, no sales or corporate income taxes can be collected if production is not taking place at an economically remunerative level — especially if it is not taking place at all.

In addition to such basic maintenance and care operations, which require an increasingly larger proportion of dwindling foreign exchange resources, the servicing of past debts also threatens to turn an already precarious situation into a near disaster. Some developing countries are already in the tragic situation where over 100 per cent of their annual export earnings are needed to service their past external debts.

Surely rational minds expect such countries to meet their external obligations only at their own peril. Yet that is what the financial pundits insist upon like a dogma, namely that external debt obligations be met, and promptly.

The role of external forces

There is no doubt that the root cause of such external payments crises is primarily external. Those who are looking for a scapegoat for a system that has become increasingly unworkable and unjust would like us to believe that the main source of the problem is the domestic policies of the developing countries concerned. The World Bank Report on Sub-Saharan Africa has aptly demonstrated in its statistical appendix that regardless of their domestic policies, of their free enterprise or planning and controls, the Sub-Saharan economies have all been in a very serious bind. In fact, those Sub-Saharan African countries that have *not* left their economies to the vagaries of market forces have done just as well in income per capita growth-rates, as well as superbly better in the provision of basic social services like education, health and rural water supply.

Thus, such evidence does unambiguously suggest that the economic difficulties bedeviling the developing countries are largely outside their control. The high cost of imported energy, the rapidly increasing cost of imports as a result of world inflation, high interest rates and the declining prices of major exports, have all been decisive. In other words, the economic difficulties of the Third World have their origin in an economic system that forces them to sell the little they produce (exports) cheaply and purchase their critical requirements from abroad (imports) dearly. No one can operate viably for long under such an arrangement.

In light of such compelling circumstances and evidence, the imperative for reform of the international monetary institutions, primarily the International Monetary Fund and the World Bank, in order that they may better respond to the world economic crisis unfolding before us, can hardly be overstated. Indeed, as long as the developing countries are unable to provide all their basic requirements within their borders or out of their own resources, they will continue to depend on trade and exchange to provide them with the requisite machinery, equipment, industrial raw materials and even some agricultural products.

Thus, what can be or is to be traded and at what prices and other terms are not irrelevant issues. I begin from the basic assumption that the developing countries will continue the struggle to make the world economy a just and equitable one. The option of withdrawal to a subsistence and non-industrial economy is irrevocably unavailable to us.

The essence of reform of the International Monetary Fund and the World Bank stems from the fact that these institutions as constituted at present appear less than able to cope with the current economic crisis, especially the crushing impact of such a crisis on the developing countries. The elements of reform are essentially three-fold: decision-making process; quantum and automaticity of resources; and conditionality.

The decision-making dilemma

As is well known, the majority of developing countries, especially the African countries, were not present at Bretton Woods in 1944 when the IMF and World Bank were created. Since they were then still under colonial domination, their interests could not have been adequately catered for. As a result, decision-making powers are concentrated among a very few powerful industrial countries. It is like a modern corporation where voting is in accordance with shares in that corporation. Thus, a large number of member countries representing the majority of the world population are semi-disenfranchised.

Consequently, the push towards democracy of decision-making in these two sister institutions, along the lines of United Nations institutions, is an important aspect of reform. We are, of course, acutely aware of the cruel fact that those who hold most power in these institutions have to agree to share it with the rest of the membership and this is not going to be easy. But that only makes the task that much more difficult. It is not a case for giving up altogether. It is quite clear that decisions which affect the lives of millions of people around the globe cannot be left to be a prerogative of a few selective countries. The argument that those who pay have to have a greater say is no different from the argument that would deny the less prosperous provinces or states of a nation the right to participate fully in the management of the affairs of their nation. In the twentieth century such an argument would be retrogressive and unacceptable.

Regulating resources

The second aspect of reform is the quantum of resources and their automaticity. It is quite clear that in view of the enormity of the problems facing the developing world, the quantity of resources available from the IMF and World Bank is far from adequate. Similarly, those developing countries in dire need of external resource inflow should be assured that such resources will be available to them almost automatically, in the same manner that a disaster-stricken area within a country expects the rest of that country to come to its aid as a matter of course. What is disturbing is that not only is a developing country often denied the timely assistance required, but also, even when such assistance is made available, it comes too late and in doses which can hardly make an impact. Furthermore, equally disconcerting, there is sometimes also no relationship whatsoever between the quantity of resources a particular country receives from outside and its ability to use those resources effectively and for the benefit of its people. Thus, somewhere along the line, principles stop and real politics take over and in the process it is the weaker that suffer most.

The politics of conditionality

The third area of reform is what may be called conditionality. Clearly, no one is saying that assistance from the international monetary institutions should be provided without any kind of conditions attached. In the first place resources, whether external or domestic, must be used only for the purpose intended. Ironically, this kind of condition creates the least controversy and is seldom asked for or insisted upon by external aid agencies in any case.

It is, however, the conditions that tend to exploit the difficult situation in a developing country, in order to change its socio-political objectives, which are most objectionable. Thus, as a condition for assistance, a developing country is often required to scrap public enterprises and hand them over to the private sector, to abandon price controls, agricultural subsidies, free medical and other social services, to take these things away from a population which everyone agrees is already too deprived.

The political and ideological slant of such conditionality is beyond doubt. Where a country has submissively endorsed and implemented such an austerity program, social disorder has almost always been inevitable. What is worse, developing countries desperately in need of external resources are forced to adopt policy measures which have either been discredited or are still the subject of unsettled and intense professional debate even in the advanced industrial countries where they are supposed to make a great deal of sense.

The tragedy in all this is that no one seems to pay any attention to what some of the developing countries are saying. To call it indifference or callousness is probably an underestimation.

Power — and responsibility

It is quite clear from what I have been saying so far that the three elements of reform are quite interrelated. No amount of rational argument against conditionality, for instance, is going to make much impact until the power structures of the international monetary institutions have been radically changed in favour of the majority. As may be obvious to all of you, I have not examined South-South co-operation as a substitute to the present international monetary institutions, or even international economic co-operation generally.

My own candid opinion is that South-South co-operation, important as it is, can only be a crucial supplement but never a substitute. Such a defeatist withdrawal would only offer an alibi to those who already know that more than anything else, *they* are responsible for the present plight of the developing countries, and hence have a moral responsibility to do something about the misery of those countries. It should not be the business of developing countries to let those responsible for their economic troubles off the hook.

The Push for Fiscal Balance: An IMF Response

David Finch

David Finch, an Australian economist, has worked with the IMF since 1950. Most recently he has served as director of the IMF's Exchange and Trade Relations Department in Washington. He was personally involved in IMF negotiations with several Third World countries — including meeting with the Manley administration in Jamaica.

It is very clear that the world isn't working well. I don't think there is any doubt of that, and I think the developing countries are in one of the most acutely difficult phases they have seen since the 1930s. Interest rates are very high — and in real terms much higher than they have ever been in the last 30 years. As countries struggle to cope, they find that their markets are being restricted.

It is not going to be easy to see a way through these problems in the next few years. At this present juncture it is a very difficult thing to be a government in a developing country and, for that matter, in an advanced country. Virtually all of the major governments promise more than they can deliver and they see their public opinion polls starting to shift again even as they struggle to deliver what they've promised in a world that is just not working out the way they would like. I don't think it is for the Fund or the World Bank to remedy the situation either. I don't think we are *that* important. We can do some things in this area — and I hope that we are struggling with intelligence to make the message known — but quite literally we do not think we have some solution that is going to change the situation.

I'm afraid that I would differ with the Tanzanian Minister in one respect: I don't think there is any alternative that is particularly attractive. The prospect we hold forth is one of trying to understand where the constraints are, trying to explain them to people, trying to get people to wait patiently for the changes that will come. I have no doubt whatever that in five or ten years' time we will look back on this period and wonder why we despaired about it. We will wonder why we did not believe in the technological improvements taking place throughout the world, why we did not see that those improvements were going to solve the problems. And why we struggled so hard to ignore the adjustments needed, never expecting them to pay off when in fact they would.

But so much for my philosophical approach. Let me move to the more immediate things. It is quite clear that in the IMF/ World Bank annual meetings we have seen a new range of countries coming into very severe difficulties. Mexico is an example. Conditions in the world overwhelmed the Mexican administration, although clearly there were contributing causes within the government's control. There had been expenditure increases which went beyond what the Mexicans would now regard as reasonable; they expected oil to continue to go up in price and they expected it would be easy to continue borrowing. It turned out to be different and adjustment has now to be made to this reality. What is the role of the Fund in this? When people talk about the harshness of conditionality, this has nothing to do with the Fund. Life is hard in Mexico right now, without the Fund having done a thing.

What can the Fund do to help a country like Mexico? There are two aspects. The Mexicans would regard money as the most important one. When a country is faced with a withdrawal of resources, when it finds that it cannot keep the imports coming, it is a great step forward for the nations of the world to band together in an institution like the Fund, to provide money in difficult circumstances and in accordance with the rules of the system. So we think that the most important thing for us to do in the case of such countries is to provide them with the resources they so desperately need, within the limits laid down for us.

The difficulty here is that no one empowered the Fund to dispense these resources as a gift. No one passed them over to our executive directors to distribute as they think fit to ease the ills of the world. The Fund is a co-operative, set up with the idea of lending to countries when they have a patch of difficulty — but with the clear expectation that the money can be paid back to the Fund to be made available to others. The revolving character of the Fund is essential. The original Articles made it clear that resources would be used to tide countries over a fairly short cycle, with repayments in three to five years. We have gone out to as far as ten years for some facilities but it is within that sort of revolving arrangment that the co-operative was planned.

Now this point becomes even more directly evident when the Fund goes out to borrow from, say, the Saudi Arabian authorities. The Saudis are not giving the money away; they regard themselves as having a depleting resource: They need to be accumulating capital from it. They lend it to us in the confident belief that it is going to be in safe hands, that it will be available to them when their oil is depleted, and that they will have an asset that is still worth what it was when they originally lent it. One role of the Fund as a co-operative is to take money from those who have a surplus and lend it to those in temporary deficit.

The servicing of debt

How are we going to decide that the resources entrusted to us and then being lent to someone else are being used constructively? We have struggled with this over the years and the principal way we do this is by trying to achieve order in the public sector finances. We pay very considerable attention to the fiscal balance in the economy. If a country gets into difficulties by overspending on things which are not contributing to the future growth of that economy, then we have to try to reach some understanding on how that imbalance is going to be corrected.

I know that, on occasion, review with the government does lead to reductions in subsidies, for example, or changes in expenditures on some social sectors. The Fund never chooses where expenditure cuts are to take place. It has to see that the overall fiscal balance is in order; it has to look at the total availability of resources, including those funds that are coming from abroad. If more is being spent than is available from external sources, payments arrears begin to accumulate. The country finds that its normal trade credits are withdrawn and the situation tends to get worse as supply dries up — of spare parts to keep the trucks going, or petroleum to run the trucks, or coal to run the electricity stations. So we spend most of our time in countries examining this overall fiscal balance. We leave the priorities, the political priorities, entirely to the government.

The general thrust is that the Fund is interested in seeing a recovery of production and exports that is sufficiently secure that a rational person would judge that the input of Fund resources is constructive. There is a judgement that when repayment is to be made the situation is reasonably likely to have improved sufficiently for the pain of repayment to be less than the pain of doing without the resources altogether. Now there is judgement in that, and that is what conditionality is about. I believe that on the whole, if you look through the record of the last five years, you would see that the Fund is being too liberal in these judgements.

A number of questions can be asked about the debt service that has arisen: Whether in fact in paying the interest charges on some of these loans, and repaying them too, are we not adding to the problems at this stage? We try to look at this aspect. We have an annual review of the conditions. We go before the representatives of our member countries in the executive board to try to explain it. We are willing to talk to any outside groups.

The plight of limited resources

Let me go on to describe some other things that follow from what I have been saying. One of the questions relates to the provision of resources. It is quite clear to us at this time — and to the vast majority of the membership — that the resources available to the Fund are too limited. The point is that when you allow for the intervening price increases and the rise in the volume of trade, quotas have shrunk tremendously.

Mexico, for example, was borrowing $18.5 billion net in 1981, whereas the maximum the Fund can lend under present rules is $1.3 billion in a year. Now the difference between those figures, when the banks cut off their lending, is just too great. We think that that has to be dealt with through an increase in quotas. It is also evident that the scale of emergency is such at present that we will need resources in addition to quotas, and there's been a question of examining the amount of borrowing we can make outside. We have been fortunate that the Saudi authorities have agreed to lend us Special Drawing Rights of $8 billion and some other governments have added another SDR $1.3 billion to that. But, against the scale of the present problems, we will need support to get more resources. It is quite clear to me that the scale of the problems is one that is overwhelming in the light of the existing resources available.

I do not want to end on the note that it is not possible to deal with the problem. Things are going to be dealt with and in a case like Mexico we will work very hard and effectively to get the co-operation of other sources of funds. We will certainly press the commercial banks to do refinancing in this case. It is not feasible for banks suddenly to end net-lending and expect to get the original terms of the contract observed. In the present circumstances, it is appropriate to give the country more time and to lend back the resources that are being taken from it if it is in debt to a very considerable degree; the banks undoubtedly understand this.

It is not possible, however, even with the best co-operation from banks, that the task can be accomplished simply by pressure on private profit-making organizations. We will also need to have the support of governments to come up with resources to ease the problem. It is one of the advantages of being an international organization that you have access to these agencies and we feel we must use that access to ease the problems of our member countries.

Towards a New System: Reform or Revolution?

Norman Girvan

Norm Girvan is a Jamaican economist who served as director of the National Planning Agency of the Jamaican government from 1977 to 1980. He is the author of Foreign Capital and Economic Underdevelopment in Jamaica *(1971), editor of* Science and Technology in the Caribbean *(1979) and was one of the major contributors of papers to the 1980 Arusha Initiative. He is currently employed at the UN Centre on Transnationals.*

I wish to address the issue of reform on two levels. First, the reform or restructuring of the International Monetary Fund itself; and secondly the reform and restructuring of the international monetary system, of which the IMF is only an institution, albeit the most important one.

The second level is the more fundamental. It calls into question the basic structure and orientation of the Bretton Woods institutions established at the end of the Second World War, and it raises a number of key questions. Among those questions is, first of all, the role of the United States in the IMF. Secondly, and linked to that, is the role of the U.S. dollar as the chief international currency, the main international reserve asset used to settle international transactions. Third is the low representation of the developing countries in the present principal international monetary institution. That representation, as you may know, approximates roughly one-third of voting power in the IMF. The fourth question is the exclusion or almost complete exclusion of socialist countries from the principal international monetary institution. And finally, there is the issue of this institution's orientation towards economic policies of a certain type; that is, policies that place priority on foreign investment and liberalization of controls on imports and foreign exchange, and emphasis on short-term stabilization as compared to long-term development.

The search for a radical alternative

The logical answer to these questions would be to find an alternative to the International Monetary Fund rather than to reform it. Such an alternative could be called, for convenience, a World Central Bank or World Monetary Institution. This would have perhaps three or four principal attributes.

First of all it would need to be universal in membership; that is, it would need to include the socialist countries as part of its membership.

Secondly, it would need to be democratic in its structure. By democratic I don't necessarily mean one-country one-vote, I mean that representation and power relations would much more closely approximate the present structure of international economic relations and their realities — as opposed to realities at the end of the Second World War, which are reflected in the present structure of the IMF.

Thirdly, such a World Central Bank would need to be in a position to issue an internationally acceptable currency, a unit internationally acceptable as a reserve asset and a means of settling international transactions. Such a unit would not be tied to the national currency of any one country.

Fourthly, such a body would have to be capable of accommodating itself to different social and economic systems and to alternative paths of development. That is to say, whereas we would need to stress the need for discipline and coherent economic management, we would have to recognize that this is a necessity irrespective of the economic system or development path. You have heard it said, for example, that the difficulties in Africa apply equally to those countries following liberal pro-market-economy kinds of economic policies, as to those which follow policies and development strategies that emphasize planning and state intervention. Within the developed world we have seen that both Poland, essentially a planned economy, and the United States, a free-market economy, show the need for proper economic management because both are suffering in their own way from the consequences of bad economic management.

Reforming the IMF

The nature of good economic management and the methods used to bring it about would be different in different circumstances and under different economic systems. At present, the underlying ideological and intellectual bias of the IMF and World Bank is to equate bad management with import controls, foreign exchange controls and the expanded role of the public sector. Conversely, good economic management is identified with the removal of such controls, with retrenchment in the public sector and encouragement of the private sector and foreign investment.

Given this bias, which is an inherent bias in the IMF's operations, it is not surprising that most developing countries find the conditionality of the IMF unpalatable and that most socialist countries have found membership incompatible with their own domestic economic and social systems.

The question is will it take a complete collapse of the international financial system to bring about such a fundamental change in the system? Only time will tell if this is the case. I hope it will not require another world war to bring about these fundamental changes. In the meantime, however, attention will be focused on more immediate questions related to reform of the International Monetary Fund itself.

For this purpose I believe that the most convenient point of departure is the position taken by the developing countries at the Belgrade conference in 1979, and the paper of the Group of 24 called "An Outline Program of Action on International Monetary Reform". The key proposal in the position of the G24 is, first of all, an expansion of the quotas of developing countries in the IMF, from roughly one-third to 45 per cent of the total voting power. Second, an expansion of balance of payments support for developing countries, with low conditionality. Third, a medium-term facility for the developing countries, providing finance on concessionary terms. And fourth, an increased allocation of Special Drawing Rights to developing countries and the linkage of the SDRs to development finance.

There is a common thread running throughout these proposals: that the deficits of developing countries are in the main not caused by internal factors or internal economic mismanagement — though of course one would not be foolish enough to assert that economic management in these countries has been perfect — but rather that the main origins and sources of these deficits are factors beyond the control of these countries; and that in addition the development process itself generates balance of payments deficits. It is these deficits which require sustained resource transfers from the developed countries. Therefore, because of these two factors, balance of payments support should be linked to development financing — even though balance of payments support is not identical to development financing. Also, the conditionality of IMF balance-of-payment support should be substantially liberalized, oriented towards and sensitive to development requirements.

Conditionality: the supply-demand equation

As a member of the Jamaican government system between 1977 and 1980, I have had close personal experience with IMF conditionality, with its programs containing high conditionality. I would say the experience was not only a close one but a somewhat painful one. I think perhaps David Finch of the IMF, who sat across a negotiating table from me in 1978, would bear this out; I don't believe the experience was pleasant for Mr. Finch either. I have no particular wish to relive those painful experiences with you today, but there are, I think, three brief points I would like to make on the conditionality issue.

First of all, an extraordinary amount of press attention has been given to the proposals for an increase in the quotas of the IMF membership. This fact itself reflects the priority and emphasis accorded to the interests of the developed countries. But, while we would not of course wish to ignore the possible importance and benefits which quota increases would have for developing countries, we should remember always that the chief beneficiary of quota increases would be the international banking system.

The alternatives to a major increase in fund resources are: an increasing number of debt rescheduling exercises undertaken voluntarily or involuntarily by developing countries which are major debtors to the international banking system; the growing possibility of defaults not only on principal payments but also on interest payments to the international banking system; and a sharp reduction in trade finance and therefore a continued failure of world trade to recover with the consequent failure of the advanced industrialized economies to recover. Therefore the increase in IMF resources becomes virtually an inescapable necessity for bailing the international banking system out of its problems. As the Minister of Finance of one Third World country said, "If I owe you one dollar then I am in trouble; but if I owe you a million dollars then you are in trouble."

The second point is that the Fund places a great deal of importance on the supply side of the adjustment process. That is to say, it claims to place a great deal of emphasis in its adjustment programs on measures to increase the production of goods and services. The Fund appears to consider that these measures are as important as steps to reduce the consumption of goods and services as a means of bringing economic systems into balance. However, in my own view this alleged change in emphasis is misleading since recent Fund "stabilization" programs continue to place very great emphasis on demand management, or internal deflation, as reflected in policies to contract the supply of credit and to reduce public spending. The Fund also emphasizes doing this in a relatively short period of time, in its one to three-year programs. In fact if we are to believe the Group of 24, there has recently been a tightening in Fund conditionality, as evident in their words "an increasing resort to preconditions" and the current tendency to shift from three-year to one-year programs.

An additional point here is that the supply-side measures themselves make use of traditional techniques that have always been endorsed or proposed by the Fund, techniques involving exchange-rate changes or — to put it simply — devaluation. These traditional economic measures are aimed at increasing the profitability of export production and import-substituting production and reducing the cost of real wages in total production. With this increased profitability comes, allegedly, an increased savings and investment in the economy. These measures which are supposed to affect the supply side are, however, very similar if not identical to the measures which have traditionally been used to affect the demand side of economic adjustment. We have to ask the question of whether in fact this new recognition of the supply side is not merely the demand-deflationary measures masquerading as supply-side measures.

Socio-political objectives: new priorities?

The third point I would like to make in relation to conditionality relates to the guidelines adopted in 1979 and especially the proposition that "due regard should be paid to members' domestic, social and political objectives, their economic priorities, and the causes of their balance of payments problems." Again this part of the new guidelines has been given a great deal of publicity by IMF publications. It's supposed to indicate a new sensitivity on the part of the Fund in response to criticism that they are insensitive to the objectives of developing countries.

However, a close study of this guideline shows that it is a largely meaningless statement that can in fact be interpreted in any particular way that the Fund chooses. Indeed, paying due regard to members' social, economic and political objectives, economic priorities and causes of their balance of payments problems can actually be used as another way of justifying more discriminatory treatment rather than less. The treatment accorded to specially-favoured countries can be justified by the argument that the IMF is responding to special circumstances.

As the Minister of Finance of Tanzania, Amir Jamal, pointed out in his statement at this meeting, the limited IMF resources still seem to be concentrated in three groups of countries. First, those which have militarily strategic significance in the world's geopolitical structure. Turkey would be an example of this. Secondly, those with very heavy debts that threaten the world's monetary system, and of course Mexico would be an example of this. And thirdly, those which have the requisite managerial and infrastructural equipment and are capable of relatively short-term adjustment due to reasonably balanced internal-external linkages. As Mr. Jamal points out, this leaves many poor developing countries altogether on the margin. Because the IMF does not have the resources to meet their needs, it asks for sharp, almost body-blow adjustments, which it must know either will not be acceptable or if accepted will lead to non-compliance with the performance criteria.

Towards a new system

I would like to make the following overview points. First of all, fundamental reform of the international monetary system requires the establishment of a wholly new institution to replace the IMF. This must be an institution with universal membership and with an altogether different character and orientation. The position that the developing countries have now adopted is perhaps a few steps behind this fundamental and radical approach. They have called for fundamental changes in the structure and operations of the IMF itself, changes that would reflect their own interests.

The developed countries are a considerable distance behind. At present they confine themselves to asking for a substantial increase in the resources of the Fund, especially through the method of increasing the membership quotas of the Fund. They recognize the importance of this increase for the expansion of world liquidity, to oil the wheels of world trade and salvage the international banks.

Behind everybody else is the United States of America, opposing anything other than a modest increase in the quotas of the Fund. The position of the present United States administration and that country's pre-eminent position in the decision-making processes of the Fund therefore stand as the chief stumbling blocks before even minor or modest changes in the institution.

Reforms, however, should go beyond quota increases to the very nature and orientation of the IMF, and even possibly to its very existence in the present form. Given the opposition of the chief decision-making authority, one must look at weaknesses in the overall system. The chief areas of weakness are the present instability in the world financial system, the huge deficits of the developing countries and the inadequacy of the conventional means of financing those deficits, plus the crisis in the advanced industrialized countries and the inadequacy of the present system to serve the interests of the developing countries.

Unfortunately, it would seem to require some major event or series of events of a cataclysmic nature — like the one that took place in the 1930s — to open the way towards the fundamental reforms that are necessary, or towards the establishment of a new system.

Statement from UNCTAD VI

Amir Jamal

This paper was delivered by Amir Jamal, Tanzanian minister without portfolio in the office of the President, as a statement at the Sixth Session of the United Nations Conference on Trade and Development (UNCTAD VI) held at Belgrade, Yugoslavia in June 1983.

At this point in time, we must avoid at all costs talking ourselves into a global depression. The almost unprecedented recession has been cruel enough. But neither should we delude ourselves into thinking that we can talk our way out of the present crisis. Flashes in the pan may look scintillating, especially when election time draws near. The danger is that valuable time may be lost, with irretrievable damage to all.

There seems to be reasonably common agreement that action is needed on two tracks simultaneously. There are certain immediate measures that cannot be delayed any longer. Already it is quite late, especially for the least developed countries. They need balance of payment support, as well as quickly disbursable import support to rehabilitate their capacity — thus enabling them to restore the lost momentum of development. At the same time the issue of remunerative prices of their commodities should now be pursued. And for all developing countries, access to markets and debt settlement are matters of urgency.

It must be stated at the outset that the developing countries have the primary responsibility to manage their economies in a manner conducive to their development, in conformity with their own values. Indeed from their very first days of political independence it becomes necessary to exercise that responsibility. The immediate task is to embark on a long, long journey of structural adjustment on a continuous basis.

And the less developed an economy, the more imperative the need for structural changes on the entire front constituting the development process. Quite often structures need to be built for the first time, because they were needed and not there. Education, health, water supply, village development, roads, communications and transport, agricultural support services, import substitution, processing of raw materials — all this and much more calls for structural adjustment. We hear so much about such adjustment these days! The developing countries have been doing nothing if not structural adjustment ever since the first day of their independence.

But the cause of the malaise afflicting the world economy does not lie with the poor developing countries, especially those who rely for their existence for the most part on primary commodities and the early stages of their processing. Nor do the large land masses of Asia and Latin America, with their large concentration of population, seem to have affected the world economy adversely. If anything, without their participation in world trade together with those of the least developed, the economies of the industrialized countries would have been under still greater strain. So what happened? How?

The OECD, the UNCTAD Secretariat and several other economic analysts have pointed at low productivity, inadequate research and savings, rigidities in production structures, too many market decisions of a short-term nature jeopardizing long-term investment plans — including investment in structural changes — as some of the factors that have been at play. Could it be that the rules of international trade and exchange established by the industrialized countries themselves were flaunted beyond an acceptable margin?

Could it be that certain transnational consequences and implications of pursuing basically national policies wedded to the free-play market forces have produced irreconcilable contradictions? That in the last analysis this meant the building-up of multiple surplus capacity structured for quick mass consumption, thus leading inevitably to high levels of unemployment?

Could it be that arms manufacture based on an ever-rising level of technology became an additional factor in the structural distortion caused by the progressive transnationalization of the world economy, without corresponding transnational political control of that process?

And could it be that the incompatibility of institutional capability with fiscal and monetary policies, and the structural disorientation of the economies of the industrialized countries inevitably led, among other things, to the enormous overhang of hundreds of billions of dollars of credit and debt balances which are equally asymmetrical structurally?

And finally, could it be that in this forest of thick weeds, basic human values have been the first to be smothered beneath?

A *prima facie* conclusion is hard to escape, namely that the slow and somewhat tortuous evolution of a practicable international order that was potentially premised through the establishment of the Bretton Woods institutions was decisively interrupted by the pursuit of nationalistic objectives, based on the possession of technological and military power. This meant abandoning the logic, even if one ignored the ethics, that motivated the founders of the Bretton Woods institutions and that pointed towards steady surrendering of sovereignty to steadily increasing international control and surveillance in the field of trade and exchange, with all its implications for human evolution.

That logic, with its ethical component, led the industrialized countries under the inspiration of the United States to establish the International Development Association in 1960. This was a historic milestone in human evolution. And so was the UN General Assembly decision to convene the United Nations Conference on Trade and Development. Not only did the poor developing countries find cause for hope, they were actually beginning to receive some predictable form of material assistance with which to connect themselves one day with the international chain of trade and exchange as part of a larger human community. But then somewhere, somehow, the process was not only interrupted but actually detracted onto another and seemingly altogether unregulated orbit.

The case of Tanzania

As a poor developing country, Tanzania, like many other poor developing countries, had perceived at an early stage the importance of managing its economy within the overall limits of its resources and such resources as were made available to it by other progressive, enlightened societies. The IDA has been a source of real help in building our physical and social infrastructure. Together with other helpers, it was possible for us in the 1960s to compensate ourselves for what we lost in terms of trade in only one commodity, sisal. We calculated in 1971 that if the price of sisal throughout the 1960s had been indexed to the weighted price of our imports of essential manufactured goods, Tanzania would have been left with a little surplus even if it had not received any assistance at all. And of course, with the resources that it actually did receive, Tanzania would have had greater capital formation — with all the incremental return to the economy that would have thus accrued.

Even so, from 1961 to 1977 Tanzania was able to balance its budget on recurrent account, while relying on grants, soft loans of the IDA type and internal savings to finance its development effort. With some considerable difficulty and despite prolonged drought in 1973-74, we succeeded in absorbing the first rise in the price of oil. Later, from 1977 onwards, within a short span of less than three years we were afflicted with the overnight loss of access to vital transport and communications services following the collapse of the East African Community; the completely unforeseen aggression on our territory calling for instant mobilization of all our resources, meagre as they were; the second oil shock; and very heavy flooding. All this constituted a body blow to our economy which deflected us from our painfully laid course, and the deepening world economic crisis did nothing to make things any easier.

Our own errors of commission and omission, which at the best of times for a developing country could not have been avoided in one form or another, compounded our problems. A whole burden of adjustment fell upon us, even though a very large component of the causes related to factors outside our control. With recourse to private banking quite out of the question, we hoped that the World Bank and the IMF would give us assistance and understanding. Instead, we encountered an insistence on applying to us a set of criteria with which even more developed countries would have quite some difficulty in complying.

We had already perceived that while the IMF was a most useful source of technical assistance, the premises on which it was established made its operational policies relevant only to industrialized societies endowed with a critical quantum of financial and fiscal infrastructure in addition to physical infrastructure. We were captive of historical underdevelopment, with only rain-fed agriculture and no assurance of adequate rainfall or of absence of pests or of remunerative prices, and with the task of building physical and social infrastructure still ahead of us. We were thus only too aware of the immense task of differentiating a balance of payment problem arising from short-term disequilibrium in income and expenditure in both fiscal and external trade accounts, and a negative balance of payment outcome due to our inherited circumstances.

We realized that with so many gaps in our economic structure, monetary policies could only yield results over a period of time — that is after we had made adequate investment in a broad spectrum of priority areas including roads, transport, education, health, water supply, credit institutional network and the like. In short, a per capita income of $200 was no qualification for a classical IMF program with its litany of prescriptions related to exchange rates, cuts in social expenditure and so forth.

In the 1970s we found ourselves taking the first faltering steps in some light industrial activities aimed at import substitution. It was neither politically nor economically feasible to remain content with only production of primary commodities. We had to make efforts to begin the escape from that historical bondage. And we believed that a policy of meeting basic needs through the establishment of industrial activities would receive international understanding and support. We entered a new phase in which the profile of our external trade was to change from year to year, to the extent we succeeded in adding value, through processing and manufacturing, to our primary commodities, themselves hostage to weather conditions.

Having embarked upon the task of restructuring our economy in order to carry out import substitution and to add further value to our own raw materials, we came face to face with the contradictions inherent in having to reconcile the needs of short-term external and internal equilibrium and the much longer process of restructuring our economy.

The failure of the IMF

If I have referred to the economy of my country, I have done so to make a number of important points:

- First, developing countries are in a continuous process of structural adjustment.
- Second, an economy large or small develops a strain in one area or another from time to time. When this happens, it is the function of responsible management to take remedial action. In order to do so, it becomes necessary to lean on the rest of the economy to find resources needed to take that remedial action. When an economy receives such a total all-pervasive blow as I have described it has no alternative to seeking assistance from outside.
- Third, a least developed country does not get any commercial bank loans. It is not considered credit-worthy. It can only seek assistance from friendly countries and seek a short-term facility from the IMF and long-term structural adjustment loan from the World Bank out of its quite limited funds — only 10 per cent of World Bank total lending being available for this purpose.
- Fourth, there is a limit to what assistance friendly countries can give in addition to the commitments already made which are intended to assist development rather than meeting balance of payment needs.
- Fifth, the IMF does not recognize the particular category of the least developed countries. It insists on applying criteria or conditionality as if a social and financial infrastructure comparable to that of an industrialized country was in place and responsive to monetary and fiscal measures, when in actual fact there are constraints at practically every step along the way — be they lack of feeder roads, or sparseness of bank facilities, or uncertain weather, or unpredictable appearance of pests, or erratic world market prices, or fluctuating rates, or high interest rates, not to mention availability of fuel, transport equipment and spare parts in the first place in addition to improved seed, fertilizers and so on.

• Sixth, the World Bank will not commit even the very limited funds available to it for lending towards structural adjustment unless the poor developing country first concludes an arrangement with the IMF and its unrealistic terms of conditionality.

Finally, there is a cruel contradiction between the very short-term framework of an IMF program, and the medium- and long-term framework of a structural adjustment program. In order to obtain an improvement in both external and internal accounts in the shortest possible time, under an IMF program a poor country has no choice but to try to make the most of the existing tracks in its economy. There is no way a country can seriously pursue long-term changes in its structures and at the same time struggle to obtain short-term results by concentrating on the micro-economic activities based on the existing profile of its economy.

I must admit I felt greatly perplexed and also somewhat depressed by what the managing director of the IMF has told UNCTAD. Evidently, he was not prepared for the IMF to give recognition to the special needs of the least developed, as the rest of the entire international community had done. He was happy that 20 out of 27 countries which had concluded stand-by arrangements had shown improvement in their economies in the first year.

Apart from the question as to how many of these countries were in the group of the least developed, it would be instructive to know whether the governments of these countries imposed their decisions on the people or whether the policies were given consent through the functioning of democratic process; or whether policies produced successful outcome because they were applied in an environment which was just preceded by chaos and disorder — thus rendering the population willing to try almost anything that might have some promise of working.

We were told by the IMF managing director that he expected the non-oil developing countries to pick up a growth rate of about 2.5 per cent in 1983 while their current account deficit would decline to less than $70 billion. Again, not a word about the prospects for the least developed countries which, most unfortunately, are not expected to register any growth at all.

And it is not clear if the decline of the current account deficit is due to depressed imports or greater real earnings through exports, or due to relative decline in interest rates from their unbearably high levels of 1982. The IMF is cautioning the industrialized countries against reflating their economies too early, which leads one to the question of whether the Fund shares the now almost universally held view that long-term economic growth for the industrialized countries is predicated on early revival of the economies of developing countries. Mr. Witteveen, the illustrious predecessor of the present managing director, recently commented:

With present high unemployment rates and low capacity utilization, surpluses in oil and other raw materials markets and pervasive deflationary pressures in the world financial system, the risk that a somewhat higher increase in money supply would rekindle inflation is practically non-existent. This should be explained clearly and forcefully to overcome dogmatic and unrealistic monetarist fears.

A very responsible body of opinion now advocates a special allocation of a substantial quantum of SDRs specifically aimed at stimulating development of the relatively underdeveloped.

Even if the international community does not wish to concern itself with the problems and difficulties of Tanzania, could it avoid asking itself those questions I have posed with regard to the evolution of the international economic system, and the digression of its logical and ethical evolution? While the IMF "disciplines" Tanzania and other similarly-placed developing countries who, we insist, have not contributed to the malaise in the international economy, the international community has not much time left for diagnosing the illness and taking the necessary remedial measures.

Quite apart from the fundamental questions related to equity in the decision-making process and in the treatment of historically disenfranchised developing societies, has the IMF achieved the purpose for which it was established? The primary function of the IMF was to ensure that the legitimate balance of payment needs of the world's trading nations were met as and when necessary, and that this basic purpose was to be achieved in the context of a sustained growth in world trade. The responsibility to achieve and maintain an equilibrium in the community of trading nations was premised on the self-evident fact that there could not be balance of payment surplus at one and the same time for all countries engaged in trade and exchange. It was obvious from the start that adequate resources would have to be placed at the disposal of the IMF from its inception, and that these resources would have to be increased in proportion to the growth of world trade, if the IMF was to serve the purpose for which it was created.

What actually happened? In 1950, against world exports of $57.2 billion, the IMF quota resources amounted to $8.04 billion: a ratio of 14 per cent. In 1960, world exports reached $113 billion, against IMF quota resources of $14.74 billion: a ration of 13 per cent. In 1970 world exports amounted to $282 billion against IMF quota of $31.85 billion: or a ratio of 11.3 per cent. In 1980, world exports amounted to $1,869 billion whereas the IMF quota inclusive of SDR allocation amounted to $98.18 billion: or a ratio of 5.25 per cent.

Quite clearly the IMF has been forced to abdicate its due function because it was not given the required resources. At the same time its function was all but taken over by private banks with their own terms of reference within the framework of their shareholders' mandate.

Global costs — global benefits

It is of course true that history does not offer any retrospective options. But I believe it is possible and indeed necessary to draw some important conclusions.

I say this in all humility and do not wish to be misunderstood. It seems that the step-by-step, necessary adjustment in both the Articles of Agreement and in the resources of the Fund have not kept pace with either the dynamic requirement of the logic of the Fund's establishment or with the objective needs of the international community from year to year. It is possible to visualize quite a different scenario for the sixties and seventies if an adequately resourced Fund had been truly sensitive to developments at both the extremes.

At one end a wholly identifiable new group of countries was just barely making faltering entry into the complex field of finance and fiscal management of their just recently monetized economy. At another end, a powerful combination of capital and technology was leading to fiscal and monetary behaviour both within and across national boundaries quite contrary to IMF tenets. An IMF that was truly committed to the goal of maintaining a continuing equilibrium in the world economy would have leaned much more towards the needy, fragile incipient economies. At the same time it would have demanded early compliance from forces which were cutting loose from the responsibility implied in the role of a particular currency being a *de facto* international trading and reserve unit.

An orderly organic development of the Fund's policies and performance, with due regard for the needs of resources to match its responsibilities, would have in the end enabled more orderly growth of trade, more sustained development, orderly exchange rate regimes, less unemployment and more effective containment of private banking, which even the banks themselves would have come to appreciate in due course.

An international conference participated in by all the countries of the world, to deal with money and finance for trade and development is now an urgent need. Both superpowers have a major role to play in the world economy. A great power, more than most, realizes its true limits. In the event, its own security cannot be assured without the security of all the rest. Deliverately limiting one's power is a manifestation of mature power. Limiting it in order to advance collective security through collective participation makes it humane power.

As for private investment, least developed countries are in a very peculiar situation. They need both capital and technology. And they need management skills to be developed. But an investor with these resources asks to be provided with such services as electricity, telephones, water supply, sewerage, well-maintained roads, transport services, physical security and a minimum of social amenities, to mention a few prerequisites. Each one of them has a high foreign exchange content, both in terms of initial capital and subsequent maintenance. Unless private investment can yield sufficient returns to make significant contribution to these sectors in addition to meeting the recurrent requirements of the enterprise itself, the whole exercise on the face of it is much less than a zero sum affair for a least developed country.

Unfortunately, many of the basic questions raised in UNCTAD I still remain to be resolved. The question of remunerative prices of primary commodities — which it was hoped would be meaningfully dealt with through a comprehensive Commodity Fund — still remains with us. Even in its diminished form, the Common Fund has not seen the light of day. The transition from primary production to industrialization needs time and resources. IDA is now poised on a thin razor's edge with a real risk of undoing all the good it has done. The debt of the developing countries needs urgent attention if it is not to contribute to inflation or to the collapse of private banking. Energy has assumed a time and resource dimension unforeseen in 1964. The poor countries are going to the wall. The unemployed in the industrialized world as yet do not see any glimpse of light.

And all this when intelligent synchronization of capacity in the industrialized world with the unmet needs of basic goods for development in the poor countries is altogether within the resourcefulness of humankind. All this enormous pain, when a 2 per cent reduction in defence expenditure by the industrialized countries would meet the minimum unsatisfied needs of poor developing countries. Ninety-eight tanks instead of a hundred, ninety-eight bombs instead of a hundred, ninety-eight missiles instead of a hundred. Is this such a huge sacrifice?

In the end the issues facing the international community are not just economic. Indeed they are fundamentally political. The issues concern the human race — our well-being, our self-respect. Even as we deliberate here, three freedom fighters went to the gallows in racist South Africa because they chose to take all the risks they could for the sake of asserting dignity. When we plead for an equitable deal in commodities, in trade, in liquidity adjustment to safeguard the process of development, we are concerned with humanity and its well-being.

These are not abstract subjects we are deliberating on. The manner and the speed with which we deal with these urgent matters which cumulatively constitute the core of the world crisis, will determine whether democratic values will have a chance of firm roots in the yet developing societies or whether authoritarianism, repression and trampling of basic human rights will be the order bequeathed to our children.

I trust no one wants the scenario of Horatio, who at the end of *Hamlet* looked over the dead bodies of Hamlet, Laertes and the King and Queen of Denmark and said in Shakespeare's inimitable words:

And let me speak to th' yet unknowing world,
How these things came about. So you shall hear
Of carnal, bloody and unnatural acts, of accidental judgements,
Casual slaughters of deaths put on by cunning and forced cause,
And in this upshot, purposes mistook
Fall'n on th' inventors' heads.

Indeed, we are all in one boat. We need to be extremely careful that the distribution of weight through the various structures of that boat does not become so uneven as to endanger its seaworthiness, in high or low tide. Courage and imagination, as much as careful calculation of global costs and global benefits, need to be our equipment in these crucial days.

Glossary

ADFU — the Apex Development Finance Unit of the Central Bank of the Philippines, established in order to channel World Bank loans to Philippine financial institutions through one central national institution.

AID — Agency for International Development: the U.S. government agency established in 1961 to disperse social development assistance to other governments; it has at times been associated with the CIA.

Apex loan — a World Bank loan made to the Apex Development Finance Unit of the Central Bank of the Philippines, which in turn acts like the World Bank in dispersing portions of the loan to (at present) six lower-level financial institutions; see also ADFU.

BIS — Bank for International Settlement: the powerful international bank, based in Basel, Switzerland, which handles transfers between the national central banks and is increasingly involved with emergency loans to developing country debtors; it was established in 1930 to facilitate the looting of Germany under the terms of the 1919 Versailles Treaty and is owned by its constituent central banks.

Balance of payments — the record of all of a nation's international economic transactions; those which create credits for the country (exports, capital inflows, etc.) are counted as positive items; while those which create debits (imports, capital outflows, etc.) are counted as negative items; when the credits exceed the debits the balance of payments is said to be in surplus, and when the opposite is true it is in deficit; when the two are equal it is in equilibrium.

Balance of trade — the difference between the sum of a nation's exports of goods and services (counted as a positive item) and the sum of its imports of goods and services (counted as a negative item).

Bretton Woods — the New Hampshire town which was the site of the UN Monetary and Financial Conference organized to plan economic and financial co-operation for the postwar years; held in July 1944 with 44 nations participating, the conference planned the IMF and IBRD. See also IBRD, IMF.

CIDA — Canadian International Development Agency: the federal government agency in charge of dispersing social development assistance; its budget of over $1.5 billion is distributed annually to more than 80 Third World recipient governments, with emphasis on Asia and Africa.

Compensatory Finance Facility — an IMF facility that provides shortfall credit, with low conditionality and of three to five years' duration, to compensate countries for sudden declines in their foreign exchange earnings from their major export commodities; see also foreign exchange, conditionality.

Concessional loans — loans for development purposes made at below-market interest rates and with other special terms; often available only to the poorest countries.

Conditionality — refers to the criteria that the World Bank and IMF attach to their loans and credits, over and above the obligation to repay and cover interest charges; these criteria extend over a far wider range of economic policy than that related directly to the loan or credit in question, and are criticized by many Third World governments for being onerous and counter-productive to development.

Debtor power — in the dynamics of north-south negotiations, this refers to the potential of the debtors, the south, at some point to refuse to pay, and their potential power in so doing to form a debtor cartel: "If you owe the banks $10 million the banks own you; if you owe the banks $10 billion you own the banks"; see also NICs.

EFF — Extended Fund Facility: an IMF facility which provides an extension of the stand-by agreement under strict conditionalities, usually three year agreements used by countries forced to undergo major structural economic changes; see also stand-by agreement, conditionality.

EOI — export-oriented (or -led) industrialization: where the primary emphasis of development policy is to extend production for the export market rather than to service domestic needs directly.

EPZs — Export-processing zones: special areas created by some of the poorest countries, where no import duties are charged on industrial inputs imported and no export duties are charged on manufactured or semi-manufactured goods exported.

Eurodollars or **Eurocurrency** — claims on the U.S. banking system, held in banks in Western Europe; these claims are loaned and borrowed by banks in much the same way as a currency is used within a particular nation.

FIRA — Foreign Investment Review Agency: a Canadian government body set up to screen applications of foreign firms wishing to invest in Canada; established in 1973.

Floating interest rates — arrangements under which the rate of interest on loans is recurrently adjusted on the basis of shifts in the inter-bank interest rates.

Foreign exchange — any holdings by one country of another country's currency, or claims on that other country's currency.

G-7 — Group of Seven: the seven leading industrial states whose leaders meet recurrently: Britain, Canada, France, Germany FR, Italy, Japan, United States.

G-10 — Group of Ten: operating since 1962 as a caucus of the major developed countries within the IMF and World Bank, this group includes those countries which contribute to GAB; at times referred to as the Paris Club, it effectively controls the IMF and World Bank; members are: Belgium, Canada, France, Germany FR, Italy, Japan, Netherlands, Sweden, U.K., U.S.A.; see also G-7, GAB, quotas.

G-24 — Group of 24: the developing country caucus within the IMF and the World Bank, representing the position of the Group of 77 on all issues related to these two institutions; established in 1972 in order to counterbalance the positions of G-10; see also G-10, G-77.

G-77 — Group of 77: developing countries that came together in the early 1970s to present a unified voice at the United Nations and other international bodies on all negotiations on international development issues; now numbering over 120 members the group first caucuses to arrive on a common statement, which is then presented by their appointed spokesperson; see also G-24.

GAB — General Arrangements to Borrow: IMF funding arrangements restricted to the ten industrialized countries; the purpose of this is to safeguard the IMF's regular funds from being overwhelmed by simultaneous demands from countries with substantial quotas; see also G-10.

GATT — General Agreement on Tariffs and Trade: a UN body set up to co-ordinate trade policy among countries in the hope of avoiding the "beggar-thy-neighbour" import restrictions of the 1930s; GATT has overseen a gradual lowering of barriers to international trade; see also Bretton Woods.

GDP — Gross Domestic Product.

GNP — Gross National Product.

Green Revolution — refers to a considerable increase in Third World agricultural production resulting from the introduction of new seeds (primarily wheat and rice) and a capital-intensive approach to agriculture.

IBRD — International Bank for Reconstruction and Development: also known as the World Bank, it was established at Bretton Woods in 1945 by 28 countries as a specialized agency of the UN to promote the economic development of member countries; see also Bretton Woods, IMF, quotas.

IDA — International Development Association: a World Bank body established in 1960 as a source of concessional

finance for the poorer developing countries; see
concessional loans, IBRD.

IMF — International Monetary Fund: established in 1945 by
29 governments to promote international monetary
co-operation; as an independent body the IMF co-operates
in a program of mutual assistance with the UN and other
international bodies; based in Washington, with a staff of
1,400 and 141 member countries; borrowing ability and
voting rights are determined by the "quota" paid to the
Fund by each member, which again gives dominant power
to the U.S. and European Economic Community; see also
Bretton Woods, IBRD, and quotas.

International Finance Corporation — a World Bank
subsidiary, which seeks to promote growth in the private
sector of developing countries by providing equity capital
as a means of helping to mobilize complementary local
and foreign investment.

International liquidity — the sum of all foreign exchange
and gold reserves and all readily available international
credits.

ISI — Import-substitution industrialization: where local
industry is protected from the competition of imports in
order that it may manufacture previously imported goods
to meet the needs of the domestic market.

Keynesianism — in popular usage refers to propositions
associated originally with the late John Maynard Keynes,
to the effect that increased deficit-financed government
spending is the appropriate major instrument for
alleviating an economic depression, by thus creating an
increase in aggregate demand for goods and services,

LDCs — Less Developed Countries: a catchphrase used to
designate those lower-income countries of the "South",
usually former colonies of European nations; also, referred
to at various times as *developing, underdeveloped* or
Third World nations. More recently, with increasing
industrialization in some of these countries, they have also
been divided into those with *low-income economies* (the

majority still of Third World nations) such as Tanzania,
India and Vietnam; and *middle-income economies* such as
Brazil, South Korea and Malaysia.

LIBOR — London Interbank Rate, the variable,
market-determined rate for borrowing U.S. dollars.

MDBs — Multilateral development banks; for example, the
African Development Bank and the Asian Development
Bank.

Monetarism — a popular label for an economic theory,
influential in right-wing circles in the U.S. and Britain,
which would rely on monetary instruments and control of
the supply of money as the major macroeconomic policy
resource to constrain or stimulate the economy.

NEP — National Energy Policy: the Canadian government
policy introduced in 1980 to increase Canadian
participation in and control of the production and export
of energy in Canada.

NICs — Newly industrialized countries: Third World nations
such as Brazil, Mexico, Nigeria, Taiwan, South Korea, and
Malaysia, which have achieved sustained rates of growth
in their industrial output and also have the potential of
debtor power; see also debtor power.

NIEO — New International Economic Order: a set of reforms
advocated by developing countries, particularly in the
1970s when the NIEO was a major theme of international
negotiations; rich country opposition successfully blocked
the introduction of almost all of these reforms.

OECD — Organization for Economic Co-operation and
Development: established in 1961 to promote economic
and social welfare throughout the industrialized, capitalist
countries by co-ordinating policies and harmonizing
members' aid efforts to developing countries; the 24
members are: Australia, Austria, Belgium, Canada,
Denmark, Finland, France, Germany FR, Greece, Iceland,
Ireland, Italy, Japan, Luxembourg, Netherlands, New
Zealand, Norway, Portugal, Spain, Sweden, Switzerland,
Turkey, U.K., U.S.A.

OPEC — Organization of Petroleum Exporting Countries: established in 1960 to unify the petroleum policies of members and to safeguard the individual and collective interests of member countries in counter-balance to the big seven oil companies: its 13 members are: Algeria, Ecuador, Gabon, Indonesia, Iran, Iraq, Kuwait, Libya, Nigeria, Qatar, Saudi Arabia, United Arab Emirates, Venezuela.

Quotas — a popular term for a member's contribution to the subscribed capital of the World Bank and the IMF; it is capital based broadly on the member's economic strength, its gold and dollar reserves, its average imports, the variability of its exports and their ratio to national income; a member's quota determines its voting strength in each institution; see also IBRD, IMF.

Reserve currency — a currency held by one country and as a means for settling international accounts. It is held as a form of international liquidity available in the event of a balance of payments shortfall.

Roll-over of debt — when loans coming due are deferred or renewed for a further period of time, usually at different interest rates depending on trends in those rates since the original loans were arranged, and often with heavy additional fees.

SDRs — Special Drawing Rights: an IMF reserve asset created as an international unit of account, with a value linked to five major currencies (dollar, mark, yen, franc and pound); used under special conditions to provide an additional source of liquidity beyond gold, U.S. dollars and other key currencies, to settle international accounts; established in 1969, SDRs may be used by fund members experiencing balance of payments difficulties, to obtain convertible currencies from other members.

Stand-by agreement — an arrangement with a member-country in balance of payments difficulties, whereby the country is guaranteed access to an agreed-upon amount from which it can choose to draw; the agreement is usually for one to two years with conditionality; see also balance of payments, conditionality, EFF.

Structural adjustment loan — a form of lending recently introduced by the World Bank and designed for countries faced with the necessity of making significant structural changes in their economies in order to overcome severe and persistent foreign exchange deficits: this form of loan, offered with high conditionality, creates a reduction in the level of protection for domestic industry and a reorientation of policies towards export promotion; see also foreign exchange.

Terms of trade — the rate at which a country's exports can be exchanged for its imports; when its terms of trade improve, a given quantity of exports will buy more imports than before.

Tranche — a portion of an IMF credit to a country, distinguished from other "tranches" by different levels of conditionality.

Trust Fund — an IMF fund that makes available interest-free loans over a ten-year period, with low conditionality.

UNCTAD — United Nations Conference on Trade and Development: established in 1964 to meet the demands of the Third World members for a UN agency dealing with trade and development issues sympathetic to their aspirations.

World Bank — see IBRD.

Further Reading

Abdalla, Ismaïl-Sabri, "The Inadequacy and Loss of Legitimacy of the International Monetary Fund," *Development Dialogue* 2, 25-54, 1980.

Assman, Hugo, ed, *El Banco Mundial: Un Caso de "progresismo conservador,"* San Jose: Departamento Ecumenico de Investigaciones, 1980 [With contributions from Cheryl

Payer, Joseph Collins, Frances Moore Lappé, Robert Carty, *et al.*]

Ayres, Robert L., *Banking on the Poor: The World Bank and World Poverty*, Cambridge: MIT Press, 1983.

Beckford, George and Michael Witter, *Small Garden ... Bitter Weed: Struggle and Change in Jamaica*, Morant Bay, Jamaica: Maroon Pub.; London: Zed Press, 1982.

Bello, Walden, and Elaine Elinson, *Elite Democracy· and Authoritarian Rule*, San Francisco: Philippine Solidarity Network, 1981.

Bello, Walden, David Kinley and Elaine Elinson, *Development Debacle: The World Bank in the Philippines*, San Francisco: Institute for Food and Development Policy; San Francisco: Philippine Solidarity Network, 1982.

Block, Fred L., *The Origins of International Economic Disorder: A Study of United States International Monetary Policy from World War II to the Present*, Berkeley: University of California Press, 1977.

Carty, Robert, "Chile: Miracle or Mirage," Toronto: Taskforce on the Church and Corporate Responsibility, 1981; *LAWG Letter*, 7 (5-6), 1982.

Carty, Robert and Virginia Smith, *Perpetuating Poverty: The Political Economy of Canadian Foreign Aid*, Toronto: Between The Lines, 1981.

Centre for International Policy, (Washington, D.C.), "A Billion Dollars for Southern Africa," *International Policy Report*, April 1983, 7 pp.

—— "Central America: The Financial War," *International Policy Report*, March, 1983, 11 pp.

Cline, W.R. and S. Weintraub, eds., *Economic Stabilisation in Developing Countries*, Washington, D.C.: The Brookings Institute, 1981.

Commonwealth Secretariat, *Towards a New Bretton Woods: Challenges for a World Financial and Trading System*, Report by a Commonwealth Study Group led by G.K. Helleiner, London: 1983.

Dell, S. and R. Lawrence, *The Balance of Payments Adjust-*

ment *Process in Developing Countries*, New York: Pergamon, 1980.

Deu, S., "Stabilisation: The Political Economy of Overkill," *World Development* 10 (8), 1982.

Dziobek, Claudia, "Mexican Economy: Creative Financing to the Rescue," *NACLA Report* 17 (1), 40-44, 1983.

Faalawd, Just, ed., *Aid and Influence: The Case of Bangladesh*, London: Macmillan, 1981.

Fagen, Richard and Olga Pellicer, eds., *The Future of Central America: Policy Choices for the U.S. and Mexico*, Palo Alto: Stanford University Press, 1983.

Feder, Ernest, "The World Bank and the Expansion of Industrial Monopoly Capital Into Underdeveloped Agricultures," *Journal of Contemporary Asia* 12 (1), 34-60, 1982.

Feinberg, Richard, *The Intemperate Zone*, New York: W.W. Norton; Toronto: Geo. McLeod & Co., 1983.

Frank, André Gunder, *Reflections on the World Economic Crisis*, New York: Monthly Review, 1981.

Freeman, Linda, "Canada and Africa in the 1970s," *International Journal* 35 (4), 1980.

Girvan, Norman, "Dependency Economics in Latin America and the Caribbean: Review and Comparison," *Social and Economic Studies* 1-33, 1973.

——, *Foreign Capital and Economic Underdevelopment in Jamaica*, Kingston, Jamaica: Jamaica Institute of Social and Economic Research, University of the West Indies, 1971.

——, "Swallowing the IMF Medicine in the 'Seventies," *Development Dialogue* 2, 55-74, 1980.

Girvan, Norman and Richard Bernal, "The IMF and the Foreclosure of Development Options: The Case of Jamaica," *Development and Peace* 2 (2), 137-150, 1981.

Girvan, Norman, Richard Bernal and Wesley Hughes, "The IMF and the Third World: The Case of Jamaica, 1974-80," *Development Dialogue* 2, 113-155, 1980.

Green, R.H., and D.G. Rwegasira and B. Van Arkadie, *Economic Shocks and National Policy Making: Tanzania in the 1970s*, The Hague: Institute of Social Studies, 1980.

Hayter, Teresa, *Aid as Imperialism*, Harmondsworth: Penguin Books, 1971.

——, *The Creation of World Poverty: An Alternative View to the Brandt Report*, London: Pluto Press, 1981.

Helleiner, Gerald K., ed., *For Good or Evil: Economic Theory and North-South Negotiations*, Toronto: University of Toronto Press; Oslo: Universitetsforlag, 1982.

——, *International Economic Disorders: Essays in North-South Relations*, University of Toronto Press, 1981.

Honeywell, Martin, ed., *The Poverty Brokers: The IMF and Latin America*, London: Latin America Bureau [1 Amwell St., London ECl, England], 1983.

Hooke, H.W., *The International Monetary Fund: Its Evolution, Organization, and Activities*, Washington, D.C.: IMF, 1982.

IBRD, *Accelerated Development in Sub-Saharan Africa: An Agenda for Action*, Washington, D.C.: 1981. [The Berg Report]

IDS Bulletin (Sussex), "Accelerated Development in Sub-Saharan Africa: What Agendas for Action?" 14 (1), 1983.

Independent Commission on International Development Issues, *Common Crisis; North-South: Cooperation for World Recovery*, London: Pan Books, 1983. [The Brandt Report]

——, *North-South, a Program for Survival: Report of the Independent Commission on International Development Issues*, London: Pan Books, 1980. [The Brandt Report]

Killick, Tony, ed., *Adjustment and Financing in the Developing World: The Role of the International Monetary Fund*, London: Overseas Development Council; Washington, D.C.: International Monetary Fund, 1982.

KSP, [Philippines] Comite mg Sambayanang, "Health, the Fruit of Struggle," *KSP Kilusan* 2 (1), 32 pp., 1983. [Admiraal van Gentstraat 26 bis, 3572 XL Utrecht]

——, "In the Face of Adversity," *KSP Kilusan* 1 (1-2), 56 pp., 1982.

——, "Seeds of Intervention," *KSP Kilusan* 2 (2-3), 40 pp., 1983.

La Feber, Walter, *Inevitable Revolution: The United States in Central America*, New York: Norton, 1983.

Latin America Working Group, "Brazil: Structures of Repression," *LAWG Letter*, 7 (3-4), 1982.

———, "The Brazilian Debt Crisis", *LAWG Letter* 8 (2), 1983.

Loxley, John, "The Berg Report and the Model of Accumulation in Sub-Saharan Africa," in J. Barker, ed., *Agriculture and Politics in Africa*, Beverley Hills: Sage, forthcoming.

———, *Growth, Equity and Structural Adjustment in the LDCs*, Ottawa: North-South Institute, forthcoming.

———, *External Finance and Structural Adjustment in Third World Countries*, Ottawa: North-South Institute, 1984.

———, "Low Income Countries and the International Financial Crisis," Commonwealth Study Group on International Financial Reform, London: Commonwealth Secretariat, forthcoming.

———, "The Performance of Low Income Countries under IMF Standby Agreements: Empirical Evidence and Policy Implications," Commonwealth Study Group on International Financial Reform, London: Commonwealth Secretariat, forthcoming.

———, "Regulation and Restructuring: Responses to the International Financial Crisis," in *Proceedings of the Marx Centennial Conference*, University of Manitoba, March, 1983, forthcoming.

Manley, Michael, *Jamaica: Struggle in the Periphery*, Oxford: Third World Media Ltd., 1982.

Marcussen, Henrik S. and Jens E. Torp, *Internationalization of Capital: Prospects for the Third World: A Re-examination of Dependency Theory*, London: Zed Press, 1982.

Martel, Julian, "Domination by Debt: Finance Capital in Argentina," *NACLA Report* 12 (4), 1978.

Moffitt, Michael, *The World's Money: International Banking from Bretton Woods to the Brink of Insolvency*, New York: Simon and Schuster, 1983.

Multinational Monitor, "The Rule of the IMF," 4 (1), 1983.

Mwansasu, Bismarck and Cranford Pratt, *Towards Socialism in Tanzania*, University of Toronto Press, 1979.

Naylor, R.T., "Reaganism and the Future of the International Payments System," *Third World Quarterly*, 1982.

Omvedt, Gail, "India, the IMF and Imperialism Today," *Journal of Contemporary Asia* 12 (2), 131-144, 1982.

Parboni, Riccardo, *The Dollar and Its Rivals*, trans. by Jon Rothschild, London: NLB, 1981.

Payer, Cheryl, *The Debt Trap: The IMF and the Third World*, New York: Monthly Review Press, 1974.

——, *The World Bank: A Critical Analysis*, New York: Monthly Review Press, 1982.

Pearce, Jenny, *Under the Eagle: U.S. Intervention in Central America and the Caribbean*, London: Latin America Bureau, 1981. [See M. Honeywell]

Plumtree, A.F.N., *Three Decades of Decision: Canada and the World Monetary System, 1944-75*, Toronto: McClelland & Stewart, 1977.

Pratt, Cranford, "From Pearson to Brandt: Changing Perceptions on International Development," *International Journal* 35 (4), 1980.

Robinson, H. Lukin, *Canada's Crippled Dollar: An Analysis of International Trade and Our Troubled Balance of Payments*, Toronto: James Lorimer, 1980.

Rwegemamu, Justinian F., "Restructuring the International Monetary System," *Development Dialogue* 2, 75-91, 1980.

Sampson, Anthony, *The Money Lenders: Bankers and a World in Turmoil*, London: Hodder and Stoughton, 1981.

Southeast Asia Resource Centre, "The Philippines in the 1980s," *Southeast Asia Chronicle* 83, 1983.

——, "The World Bank," *Southeast Asia Chronicle* 81, 1981.

The South-North Conference on 'The International Monetary System and the New International Order', "The Arusha Initiative: A Call for a United Nations Conference on International Money and Finance," *Development Dialogue* 2, 10-23, 1980.

The South-North Conference on 'The International Monetary System and the New International Order', "Background

Notes on the International Monetary Fund," *Development Dialogue* 2, 95-112, 1980.

Stallings, Barbara, "Privatization and the Public Debt: U.S. Banks in Peru," *NACLA Report* 12 (4), 1978.

Taskforce on the Church and Corporate Responsibility,[129 St. Clair Ave. W., Toronto M4V 1W5] "Canadian Economic Relations with Countries that Violate Human Rights: A Brief to the Subcommittee on Latin America and the Caribbean of the Standing Committee on External Affairs and National Defence," House of Commons, June 1982, 41 pp. and App.

———, "Canadian Policies Towards South Africa: An Exchange Between the Secretary of State for External Affairs and the Task Force," *Canadian Journal of African Studies* 17 (3), 1983.

U.S. Department of the Treasury, *Assessment of U.S. Participation in the Multilateral Development Banks*, Washington, D.C.: 1982.

Van de Laar, Aart, *The World Bank and the Poor*, Boston: Martinus Nijhoff, 1980.

Wachtel, Howard, *The New Gnomes: Multinational Banks in the Third World*, Washington, D.C.: Transnational Institute, 1977.

Warrian, Peter, "Trade Union Response to the Recession," in W.J. Megaw, ed., *Prospects for Man.* Toronto: York University Centre for Research on Environmental Quality; Prospects for Man Symposium, York University, (1979), 1982.

Warrian, Peter and David Wolfe, *Trade Unions and Inflation*, Ottawa: Canadian Centre for Policy Alternatives (Box 4466, Station "E", Ottawa K1S 5B4), 1982.

Weinert, Richard, "Nicaragua's Debt Renegotiation," *Cambridge Journal of Economics* 5, 187-194, 1981.

Williamson, John, ed., *IMF Conditionality*, Washington, D.C.: Institute for International Economics, 1983.

World Bank, *IDA in Retrospect: The First Two Decades of the International Development Association*, Oxford University Press, 1981.

The Political Market for Protectionism in Industrial Countries, Staff Working Paper, No. 492, Washington, D.C.: 1981.